BAPTIST CHURCH COVENANTS

CHARLES W. DEWEESE

BROADMAN PRESS
NASHVILLE, TENNESSEE

To five professors of graduate studies at The Southern Baptist Theological Seminary, Louisville, Kentucky, 1970-1973, who nurtured and shaped my interest in the biblical and Baptist emphasis on a regenerate church membership:

James Leo Garrett, Jr.
E. Glenn Hinson
W. Morgan Patterson
Frank Stagg
C. Penrose St. Amant

©Copyright 1990 ● Broadman Press
All rights reserved
4265-87
ISBN: 0-8054-6587-1
Dewey Decimal Classification: 286
Subject Heading: BAPTIST CHURCHES // CHURCH COVENANTS
Library of Congress Card Catalog Number: 89-29513
Printed in the United States of America

Unless otherwise stated, all Scripture quotations are from the *Revised Standard Version of the Bible,* copyrighted 1946, 1952, ©1971, 1973. Scripture quotations marked KJV are from the King James Version of the Bible.

Library of Congress Cataloging-in-Publication Data

Deweese, Charles W.
    Baptist church covenants / Charles W. Deweese.
    p. cm.
    Includes bibliographical references.
    ISBN 0-8054-6587-1 :
    1. Covenants (Church polity)--History of doctrines. 2. Baptists-Government. I. Title.
BX6340.D49 1990
262'.06--dc20

                                                89-29513
                                                   CIP

262
Dew

Contents

Foreword

Baptists worldwide have written and used hundreds, and perhaps thousands, of church covenants since initiating that development in England in the early 1600s. They have viewed covenants, along with believer's baptism and church discipline, as means of nurturing and safeguarding the New Testament emphasis on a regenerate church membership. Covenants deserve careful evaluation because they helped shape Baptist church membership standards and practices. Thus, this book tells the emerging story of Baptist church covenants by displaying their history (including background influences), interpreting their role and impact, presenting an international sampling of major and representative covenants, and suggesting guidelines for writing and using covenants today.

Baptist Ideals for Church Membership

The rise of the Believers' Church was one of the most important developments in Christian history. This movement began among the Czech Brethren in the 1400s and continued through the Continental Anabaptists of the 1500s. Baptists arose in the early 1600s as a dynamic extension of the movement. The Believers' Church has been variously defined as "a church which strives to practise regenerate church membership"[1] and as "the covenanted and disciplined community of those walking in the way of Jesus Christ."[2]

Alongside believer's baptism, congregational polity, the associational principle, and the separation of church and state, the concept of a regenerate church membership has always been a distinguishing mark of Baptists and has permeated historical Baptist teachings on the nature of the church.[3] Although the idea of a regenerate church membership existed in Protestantism prior to their rise, Baptists led the way in contributing the doctrine to Protestant growth.[4]

Early Baptists based their church membership ideals and practices upon New Testament patterns. They reached four basic conclusions: (1) admission standards for membership should be high; (2) believer's baptism is essential for membership and helps safeguard the regenerate nature of church life; (3) church members should consistently meet biblical requirements for doctrinal soundness, moral purity, spiritual growth, covenant relationship, and active ministry; and (4) discipline should be administered for serious failures to meet the covenantal expectations of church membership.

For centuries, in their confessions of faith and other writings, Baptists have insisted on a regenerate church membership. Regeneration means being "born anew" (John 3:3,7; 1 Pet. 1:3,23) by the Holy Spirit. The initiative for regeneration comes from God and is not derived from human effort. God "saved us, not because of deeds done by us in righteousness, but in virtue of his own mercy, by the washing of regeneration and renewal in the Holy Spirit" (Titus 3:5). A regenerate person is one who has received "baptism into death" (Rom. 6:4) has become "a new creation" (2 Cor. 5:17), and "overcomes the world" (1 John 5:4).

What, therefore, is the biblical relationship between the regenerate and church membership? In the New Testament only those persons who repent of sin, commit their lives to God in Christ, and experience the "new birth" are eligible candidates for believer's baptism and church membership. Thus, Baptists have concluded in their definitions of the church both that the church can achieve its mission for God only if comprised of the regenerate and that the regenerate can fulfill their covenantal obligations to God only within the context of the church. In 1611 Thomas Helwys, soon to become the pastor of the first Baptist congregation in England, led several laypeople in jointly writing a statement of faith. As the first English Baptist confession, this statement described the church as a company of faithful Christians who have separated from the world, confessed their sins, acknowledged their faith in God, and knit themselves to God and one another by baptism.[5] These same elements have characterized Baptist views of the church since that time.

In their efforts to highlight the importance of responsible church membership, early Baptists concluded that since God had created the church to help meet His purposes for His people, the church had both a right and a duty to maintain biblical standards by expecting certain qualifications of its members. Baptists injected responsibility and account-

ability into church membership so that each congregation could reflect
biblical ideals and make an effective impact on the world through witness, ministry, missions, education, worship, stewardship, and other
means.

The doctrine of a regenerate church membership is exceedingly important to Baptists. To illustrate, three writers between 1901 and 1908 variously described this conviction as "the prime plank in our doctrinal and
practical platform," as the principle which "more than anything else,
marks our distinctiveness in the Christian world today," and, along with
"the equality and priesthood of believers," as "the ecclesiastical significance of the Baptists."[6] In sharp contrast, a noted Baptist professor recently termed this historic Baptist conviction "a vanishing distinctive—
at best, a molested ideal; at worst, a mangled fiction."[7] That indictment
alone provides sufficient justification for Baptists to assess the problem
carefully and to evaluate possible remedies for it. This book is intended to
provide constructive contributions in these directions.

A dilemma facing contemporary Baptists in America is how to recon-
cile mounting trends toward an uncommitted church membership with
doctrinal statements that require a committed membership. The stakes
are high, and the regenerate quality of much Baptist church life is at risk.
Evidence of the problem includes baptizing thousands of preschoolers,
frequent requests for rebaptism by persons already baptized as "alleged"
believers, little concern for candidates' qualifications for membership,
weak admission standards and procedures, inadequate attention to defining and carrying out membership responsibilities, decreased use of covenants and discipline, large numbers of nonresident members, and numerous inactive resident members. As one Baptist historian recently
claimed,

> Sadly for those who espouse a high quality of church membership,
> Baptists have lately experienced the same patterns of membership defi-
> ciencies that other Christian groups have. Typically, Sunday services
> do not exceed one-third of the membership roster and covenant respon-
> sibilities often go unheeded.[8]

Baptists today can profit by taking a fresh look at the strengths and
weaknesses of how Baptists historically have viewed and practiced responsible church membership. Specific concerns deserving renewed attention include qualifications of candidates for church membership, ad-

mission procedures for membership, covenantal expectations of church members, and accountability for meeting biblical standards of membership.

The Bible and Baptist history urgently appeal for today's churches to cultivate a truly regenerate membership. Failure to do that can easily shatter the Baptist witness in the modern world and neutralize a conviction that has characterized Baptists for centuries. Acceptance of that responsibility can upgrade church membership standards and increase the integrity and quality of Baptist church life.

The Covenant Idea

Baptists have typically applied various kinds of covenants to many facets of their experience. Seven twentieth-century examples illustrate this variety.[9] In 1937 the Southern Baptist Convention adopted a Convention-wide prayer covenant. The National Baptist Convention, U.S.A., Inc., adopted as a standard guide for its churches a 1963 manual on church administration which contained a covenant for church choirs. In the 1970s, the American Baptist Churches in the U.S.A. reorganized their entire denominational structure around a covenant through which local churches and denominational organizations agreed to accomplish their common purposes. In 1979 the editor of *The Deacon* (quarterly publication of The Sunday School Board of the Southern Baptist Convention) observed that an increasing number of Southern Baptist churches were writing deacon covenants. In 1982 *The Baptist Program* (monthly publication of the Executive Committee of the Southern Baptist Convention) published a major article focusing on a suggested covenant for a pastor-church relationship. In 1986 the Sunday School Board published a guide for shared ministry worship planning which gave significant attention to a believer's ministry covenant. In the 1980s the Board began publishing materials promoting covenant marriage.

A church covenant, however, differs from all seven of these covenantal expressions. A church covenant is a series of written pledges based on the Bible which church members voluntarily make to God and to one another regarding their basic moral and spiritual commitments and the practice of their faith. A covenant deals mainly with conduct (although it contains some doctrinal elements), while a confession of faith centers more heavily on beliefs. The basic meaning of a covenant resides in divine/human relationships in the context of church membership.

Through the centuries Baptist churches have tended to write and/or adopt church covenants and confessions of faith in tandem as basic constitutive documents of their congregational life. This process has sought a balance between faith and practice, words and deeds, beliefs and behavior, doctrine and conduct.

Church covenants entered the Baptist experience as early Baptists sought ways to help make church members responsible to the Lord, to one another, and to their Christian commitments. Through covenants Baptists defended high ideals for church membership and presented positive and practical approaches to ensure a regenerate membership. Such actions and relationships made a significant impact on the quality of church life.

Through the centuries Baptists have regularly included covenantal themes in their definitions of the church. Many major Baptist confessions of faith have clearly identified covenanting as integral to the nature of the church. For example, *The Baptist Faith and Message* (1963) statement of the Southern Baptist Convention affirmed that "A New Testament church of the Lord Jesus Christ is a local body of baptized believers who are associated by covenant in the faith and fellowship of the gospel . . . ."[10]

Valuable precedents from the Baptist past and the imperative need for consistency between statements of faith and practical living compel Baptists today to take seriously the covenantal commitments inherent in their doctrine of the church. This will add increased substance to Baptist church life. New allegiance to biblically based covenantal pledges can help Baptists achieve consonance between their ideals and their discipleship.

Baptists of the twentieth century have generally given less priority to covenants than their denominational ancestors. This neglect prompted the writers of a major Baptist church manual to claim in 1963 that "Few people know the significance of the covenant idea in the history of their churches, and little attempt is made to impress upon them the significance of their words when they read this document together."[11]

A church covenant has close ties with Christian ethics. In the early 1960s, a major Baptist theologian claimed that "the absence in some churches of any serious doctrinal or ethical standards for membership has cheapened the meaning of church membership."[12] It is precisely at the point of highlighting "ethical standards of membership" that a church covenant can assume importance. A covenant does not create ethical standards and obligations; it condenses and reflects biblical ethics.

Ties between covenants and ethics demand new exploration in view of a list of recent trends in religion compiled by the Discipleship Training Department of the Sunday School Board. "The No. 1 trend of religion in America," the report stated, "is the spiritual hunger for depth and meaning in the lives of Christians. But at the same time, the level of ethics is declining. Little difference is found in the ethical views and behaviors of those who go to church and those who don't."[13]

Faithful attention to the contents of a carefully formulated, biblically based covenant can deepen the quality of a church's fellowship, sharpen a church's awareness of vital moral and spiritual commitments, clarify biblical standards for Christian growth, and create and maintain a disciplined church membership. As one pastor has affirmed, to worship God and study the Bible regularly, to serve Christ consistently, to give self and money sacrificially, to live morally under the lordship of Christ, and to witness compassionately are all disciplines which "should be viewed as covenants between the Christian, Christ, and fellow Christians."[14] Ideally, these kinds of disciplines form the heart and substance of a church covenant.

Few documents demonstrate more incisively the issues at stake in this book than the 1846 circular letter of the Meredith Baptist Association in New Hampshire. Focusing on "Individual Responsibility of Church Members," this timely piece of associational advice regarding the seriousness of making and keeping covenantal vows serves as a launching pad for the remainder of this volume:

> The religion of Jesus Christ is consistent in all its parts. There is no disagreement between the principles it inculcates and the practice it requires. Primitive saints first gave themselves to the Lord, and then unto one another by the will of God. Responsibility was shared alike. So, brethren, when you gave yourselves to the Lord it was in a covenant never to be broken. Such was your sense of responsibility, that, without any reserve, you consecrated your all to God—your time, your talents, your property, your intellectual powers, and all your moral influence. The vows you then took upon you, you assumed deliberately, freely and cheerfully, while a cloud of witnesses compassed you about. The world, saints, angels, God, gazed on you, while you dedicated yourselves, to Christ and the church.
>
> Brethren, can you ever forget those solemn vows? When you joined

yourselves unto the Lord, and unto his people by the will of God, did
you divide your responsibilities among those with whom you connected
yourselves in church fellowship, so as, in fact, to diminish your previous personal obligation? Far otherwise; the moment you crossed the
threshold of the church your responsibilities were greatly increased;
they sprung out of your new relation; they were imposed by your new
privileges. From that memorable hour you have been bound to make
the glory of God and the salvation of the world the constant aim and
effort of your life, according to your opportunities and the measures of
your moral capacities; and this obligation will ever remain unalterably
the same; it will be recognized and acted on in the decisions of the Last
Day.[15]

Two lengthy histories of church covenants have previously appeared.
In 1904 the American Baptist Publication Society published Champlin
Burrage's *The Church Covenant Idea: Its Origin and Its Development.* By
including and assessing numerous covenants, this writing helpfully dem-
onstrated covenantal use among such groups as the Continental Anabaptists of the 1500s the Scotch Reformers of the 1500s and 1600s, the
English Separatists and Independents of the 1500s and 1600s, and the
Congregationalists in England and America in the 1600s and 1700s. The
work also discussed and printed many English and American Baptist
covenants of the 1600s and 1700s.

In 1973 the author completed a doctoral dissertation (unpublished)
entitled "The Origin, Development, and Use of Church Covenants in
Baptist History" (The Southern Baptist Theological Seminary, Louisville, Kentucky). This writing pinpointed antecedents for the Baptist use
of covenants, described covenantal patterns among Baptists in England
in the 1600s and in America in the 1600s-1900s, and included the texts of
twenty-eight covenants of Baptists in America dated from 1663 to 1971.

Recognizing an important debt to both of these writings, I believe a
new work on Baptist church covenants is needed and can provide the
most comprehensive treatment yet, especially among Baptists in the
United States, Canada, and selected other countries in the 1800s and
1900s. A new treatment can blend into a single account the broader scope
of covenanting in the Baptist experience. And it can print in one place the
largest and most internationally representative collection of such covenants ever published. Any contribution which this book can make to a
resurgence of attention to and implementation of the basic Baptist ideal
of a regenerate church membership will make the project worthwhile.

William L. Lumpkin's *Baptist Confessions of Faith* (Judson Press, 1959; revised 1969) provided an excellent collection and analysis of confessions used by Baptists in England, the United States, and selected other countries, thus highlighting the significance of doctrinal convictions to Baptist religious experience. Perhaps a comparable treatment of Baptist church covenants can sharpen Baptist focus on the biblical meaning of regenerate church membership, on biblical requirements for Christian conduct, and on the application of biblical ethics to all phases of Christian discipleship. Perhaps a renewed integration of confessions and covenants in church life can help Baptists gain a more balanced perspective between faith and practice. At times in the Baptist story, excessive attention to orthodoxy has seemingly fed controversy and detracted from the biblical authority for Christian attitudes and behavior. Covenantal renewal can help correct this kind of faulty Baptist vision and reestablish meaningful confessional and covenantal relationships.

Chapters 2—5 contain many cross-references to the texts of seventy-nine covenants printed in chapter 6. Thirteen of these covenants relate to Baptists in England and Wales, forty-nine to Baptists in the United States, eight to Baptists in Canada, and nine to Baptists in other countries (Jamaica, France, China, Australia, Republic of Cameroon, New Zealand, South Africa, Sweden, and Russia). Relating historical development and interpretation to primary-source documents will hopefully enhance the usefulness of the book. Texts of covenants in chapter 6 reflect original spelling and punctuation with the single exception that "ye" has been changed to "the." Additional paragraph breaks have been added to some covenants to aid readability. The source of each covenant appears at the end of its text, along with required permission statements and occasional explanatory comments.

Acknowledgments

Special appreciation goes to the trustees and executive director (Lynn E. May, Jr.) of the Historical Commission of the Southern Baptist Convention for their support of my interest in church covenants during my years of employment with the agency. That support began prior to my employment when the agency presented to me in 1972 the Davis C. Woolley Memorial Award for the Study of Church Covenants and culminates in the publication of this book.

The author is indebted to many for assistance with ideas and/or research, but the following people offered special help: Pat Brown (librarian), Bill Sumners (archivist), and Mary Jo Driskill (microfilm technician) of the Southern Baptist Historical Library and Archives in Nashville, Tennessee; John Binder, executive director of the North American Baptist Conference in Oakbrook Terrace, Illinois; Beverly Carlson, administrator/archivist of the American Baptist Historical Society in Valley Forge, Pennsylvania; Judith Colwell, librarian of the Canadian Baptist Archives at McMaster Divinity College in Hamilton, Ontario, Canada; William Gillespie, Baptist minister, Guelph, Ontario, Canada; G. David Guston, archivist of the Baptist General Conference at Bethel Theological Seminary in St. Paul, Minnesota; Ivah T. Heneise, professor in the Department of Church History at the Baptist Theological Seminary of Haiti in Limbe, Haiti; D. Hugh Matthews, tutor at South Wales Baptist College in Cardiff, South Glamorgan, Wales; Don A. Sanford, historian of the Seventh Day Baptists of USA and Canada in Janesville, Wisconsin; Allen Schmidt, executive director-treasurer of the Canadian Convention of Southern Baptists in Cochrane, Alberta, Canada; Carl W. Tiller, interim director of the American Baptist-Samuel Colgate Library of the American Baptist Historical Society in Rochester, New York; and Jarold K. Zeman, professor of church history at Acadia Divinity College in Wolfville, Nova Scotia, Canada.

Permission is gratefully acknowledged to the Historical Commission of the Southern Baptist Convention for the use of parts of three writings by the author: two articles which first appeared in *Baptist History and Heritage* ("Southern Baptists and Church Covenants," January 1974; "Prominent Church Covenants of Maritime Baptists, 1778-1878," April 1980); and the pamphlet *Responsible Church Membership* which first appeared in the "Foundations of Baptist Heritage" series (January 1989).

Certain material is adapted from chapters 1 and 2 of the 1978 Judson Press book by the author entitled *A Community of Believers: Making Church Membership More Meaningful.* Used by permission of Judson Press.

Permission is further gratefully acknowledged to the Baptist Historical Society (4, Southampton Row, London, England WC1B 4AB) for the privilege of reprinting four church covenants which originally appeared in *The Baptist Quarterly* (January 1926, pp. 41-44; January 1934, pp. 24-26; January 1935, pp. 228-30, 234).

Unless otherwise noted, all biblical quotations used in this volume are from the *Revised Standard Version.*

This book is a modest contribution toward understanding an important dimension of the Baptist pilgrimage. I do not consider this writing the final word on church covenants. The unfolding story of covenants will always be in transition and in need of constant revision and retelling. Hopefully, this work will stimulate more research into the covenantal traditions of Baptists around the world. I welcome new information, other viewpoints, and correction from any reader.

Charles W. Deweese

1
Covenantal Backgrounds

Covenant-making characterized the Judeo-Christian heritage long before Baptists broke into history in the early 1600s. The Bible, the Dead Sea Scrolls, and the records of church history up to the Reformation provide remarkable illustrations of how God's people committed themselves to Him through bold covenantal pledges. Making vows to God served as long-range antecedents for the Baptist use of covenants. More immediate precedents emerged in the life of the Continental Anabaptists and the English Separatists. The actual impact of these latter two traditions upon the early English Baptist use of covenants will be assessed in chapter 2. Since one can best understand Baptist church covenants in the light of major background influences, chapter 1 describes important covenantal contexts to which Baptists are indebted.

The Bible and the Dead Sea Scrolls

Covenantal concepts permeate the Old Testament. Some covenants occur between people. Military, political, marital, social, and certain religious covenants fit into this category. Other covenants are initiated and worded by God. But the grouping which represents the most precise antecedents for Baptist church covenants includes those covenantal statements originated by God's people as responses to His covenantal initiative.

Several examples of this last form of covenant are instructive. First, after Moses read the book of the covenant in the hearing of the Israelites, they vowed, "All that the Lord has spoken we will do, and we will be obedient" (Ex. 24:7). Second, the priest Jehoiada "made a covenant between the Lord and the king and people, that they should be the Lord's people" (2 Kings 11:17). Third, Josiah covenanted "to walk after the

Lord and to keep his commandments and his testimonies and his statutes, with all his heart and all his soul, to perform the words of this covenant that were written in this book; and all the people joined in the covenant" (2 Kings 23:3). Fourth, King Asa and his followers "entered into a covenant to seek the Lord" (2 Chron. 15:12). Fifth, the Israelites under the leadership of Ezra covenanted with God and each other to abandon the foreign women whom they had married and the children of these mixed marriages (Ezra 10:2-5). Last, the people under the governorship of Nehemiah made a "firm covenant," wrote it, and had it sealed by their princes, Levites, and priests (Neh. 9:38). They pledged to follow the law given to Moses by God and "to observe and do all the commandments of the Lord our Lord and his ordinances and his statutes" (Neh. 10:29). They specified the obligations to which they devoted themselves, most of which dealt with supporting God's house (vv. 30-39).

Old Testament covenantal practices included warnings and discipline. To illustrate, God periodically warned the Israelites not to covenant with non-Israelites (Ex. 23:32; 34:12; Deut. 7:2; Judg. 2:2). Further, God promised to administer discipline when His people broke their covenantal vows with Him (Lev. 26:14-39; Deut. 17:2-7; 29:25-28; 31:16-18; Josh. 7:10-15; 23:16; Judg. 2:20-23).

Validating covenants was basic to Old Testament religion. Such ratification or sealing of covenants included the use of circumcision (Gen. 17:9-14, 24), the sharing of gifts (Gen. 21:27; 1 Sam. 18:3-4), the employment of an oath or an oath and a curse (Gen. 21:31; Josh. 9:15; Neh. 10:29), the eating of a meal (Gen. 26:30; 31:46, 54; Ex. 24:11), the erection of pillars of stone (Gen. 28:22; 31:45, 51-52; Josh. 24:26), the preserving of a collection of laws (Ex. 24:4), the use of blood from sacrificed animals (Ex. 24:8), the use of salt (Lev. 2:13; Num. 18:19; 2 Chron. 13:5), the writing and signing of covenants (Neh. 9:38), and the shaking of hands (Ezek. 17:18).

The Dead Sea Scrolls are manuscripts found west of the Dead Sea in 1947 and afterwards. The most important are the Qumran texts discovered in several caves. The Qumran community, probably a branch of the Essenes, arose among Jews whose covenant loyalty remained unblemished during the persecution of Antiochus Epiphanes (175-163 B.C.). The scrolls show that covenant ideas remained important in Jewish theology during the interbiblical period.

The covenant idea is vital to the Qumran writings. The writings use the word *covenant* five times more often than the New Testament.[1] Further, the word appears at least thirty-five times in the *Zadokite Document,* more frequently than in any Old Testament book.[2]

The covenant concept expressed itself in a special way in the context of initiation into the Qumran community. The *Manual of Discipline* has preserved two accounts of a ceremony of initiation. The first shows that persons joining the community covenanted to follow the commandments of God.[3] In addressing "the obligation of holiness," the second states that "Everyone who is admitted to the formal organization of the community is to enter into a covenant in the presence of all fellow-volunteers in the cause and to commit himself by a binding oath to abide with all his heart and soul by the commandments of the law of Moses . . . ."[4]

Covenanters at Qumran received discipline when they failed to keep their pledges or violated the rules of the community. The most stringent discipline was exclusion, which resulted when a member of the community was found guilty of cursing God, complaining against the community, or lapsing after being in the community at least ten years.[5]

The *Zadokite Document* contains a section on the obligations of the covenant. After admonishing persons entering the covenant to live according to the injunctions of the law of God, the document lists sixteen injunctions, such as staying away from disreputable men, refraining from stealing, loving one's neighbor as oneself, and avoiding whoredom. God's covenant became effective for persons who lived these rules of holiness without failure. Persons pledging themselves to the injunctions of the law were not to depart from them even at the price of death. Also, the document mandates that parents within the covenant community should impose the oath of the covenant upon their sons when the sons reach the proper age.[6]

New Testament teachings on the idea of covenant stress that the new covenant described by Jeremiah (Jer. 31:31-34) has found fulfillment in Christ (Heb. 8:8-12; 10:16-17), who is "the mediator of a new covenant" (Heb. 9:15). The new covenant of Christ provides for the complete remission of sins (Rom. 11:27) and is confirmed in the blood of Christ (Matt. 26:28; Mark 14:24; Luke 22:20 in some manuscripts; 1 Cor. 11:25).

New Testament passages in which Christians make specific and explicit covenants with other Christians and with God concerning their obligations and conduct are limited. This form of covenant tends to be indirect, but a few possible antecedents for Baptist church covenants may be suggested. For one thing, church discipline in the New Testament era (e.g., Matt. 18:15-17) may have presupposed a covenantal standard which had been broken. And Paul's description of the church as the bride of Christ (Eph. 5:23) has obvious covenantal implications. Paul even described himself and other Christians as "ministers of a new covenant" (2 Cor. 3:6).

Church membership in New Testament times certainly included entry into a covenantal relationship with God and fellow believers. New Testament baptism may have involved a verbal covenant that the one being baptized made with the Christian community and with Christ. The person being baptized may have been expected to vow publicly to "walk in newness of life" (Rom. 6:4), to "put on Christ" (Gal. 3:27), and to make "the good confession in the presence of many witnesses" (1 Tim. 6:12). And what about the possible covenantal value of 1 Peter 3:21: "Baptism . . . now saves you . . . as an appeal to God for a clear conscience"? Without question, the baptism of Jesus gave to water baptism the new meaning of "a personal commitment to the will of God."[7]

New Testament accounts of the Lord's Supper provide some of the most significant biblical sources for understanding Baptist church covenants. The covenantal theme in the Mark-Matthew account of this event (Mark 14:24; Matt. 26:28) had the covenantal theology of the Torah as its basis. Just as the use of sacrificial blood served to ratify the mutual pledges of the old covenant (Ex. 24:8), and just as a joint meal served to complete this ratification (Ex. 24:11), the sacrificial motif in the Lord's Supper related to establishing and confirming relationships in the new covenant. God covenanted through Christ, and His people reciprocated. "The Lord's Supper is, before all, a symbol of communion, a brotherly covenant among table companions."[8]

An excellent description of the New Testament church as a community bound in covenant appeared in a letter sent from Pliny the Younger to Emperor Trajan about A.D. 112. Pliny described the Lord's Supper as an oath. In speaking of the Christians at Bithynia, he wrote: ". . . They met on a stated day before it was light, and addressed a form of prayer to Christ . . . binding themselves by a solemn oath . . . never to commit any fraud, theft, or adultery, never to falsify their word, nor deny a trust . . . ."[9]

The Early Church and the Middle Ages

The theology of baptism in the age of the church fathers centered on sharing in Christ's victory over Satan and his demonic hosts through the assistance of the Holy Spirit.[10] *"From man's side,* it [baptism] entails a vow, the meaning of the early Latin word *sacramentum."*[11] In baptism a person pledged to take seriously his personal life and to use it toward the accomplishment of God's ultimate purpose.

Several church orders, or manuals, of the early Christian centuries show that covenanting was a major part of baptism. During baptism the candidate first faced west and verbally renounced Satan and all he represented. The candidate then faced east and verbally pledged himself to God.[12] The model baptismal vow, according to one manual, was "I associate myself to Christ."[13]

The church fathers, especially those of the third through the fifth centuries, viewed baptism as a covenant with God. Gregory Nazianzen claimed that "the virtue of Baptism is to be understood as a covenant with God for a second life and a purer conversation."[14] John Chrysostom repeatedly referred to baptism as a "contract" with Christ. In describing the baptismal candidate's rejection of Satan's domination and his acknowledgment of Christ's sovereignty, Chrysostom said, "This was the signature, this the agreement, this the contract."[15]

Many church fathers viewed the Eucharist (Lord's Supper) as a renewal of the covenant first made in baptism. Soon after baptism a Christian participated in the Eucharist, which symbolized his identification with the covenant of God.[16] Cyprian interpreted the Eucharist as a pledge which fortified a Christian against Satan and his hosts.[17] As one church manual admonished, the covenantal character of the Eucharist included obligations regarding conduct: "Let those who take the Offering be exhorted by the priests to be careful to do good works, to love strangers, to labour in fasting, and in every good work to engage in servitude."[18]

During the Middle Ages monastic orders injected covenantal concepts into their common life. The Rule of St. Benedict, written in the sixth century, had superseded all other rules by the ninth century. It required that a monk promise to spend his entire life in his monastic community and to obey anything commanded of him. The monk wrote this promise with his own hand and signed it as witnesses looked on. Model Benedictine covenants included keeping "the vows of obedience, chastity, and poverty" and adhering to "steadfastness . . . , conversion of life, and perfect obedience."[19] The Rule of Saint Francis, which Pope Honorius III approved in 1223, stated that a candidate could become a monk after his year of probation was over only by "promising always to observe this way of life and Rule."[20]

Another illustration of a covenantal pledge exists in a sermon preached by Boniface, a Catholic missionary to Germany in the eighth century. Boniface reminded his listeners to consider the renunciation of Satan which they had made during their baptism, and then he warned them "to remember what ye promised unto God Almighty." He claimed that they had pledged to "believe in God," "love the Lord," "observe the Lord's Day," "give alms," "visit the sick," "give tithes to the Church," and "receive the Eucharist."[21]

The Continental Anabaptists

Continental Anabaptist communities comprised the radical wing of the Protestant Reformation. Anabaptists generally viewed baptism as the primary means of entering into a concrete covenant with God. They tended to verbalize implicit and informal church covenant-promises, which they used mainly in the baptismal setting. The favorite text of the Anabaptists in relating baptism to the covenant idea was 1 Peter 3:21. Anabaptists viewed the covenant undertaken at baptism to be the supreme form of religious voluntarism other than martyrdom. This baptismal covenant was "the pledge of a complete commitment to obey Christ."[22] Baptism was thought to be the symbol of the covenant, and the church was often designated a brotherhood of "covenanters."

In early 1525 a group of Swiss Brethren near Zurich, under the leadership of Conrad Grebel, adopted believer's baptism and founded Anabaptism. An eyewitness, probably George Blaurock, identified these first Anabaptists as "those who had properly given themselves to God, and with a good understanding had made covenant of a good conscience with God."[23] The 1527 "Schleitheim Confession" stated the views of the Swiss Brethren. Its fourth article reflected a covenantal interest. Persons reciting this article agreed to separate from the wickedness of the world and to become, or remain, obedient in faith.[24]

Balthasar Hubmaier, an influential German Anabaptist, expressed a strong concern for the covenant idea in his writings, especially in the contexts of baptism and the Lord's Supper. In 1527 he prepared a baptismal liturgy. As part of this liturgy the baptismal candidate responded, "I will," after each of three questions asked him by the administrator relating to renunciation of the devil, imitation of Christ in life and conversation, and the willingness to submit to church discipline, if ever needed. These answers constituted a covenant made just prior to baptism.[25]

Also in 1527 Hubmaier wrote a liturgy for the Lord's Supper. One section of the liturgy was a love-vow, or covenant. Here again were practical questions dealing with Christian obligations and conduct to which the participants responded, "I will." This covenanting immediately preceded the blessing and sharing of the bread and cup.[26] Besides being a grateful remembrance of the deeds of Christ in behalf of mankind, the Lord's Supper was also for Hubmaier "a love feast through which one pledges his willingness to serve Christ in works of compassion and mercy to other men."[27]

Pilgrim Marpeck, an important South German Anabaptist, viewed baptism as an affirmation of one's personal covenant with God to undertake discipleship and live obediently to God.[28] In 1530 the controversial Melchior Hofmann, who was largely responsible for introducing the covenant idea into the Low Countries, compared the baptismal covenant to that covenant which "takes place when a bride with complete, voluntary, and loving surrender and with a truly free, well-considered betrothal, yields herself in abandon and presents herself as a freewill offering to her lord and bridegroom."[29]

Menno Simons and Dietrich Philips were significant forces in the rise of Dutch Anabaptism. The covenantal relationship was a primary theme of Simons' writings. He believed that through the covenant of baptism a person entered a disciplined fellowship, promised to live in harmony with it, and practiced discipleship.[30] Philips' 1564 *Enchiridion* was a major systematic treatment of Anabaptist theology. He stressed the importance of the baptismal covenant and even beckoned his readers to remember "how fervent you were in Spirit when you entered into covenant relation with God, when you united with the Lord and his church, and there made a promise to the Most High God ... that you would serve the Lord in his church ... and walk uprightly."[31]

By way of summary, one writer has claimed that "The Anabaptist view of the church covenant enforced vigorous internal discipline, in imitation of Christ, including baptism, the Lord's Supper, a ban against association with unbelievers, non-resistance, non-swearing, cross-bearing in martyrdom, and a vocation for each member in carrying out the Great Commission."[32]

The English Separatists

The English Separatists of the late 1500s comprised the branch of Elizabethan Puritanism which sought reformation by separating from the Church of England. One of their dominant traits was an emphasis on gathered or covenanted congregations. Whereas Anabaptists generally employed informal covenants in baptismal settings, the English Separatists tended to sign their names to explicit and formal church covenant-promises, which became the basis for constituting new congregations. But even they often described baptism as the seal of the covenant. Since one writer has posited that "the church covenant came to Baptists as part of their English Separatist heritage,"[33] a look at their patterns of covenanting may be especially useful.

Robert Browne, the leading figure in the English Separatist tradition in the early 1580s, and his followers formally organized a Separatist congregation on the basis of a covenant in Norwich about 1581. He viewed the church as a company of believers who have covenanted with God, and he believed that baptism was the proper seal of a church covenant.[34]

In the late 1580s and early 1590s, Henry Barrow and others replaced Browne as the leaders of the English Separatists. In 1587, Barrow wrote that he and his followers were seeking fellowship with God's obedient servants in order "together with them to enter covenant with the Lord."[35] Barrow believed that God's covenant belonged only to the faithful, that the seals of the covenant were baptism and the Lord's Supper, and that the only person who could enter this covenantal relationship was the person who voluntarily professed his faith and vowed his obedience to God.[36]

The Barrowist congregation in London elected Francis Johnson as its pastor in 1592. Members of the church before and after this date used a church covenant-promise. The nature of the covenant expressed itself in the reports of examinations of certain members made by English authorities in early 1593. For example, the report of the examination of Abraham Pulbery stated: "Item hee saieth that hee hath made a promise to the Lord in the presence of his congregacion when hee entred thereunto that hee would walke with them as they would walke with the Lord."[37]

Three more illustrations of covenantal concern among the English Separatists need brief mention. First, Francis Johnson used a covenant in his church at Middelburg in the Netherlands in 1591. The members said,

"Wee doe willinglie ioyne together to live as the *Church* of *Christe,* watchinge one over another" and that "wee doe promisse henceforthe to keepe what soever *Christe* our Lorde hath commaunded vs."[38]

Second, the 1596 Separatist confession of faith, "A True Confession," asserted that Separatists "are vvillingly to ioyne together in christian communion and orderly couenant, and by confession of Faith and obedience of Christ, to unite themselues into peculiar Congregations."[39]

Last, the Separatist congregation at Gainsborough constituted itself in 1606 on the basis of a covenant. John Smyth, soon to become the first Baptist pastor, was a prominent member. Writing at a later date, William Bradford reflected on this covenanting experience: ". . . As the Lord's free people [the members] joined themselves together by covenant as a church, in the fellowship of the gospel to walk in all His ways, made known, or to be made known to them, according to their best endeavours whatever it should cost them, the Lord assisting them."[40]

Conclusion

Though Baptists claim that the Bible is the sole written authority for their faith and practice, denominational integrity requires acknowledging that a variety of Christian traditions have shaped the Baptist movement throughout its history. The evolving story of Baptist church covenants clearly illustrates this point. While covenantal traditions of the church fathers and the Middle Ages may have exerted only marginal, if any, influence on Baptists, one at least has to admit a Baptist relationship with and appreciation for the covenantal tendencies of diverse Christian groups since the first century.

Pinpointing precise historical evidence to demonstrate Anabaptist influence on early Baptist covenants is difficult. But the fact is that Anabaptists and Baptists share a common ancestry in the Believers' Church with its stress on a regenerate church membership, including the use of covenants. Direct English Separatist influences on Baptist covenantal patterns are much easier to document. Chapter 2 identifies the impact which Anabaptists and English Separatists may have made on English Baptist covenantal developments.

2
Covenantal Patterns of Early British Baptists

Formative views, uses, and values of Baptist church covenants originated among the English Baptists of the 1600s. Both the General (Arminian) Baptists, who arose prior to 1610, and the Particular (Calvinistic) Baptists, who appeared in the 1630s, used covenants. However, covenantal usage was not a uniform practice of churches in either group. Early English and Welsh Baptists influenced the covenantal patterns of later British Baptists (and of Baptists in America). Thus, a look at the formative covenantal traditions of British Baptists can be helpful.

Baptists also began to write their first confessions of faith in England in the 1600s. These noncreedal doctrinal statements differed from church covenants in that the latter were concerned mainly with conduct. Whereas confessions were designed to elicit a voluntary commitment to particular ways of believing, covenants were intended to produce a voluntary commitment to particular ways of practicing one's faith. The importance of the covenant adopted by John Smyth's Separatist congregation at Gainsborough, England, in 1606 rested largely on the fact that it "was not doctrinal but practical [and] that it had an immediate bearing upon life."[1] The same could be said for early Baptist covenants.

Baptist Attitudes Toward Covenants

General and Particular Baptist leaders held various views of church covenants. The earliest General Baptist leaders included John Smyth, who led the first Baptist church (formed in Amsterdam in 1608/09); Thomas Helwys, who helped found the first Baptist church in England in 1611/12; and John Murton, who succeeded Helwys as pastor.

In 1607, while a Separatist, Smyth clearly favored the use of covenants, especially in constituting new congregations. He wrote that "a vis-

ible communion of Saincts is of two, three, or mo[r]e Saincts joyned together by covenant with God & themselves," and that "the outward part
of the true forme of the true visible church is a vowe, promise, oath, or
covenant betwixt God and the Saints."[2] But Smyth's thinking changed in
Amsterdam. He stated in 1609 that "the true forme of the Church is a
covenant betwixt God & the Faithful made in baptisme" and that "the
covenant is this: I wilbe their Father . . . & wee shalbe his sonnes calling
him Father by the Spirit, wherby we are sealed."[3] As a Baptist, Smyth
placed the church covenant idea in the context of baptism. In Separatism
the covenant-promise had been indebted largely to the Old Testament,
but Smyth's concept of a baptismal covenant entrenched it within a New
Testament setting. (Thomas Grantham, who was perhaps the most gifted
writer of the early General Baptists, shared Smyth's view when in 1671
he defended the concept of a baptismal covenant.)[4]

Helwys and Murton opposed formal church covenants and did not
give believer's baptism the explicit covenantal significance that Smyth
had. One probable reason was their eagerness to distinguish the early
General Baptists from the Separatists, who made extensive use of covenants. Their views of the church also played a role. Both believed that the
proper form of a church resulted from baptism, not from a covenant.
Helwys and others claimed in 1611 that "the church of CHRIST is a
compainy off faithful people . . . separated fro[m] the world by the word
& Spirit off God . . . being knit unto the LORD, & one unto another, by
Baptisme."[5] And Murton asked in 1620, ". . . Was ever Church of the
New Testament made by a covenant without baptisme? There is not the
least showe for it."[6] Helwys and Murton did give baptism an implied
covenantal value.

Adam Taylor, noted historian of English General Baptists, claimed
that the normal means of organizing new churches among later General
Baptists was that they "generally subscribed their names to a mutual
covenant, containing a few rules by which they proposed to conduct
themselves."[7] But later General Baptists may have used covenants less
frequently than Taylor implied.[8] They clearly used covenants less often
than Particular Baptists in forming new congregations, probably because
of the attitudes and influence of leaders like Smyth, Helwys, and Murton.
But covenants did become a vital part of many of their churches, possibly
because of the influence of the Particular Baptists.

While it is difficult to produce historical evidence to show precise Anabaptist influence on early Baptist covenants, one must remember that the

Anabaptists tended to place the covenant concept in the context of baptism. John Smyth adopted this view but not until he arrived in Amsterdam, a city with numerous Anabaptist connections. Contacts with the
Mennonites in that city may well have affected Smyth's view of church
covenants. But it seems unlikely that specific Anabaptist covenants had
long-range impact on those of early English Baptists since these Baptists,
including the General Baptists, later tended to use explicit and formal
(and even signed) church covenant-promises in the act of constituting
new churches (after the pattern of the English Separatists), rather than
implicit and informal pledges confined primarily to baptism. Still, the
common participation of Anabaptists and Baptists in the Believers'
Church, which has stressed covenants across the centuries, suggests a
covenant-making linkage between the two religious traditions.

Particular Baptists apparently used church covenants more widely
than the General Baptists, but various opinions about the validity of
church covenants existed even among early Particular Baptist leaders.
For example, several writings of John Spilsbury, Hanserd Knollys, and
Thomas Collier, all of which appeared between 1643 and 1645, reflected
diverse viewpoints.

John Spilsbury, who became pastor of the first Particular Baptist
church in the 1630s, strongly approved church covenants and gave five
reasons why he believed a covenant, and not baptism, was the true form
of a church. First, a covenant is the means by which God and humankind
welcome and own each other. Second, since the covenant was the right
form of a church before the ordinances were introduced, it is still the
proper form. Third, a covenant is the relationship that gives being to a
church and maintains that being. Fourth, a covenant is that which makes
Christians members of a church and makes a church itself. Fifth, since
the church is the greatest ordinance, it cannot be constituted by any lesser ordinance, but only by God's covenant. Spilsbury further affirmed
that "baptism is one branch of the covenant," that baptism should suc-
ceed the use of a covenant, and that "a people are a church by covenant,
unto which ordinances are annexed, to confirme and establish the
same."[9]

On the other hand, Hanserd Knollys, an important London pastor,
opposed the use of church covenants. He noted that in some London
Baptist churches, the only conditions which some preachers were pro-
pounding as essential for admission into their churches were "Faith, Repentance, and Baptisme; and none other." Further, these churches did

not urge or make "any particular covenant with Members upon admittance." Finally, Knollys identified the following biblical passages as evidence that the use of church covenants was not a New Testament practice: Acts 8:12, 35-39; 16:30-33; 18:8.[10] Knollys's view was similar to that of the General Baptist leaders Thomas Helwys and John Murton.

Thomas Collier, an evangelist and church planter in the west of England, took a stance in between the extreme views of Spilsbury and Knollys. He stressed the necessity of faith, repentance, and baptism in the process of joining a church but also wrote much about the "compacting" of believers. Basing his comments on 1 Timothy 3:15, he compared a church to a house. Just as a house is not a house until its parts are fitted together, neither is a church a church until "it is brought into forme, and compact together." Then, following 1 Corinthians 12, he compared the church to a body and proceeded with the same logic.[11] Collier evidently believed in the covenant concept, even if only in a theoretical or informal manner. His position paralleled that of the General Baptist leader John Smyth.

Later in the 1600s, Benjamin Keach, the famous and influential Particular Baptist pastor of the Horsleydown Church in Southwark, England, broadened the application of church covenants by giving equal stress to their value in baptism, in forming new churches, and in admitting new members. Keach wrote in 1697 of persons seeking church membership that "when admitted members, before the church they must solemnly enter into a covenant, to walk in the fellowship of that particular congregation, and submit themselves to the care and discipline thereof."[12] Elias Keach, Benjamin's son who served as pastor of the Tallow Chandler's Hall Church in London, adopted this same attitude toward covenants. The Keach covenant (jointly printed by Benjamin and Elias in separate publications in 1697) became widespread in England and later became the most extensively used covenant among Baptists in the Middle Colonies of America both because Elias had helped form several churches there and because of the popularity there of his writing, *The Glory and Ornament of a True Gospel-Constituted Church* (1697), which contained a copy of the covenant.

Even the two major confessions of faith of the early English Particular Baptists reflected an implicit covenantal concern. The London Confession of 1644 referred to the church as being composed of those baptized believers who are "joyned to the Lord, and each other, by mutuall agreement." And the Second London Confession of 1677 designated as church members thoses persons who "do willingly consent to walk together according to the appointment of Christ, giving up themselves, to the Lord & one to another."[13]

In all likelihood, English Separatist, Independent, and Congregationalist traditions influenced the predominant Particular Baptist approach to church covenants, which included written and signed covenants used in forming new churches, admitting new members, and applying church discipline. The following illustrations show how these influences worked.

First, the seven London Baptist churches which drew up the famous 1644 confession were familiar with the 1596 Separatist confession titled "A True Confession," which clearly recommended the use of a formal covenant. The Baptists even used this confession as a model for their own. Second, Independent views on the covenant may have affected John Spilsbury's attitude toward covenantal vows. Henry Jacob's Independent congregation was organized in 1616 on the basis of a covenant. This covenant was renewed in 1630 when John Lathrop was pastor and even later under the leadership of Henry Jessey. Since the first Particular Baptist church, with Spilsbury as pastor, grew out of this covenant-oriented Independent congregation in the 1630s, Spilsbury possibly adopted his strong stress on the church covenant from these Independent antecedents. Third, throughout the 1600s, Baptists continued to be influenced by the Congregationalists, who used church covenants extensively. For example, a Congregational church in Norwich adopted a covenant in 1643. St. Mary's Baptist Church arose out of this congregation and adopted a covenant in the late 1680s. The obvious similarities in the wording of these two covenants reveal an impact of the former upon the latter.[14]

Some Baptist churches in Wales in the 1600s approved the church covenant concept, and Baptists with a Welsh ancestry influenced the development of covenants in Baptist life in New England and the Middle Colonies of America. Early Baptists in Wales apparently tended neither to write nor sign formal covenants. Covenanting seemed to be no more than a simple verbal agreement to come together as a church.[15] In the 1700s, however, they clearly wrote covenants.

To sum up, in seventeenth-century England Congregationalists used church covenants more extensively than the Baptists, and the Particular Baptists used them more than the General Baptists. English Separatist, Independent, and Congregationalist influence upon the emergence of the Baptist church covenant idea was probably wider than that of the Anabaptists. Early English Baptists did not agree on the propriety of using covenants. Some opposed covenants because they feared too close a connection between them and the covenantal theology of the Church of England which supported infant baptism. They viewed believer's baptism as that which constituted a church, not a covenant. Others, however, strongly favored church covenants, either explicit and written or implicit and verbal. Baptists often gave covenants a baptismal significance and frequently used them in forming new churches, admitting new members, engaging in covenantal renewal, and disciplining wayward members.

Nature, Content, Uses, and Values of Covenants

Many English Baptist covenants of the 1600s still exist. The oldest surviving covenant is probably that subscribed to in 1640 by the Broadmead Church in Bristol (see covenant 1 in ch. 6). Examples of others include those of the churches in Hexham, 1652;[16] Leominster, 1656 (covenant 2); Longworth, 1656;[17] Bromsgrove, 1672;[18] Amersham, 1675 (covenant 3); and Hitchin, 1681 (covenant 4). Other representative covenants include those of the Pinners Hall Seventh Day Baptist Church in London, 1686 (covenant 5); the church in Norwich, later to be called St. Mary's (date of covenant not known but probably composed before 1689);[19] the Horsleydown and Tallow Chandler's Hall Churches pastored, respectively, by Benjamin and Elias Keach (covenant 6); the Great Ellingham Church in Norfolk, 1699 (covenant 7); and the College Street Church in Northampton (the covenant was initially used in constituting a group of "Protestant Dissenters" in 1697, but it was retained by the Baptist congregation which arose from this group in 1700).[20]

Although not described as a covenant, the twenty-one duties listed in Article 25 of the 1656 Somerset Confession of Faith, principally written by Thomas Collier and adopted by the Western (or Somerset) Association, comprised what could possibly be called an associational covenant. Many of the duties in this article often appeared in covenants written and adopted by individual churches. One of the major emphases of the Somerset statement focused on the duty of a church to accept into membership only persons who had given evidence of having been regenerated. A church was to "receive none but such as do make forth evident demonstration of the new birth, and the work of faith with power."[21] A major function of most early church covenants was to support this biblical concept by highlighting it again and again among Baptists. The Somerset statement illustrated the interrelationship between confessions and covenants, beliefs and practices, doctrine and conduct that would mark developments in Baptist life.

Although there are references to covenants in Baptist churchbooks in Wales in the 1600s, "no covenants from the early period of Welsh Baptist history remain."[22] In 1668 the records of the Rhydwilym Church stated: "It being the first day of the week, the selfe same day we enterred into Covenant with the Lord and with one another Haueing submitted to baptism & laying on of hands."[23] This church was significant to covenantal developments among early American Baptists because it became the mother congregation of the Welsh Tract Church in Delaware in 1701, which was primarily responsible for introducing church covenants into the Middle Colonies. Even earlier, a group of Welsh Baptists had settled in Massachusetts and formed the Swansea Church in Rehoboth in 1663. The covenant used by that church is the oldest extant covenant of Baptists in America (covenant 14).

Twelve extant covenants used by English Baptists between 1640 and 1700 showed variations in length. Four written before 1672 consisted of only one sentence each, so simplicity characterized covenant construction in the formative years of Baptist life. Most of the covenants prepared between 1672 and 1700 were much longer and more complex, exhibiting multiple sentence structure, paragraph development, and, in some cases, division into a series of individual articles. Whereas the earlier covenants were comprised of generalized promises and statements of agreement, the later ones presented in greater detail the actual practices and patterns of conduct expected of church members.

The contents of the covenants, including the obligations to which early English Baptists committed themselves, fell into at least four distinct categories: church fellowship, church discipline, public worship and personal devotion, and pastoral and lay care.

The first category centered on the theme of church fellowship. The initial phase of this theme was the vow to "separate" from the world and false worship. Baptists then agreed to give themselves up to the Lord and to one another. This later agreement involved submitting to the "ordinances" of Christ, maintaining the purity of the truths about Christ, walking together in unity, and edifying one another. The church at Amersham pledged that it would commune neither with a person who had taken an oath and failed to repent of it, nor with a person who had married a non-Christian.

Church discipline was a second category of emphasis. When forming or joining churches, Baptists often covenanted that they would be willing to submit themselves to the discipline of their church, should this become necessary. Several covenants specified following the disciplinary pattern in Matthew 18:15-17. Discipline in the covenants was not intended simply to be a means of punishing offenders; it also had a preventive and therapeutic character. For example, the church at Amersham would not allow a person to become a member until the quality of his life and motives had been evaluated. Further, the covenant of this church claimed that the purpose of discipline was to "gaine a sole [soul] to God and hide a Multitude of sin." Finally, to ensure that disciplinary charges not be made lightly, this church made it clear that any member who brought a false charge against another member would himself be disciplined.

Public worship and personal devotion comprised the third area of covenantal concern. Church members committed themselves to worship together on Sunday and at other times. They promised to encourage the preaching of the gospel. They pledged to participate in celebrating the Lord's Supper. They vowed to pray for one another and for the well-being of the church. They covenanted to read the Bible regularly. An outgrowth of the vow to worship was the vow to use all opportunities for serving God.

Fourth, covenants encouraged a caring and pastoral attitude on the part of each church member toward every other member. Covenantal commitment to pastoral sensitivity complemented the emphasis given to discipline. To illustrate, the Keach covenant included a pledge "to warn, rebuke, and admonish one another with meekness." And members of the church at Norwich promised "to be watching over one anoether and to be counselling and advising, supporting, relieving, strengthening and comforting one anoether and as occasion shall require, be warning, admonishing and reprooveing one another."[24] Two of the seven articles in the covenant of the church at Norwich and three of the eight articles in the Keach covenant were predominantly pastoral in nature. These covenants placed a higher priority on meeting basic human needs than on other kinds of concerns.

Churches tended to use covenants in four main settings: in forming new churches, admitting new members, engaging in covenantal renewal, and disciplining errant members. Besides these settings, at least four other features characterized covenantal practices in England. First, churches often adopted and renewed covenants on days solemnized by fasting, prayer, and thanksgiving. Second, churches tended to write their own individualized covenants. Third, members tended to sign covenants when chartering new churches. Later covenantal renewal did not usually require a re-signing of the covenants. Members of one church renewed their covenant "by silence and lifting up their hands." In many instances, persons who united with a congregation after its formation also signed their names to the covenant. Fourth, congregations sometimes read covenants aloud while renewing commitments to their contents.

Covenants had many values for early English Baptists. They helped to create a sense of community among members of individual congregations. In describing covenants of the English Separatists, one scholar concluded that the concept of a contract as the foundation of church relationships "assumed an equality amongst the church members."[25] And speaking of the Separatist covenanters at Gainsborough in 1606, another scholar identified their covenant as "a source of strength—a pledge between themselves and God, and a mutual bond with one another."[26] Early Baptist covenants reflected these same concerns for the equality of believers, the brotherhood of church members, and the sonship of members to God.

Since Baptists tended to view church covenants as biblical in origin, covenants became a means by which Baptists could identify themselves with the historical "people of God." The covenant of the Great Ellingham Church, for example, indicated that the persons subscribing to it "find in holy Writ, that an Explicit covenanting . . . is the formal cause of a particular visible gosple [sic] Church" and that the covenant made by the church members was "according to the Example of the Church, in Nehemiah's time."[27]

Voluntary commitment to the contents of covenants added to their value in church life. A person became a church member by choice, not by force. Among the English Separatists, entry into church membership by way of acceptance of a voluntary covenant "minimized the possibility of a merely nominal attachment to the Christian community."[28] The same could be said for English Baptists in the 1600s.

Perhaps the most important value of covenants was their role in constantly reminding church members of the moral and spiritual duties and privileges to which they had initially committed themselves in uniting with a church. Since each church prepared its own covenant and built into it a continuing emphasis upon committed membership, the likelihood increased that each voluntary covenanter would attempt to conduct his life in alignment with his religious vows. The Keach covenant asked at the conclusion of its eight articles: "(And now can any thing lay a greater obligation upon the conscience, than this covenant, what then is the sin of such who violate it?)"[29]

Influences on Later Baptist Practices

British Baptist covenantal practices of the 1600s inevitably affected the covenantal patterns of later Baptists. A look at selected influences will illustrate this.

To begin with, churches continued to stress their autonomous right to prepare individualized covenants or to modify existing covenants to meet their unique situations. Examples relating to two issues in early Baptist life are instructive. First, although a few covenants in the 1700s continued to reflect the duty expressed in some covenants of the 1600s for church members to provide adequate financial support for their ministers, most apparently did not. Second, covenants reflected conflicting opinions over whether church membership should be open or closed.

As early as 1671, the Broadmead Church in Bristol had adopted a stewardship agreement in which they pledged "to Charge ourselves to pay yearly *These our* severall Voluntary and free Subscriptions, for the Comfortable Maintaining of a Pastor for this Congregation; and it is Concluded upon, that we will pay what we have severally engaged by Equall Proportion quarterly."[30] And the Keach covenant of the 1690s continued this theme: "We do promise according to our Ability (or as God shall bless us with the good things of this World) to Communicate to our Pastor or minister, God having ordained that they that Preach the Gospel should live of the Gospel."[31] Both the prominence of Benjamin and Elias Keach and the fact that they printed the common covenant of their churches in separate publications in 1697 "caused these documents to be copied or modified in many quarters," but the "refusal to recognize the duty of supporting a pastor was very general."[32]

The covenant signed by members of the church at Bourton on the Water in January 1719-20 (covenant 8) included an article approving financial support for ministers, but the 1735 covenant of the church at Shortwood in Gloucestershire, which was practically identical to the covenant of the congregation at Bourton on the Water, excluded the article relating to compensation for a minister.[33] The contrasting attitudes of these two churches toward an important issue show that churches persisted in maintaining the seventeenth-century Baptist belief that they should draft, adopt, and use personalized covenants, not prefabricated ones.

This principle of flexibility in designing covenants was related to the issue of closed membership churches versus open membership churches. The 1757 covenant of the church at Hog Lane in Woolrich favored a mixed membership in providing "That all those that are, or shall be convinced in their Minds, of Believers Baptism by Immersion, shall submit there-unto; and those that are otherwise minded, either as to Subject or Mode, shall also Walk according to the Dictates of their own Consciences, and that we will give no Uneasiness or Trouble to each other, or the Church . . . ."[34] The 1780 covenant of the New Road Baptist Church in Oxford echoed this sentiment, with members describing themselves as "a Protestant Catholic Church of Christ" and agreeing to accept one another in love and at the Lord's table even though "some of us do verily believe that the sprinkling of the infant children of believing parents . . . is true Christian Baptism; and others of us do believe that true Christian Baptism is that which is administered to adults upon the profession of their repentance, faith, and experience of the grace of God, by Immersion . . . ." (covenant 10).

On the other end of the spectrum, the 1790 covenant of the Baptist church in the Horse Fair, Stony Stratford, Bucks, took the singular position that only those persons would be received into membership who "we think are born again; have been baptized according to the primitive mode of administering that ordinance, and profess their hearty approbation of, and subjection to, this our solemn Church Covenant" (covenant 11). While the contemporary reader may feel that the mixed membership churches failed to receive the greatest benefit from their covenants because of their refusal to insist upon a regenerate church membership, one must at least give them credit for thinking for themselves and encouraging acceptance of one another in spite of divergent viewpoints. That spirit originated in British Baptist covenantal relationships of the 1600s and was one of the most important legacies of early Baptists.

Another influence of early British Baptists was the use of church covenants initially prepared by Congregationalists. Members of Baptist churches which evolved out of Congregationalist churches sometimes retained the covenants they had used in their former churches. This approach continued in the 1700s. For example, a Congregationalist church was formed with the signing of a covenant in 1694 and met at Clapton and at Croyden. The church periodically renewed its covenant. In 1733, the members had all become Baptists and formed themselves into a Baptist church at Great Gransden, at which time all the members signed the twelve articles of faith "as they did also the old Covenant to which had been added a Clause declaring that for the future none Should be admitted without Signing the Articles & agreeing to Baptism by Immersion."[35] Many British and American Baptist churches in the 1700s followed this same pattern, begun in the 1600s, of adopting church covenants at the same time they approved confessions of faith.

Even in America in the 1700s, especially among the Separate Baptists, Baptist churches often inherited the church covenant concept directly from their Congregationalist roots. This dependence upon another religious tradition for a major Baptist practice is only one among many evidences of cross-denominational influences that helped to shape the Baptist pilgrimage in Britain as well as America.

The early British Baptist covenantal ideal shaped ways of defining a church, admitting members into a church, and associating church covenants with church discipline. Elias Keach's popular 1697 *The Glory and Ornament of a True-Gospel-constituted Church,* which impacted Baptist life in England and America, plainly defined a church as "a Congregation of Godly Christians, who as a Stated-Assembly (being first baptized upon the Profession of Faith) do by mutual agreement and consent give themselves up to the Lord, and one to another . . . ." And all persons who are admitted as members into a church "must solemnly enter into a Covenant, to walk in the Fellowship of that particular Congregation, and submit themselves to the Care and Discipline thereof, and to walk faithfully with God in all his Holy Ordinances . . . and give themselves up to the watch and charge of the Pastor and Ministry thereof . . . ."[36]

Keach's writing and those of others, as well as the covenantal texts and practices of early British Baptists, made a decided impact upon the definitions of a church, qualifications for membership, and relation to discipline which Baptists put forward in later years, especially in America. Covenants, at times, became inseparably linked to an adequate understanding of the doctrine of the church in Baptist life.

Ironically, however, according to a major 1904 study of the history of Baptist church covenants, "In England . . . during the eighteenth century the covenant idea fell into disfavor, and . . . neither Congregational nor Baptist churches to-day make much, or perhaps any use of it."[37] That claim probably went too far because many English Baptist churches in the 1700s continued to use covenants (covenants 8, 10, 11). Baptists in

Wales in the 1700s also continued the practice (covenants 9, 12). And as recently as 1935, a study of Baptist church covenants in England noted that "To-day, many churches place in the hands of their new members a small manual, which includes a statement of the basis of the church, both as to beliefs and as to aims. While the actual word, Covenant, may not be used, the duties of the member are still put before him" [thus functioning as a covenant].[38] Then the study printed a covenant showing how "a possible covenant to-day [1935] might run" among English Baptists (covenant 13).

When the use of covenants declined among some British Baptists in the 1800s and 1900s, two key factors likely contributed. One was an increasingly negative reaction to relating covenants too closely to rigid and, at times, punitive applications of church discipline. Covenant-breakers often received the full brunt of the process of corrective discipline. In discussing early Baptist churches in Wales, a Welsh Baptist historian concluded that "there is no doubting the fact that a church derived its authority to discipline members on the grounds that a covenant had been made and broken."[39]

A Welsh Baptist association met in 1790 and approved a letter on church discipline which both encouraged its churches to use covenants and even included a model covenant for consideration by its churches (covenant 12). Following the printing of the covenant, the statement clearly tied together church discipline and church covenants: "Should any one of the church, through hardness of heart, undervalue and forget God; and despise his word, his church, and the above covenant, and return to his former sinful practices, or become worse than before; with such we are directed not to keep company, no not to eat."[40] However, the statement also related discipline to redemption by claiming that a purpose of remedial discipline was that wayward members might "be brought back into the bond of the covenant" and that restoration to membership should be given to any excommunicated member who exhibited true repentance.

Covenantal decline also likely resulted from a growing tendency of churches simply to adopt standardized, uniform covenants printed in external sources, rather than to write their own individualized statements. Throughout Baptist history covenantal value and dynamic have correlated closely with the degree of input that churches have exercised in arriving at the covenants they have used.

Miscellaneous other influences of early British Baptists upon later covenantal practices included the tendencies to base covenants on biblical teaching, to require prospective church members to pledge themselves to meet covenantal commitments, to prepare fairly lengthy covenants frequently broken down into individual sections or articles, and to sign covenants. Regarding this last item, even in Wales where "there is no firm evidence that covenants were signed" in the 1600s,[41] the pattern evidently changed in the 1700s. As examples, the Baptist church at Caerleon in 1770 drew up a covenant (covenant 9) to which the members "set our names," and the Baptists who formed a church at Wern Panteg (now Trosnant) in 1776 prepared a covenant to which they "annexed" their names.[42]

Early British Baptists sponsored the church covenant idea so effectively that covenants continue to be a part of Baptist life in Wales. And current Welsh covenantal practices illustrate another influence from early British life, namely, the tendency for churches to use covenants in various settings and in different ways. Today, for example, the Bethany Baptist Church at Risca, an English-language church, gives every new member a copy of its covenant printed on a card. This church has also adopted the custom of reading its covenant every communion Sunday. The Calfaria Church at Clydach, a Welsh-language church, prints its covenant as a part of the annual financial report distributed to every member, since the covenant contains a strong stewardship emphasis. The Caersalem Newydd Church at Treboeth, a Welsh-language church, uses a baptismal certificate on which a covenant is printed. Printed under the auspices of the Swansea District Meeting of Welsh Baptist Churches, the certificate is designed so that other churches in the same locality can use it simply by printing their own name on it.[43]

The covenant of the Caersalem Newydd Church begins by saying, "As one baptised into Christ and a member of his Church, you are expected," and then lists eight areas of expectation: regular church attendance, confidentiality regarding the church's business, forgiveness, church discipline, financial stewardship, personal ministry, congregational unity and peace, and regular attention to Bible study and prayer, both private and public.[44] Two features of this covenant which reflect early British Baptist influence are the claim that a church has a right to expect certain levels of conduct and Christian practice from its members and the strong relationship of the covenant's contents to the four major subject areas of the earliest British Baptist covenants: church fellowship, church discipline, worship and personal devotion, and pastoral and lay care.

Conclusion

British Baptists of the 1600s initiated the use of church covenants in the Baptist experience. Their attitudes toward the values of covenants varied; many churches adopted and implemented covenants, while some did not. Churches which wrote their own covenants and applied them in ways designed to support the regenerate qualities of church membership experienced significant values: fellowship grew, discipline assumed increased meaning, behavior became as important as doctrine, and commitments to God and fellow believers gained new stature. Covenantal documents encouraged and strengthened covenantal relationships. These early Baptists viewed covenants as a means of voluntarily pledging themselves to moral integrity. In an era when Baptists produced numerous major confessions of faith, the emphasis on covenants helped correct any tendency toward unhealthy preoccupation with correct belief by enhancing the ethical side of life. Put plainly, covenants functioned at their best in local churches by upgrading the Baptist ideal of appropriate conduct through magnifying biblical principles that supported the ideal.

Many early British Baptist churches wrote, signed, verbalized, renewed, defended, and recommended church covenants. They designed covenants to reflect biblical standards for church membership, conditioned entry into church life upon accepting them, evaluated the quality of churchmanship through commitment to them, and resorted to church discipline for violations of them. And they set in motion covenantal patterns that would alter the Baptist future.

3
Baptist Church Covenants in Early America

Baptist churches in early America tended to use covenants, and viewed them as significant, and sometimes essential, documents of congregational life. Accountability for the quality of church members' conduct lay at the core of the covenantal idea. Affecting the mutual duties and life-styles of church members, a covenant offered specific guidelines for relationships within the church family and spelled out the duties of individual members. Most covenants even included doctrinal elements, but Baptists normally used confessions of faith as their primary means of communicating doctrine.

This chapter will focus on Baptist church covenants in America from the late 1630s, when the first Baptist church in America was formed at Providence, Rhode Island, to 1833, when the New Hampshire Baptist Convention published a covenant that would serve as the basis for the predominant covenantal pattern among Baptists in the United States in the 1800s and 1900s. Emerging covenantal patterns prior to the Great Awakening will be treated first, followed by an examination of covenantal developments among the Separate, Particular (Regular), and frontier Baptists. General covenantal trends throughout the first two centuries of Baptist life in America will then be described.

Covenantal Patterns Prior to the Great Awakening

Besides seeking a biblical basis for covenants and responding to the influences of British Baptists, the colonial Baptists of New England "apparently were dependent on the Congregationalists not only for the idea, but also in some measure for the general expression of their church covenants."[1] Congregationalism was the key religious force in early New England, and Congregationalists used church covenants widely, after the

pattern of their peers in England. The use of a church covenant as the
basis of the local church was "a fundamental characteristic of the Congregational system."[2] The Mayflower Compact, entered into by the Pil-
grims in 1620, was a church covenant put to civic use by the Plymouth
community. The Puritan settlement at Salem consented to a church covenant in 1629. A body of Puritan leaders in Boston prepared the Half-
Way Covenant in 1662 which allowed the nonregenerate to be half-way
members of congregations, meaning that they could neither share in the
Lord's Supper nor vote in church business. Throughout the remainder of
the 1600s, most Congregationalist churches used half-way covenants as
church covenants. The texts of many these seventeenth-century New England Congregationalist church covenants still exist.[3]

Puritan writers stated the significance of church covenants for Congregationalism. John Davenport, Congregationalist pastor in New Ha-
ven, published a personal creed in 1642 which presented the Puritan doctrine of the church. This creed described as the proper way to gather a
church the need for Christians "to joyn willingly together in Christian
communion and orderly covenant."[4] Thomas Hooker, Congregationalist
pastor in Hartford, presented a clear statement of Congregationalist
principles in a 1645 writing which viewed a church covenant as an essential document in constituting a church.[5] In 1648 representatives of the
Puritan colonies completed the Cambridge Platform, which served as the
"standard symbol" of Congregationalism in Massachusetts throughout
the 1600s. According to this statement, the proper form of a visible
church "is a visible Covenant . . . call'd The Church Covenant."[6]

Although most Baptist churches in New England prior to the 1740s
did adopt covenants at their founding, the first two churches, formed,
respectively, at Providence and Newport, Rhode Island, in the 1630s and
1640s, apparently did not. In 1652 a group of Six Principle Baptists, who
stressed Hebrews 6:1-2, broke from the Providence Church and " 'joined
together in special church covenant.' "[7] In 1671 a body of Baptists
moved out of the Newport church, made a covenant (see covenant 16 in
ch. 6), and formed the first Seventh Day Baptist church in America. This
set in motion a heavy reliance upon covenants by later Seventh Day Baptists. The Newport church adopted its first covenant in 1727 (covenant
19).

The first Baptist church in Massachusetts was the Swansea church
formed in Rehoboth in 1663. The covenant of this church (covenant 14),
which is the oldest extant covenant of Baptists in America, evolved from

a Welsh Baptist setting rather than from American Congregationalism. John Miles had become pastor of a Baptist church at Ilston, Wales, near Swansea, in 1649. When the 1662 Act of Uniformity forced him from his pastorate, he and others moved to Rehoboth, Massachusetts, where they founded the Swansea church in 1663.

The First Baptist Church of Boston arose in 1665 when the members entered into a common covenant (covenant 15). The confession of faith approved by that church in 1665 showed how the congregation made the covenant central to its definition of the church: "And those that gladly received the word & are baptized are saints by Calling & fitt matter for a vissible Church. . . . And a competent number of such joyned together in Covenant & fellowship of the gospel are a Church of Christ."[8]

Messengers from the First Baptist Church in Boston assisted in organizing the first Baptist church in Maine in 1682, which was led by William Screven. This church at Kittery adopted a covenant in 1682 that clearly reflected Congregationalist influence (covenant 17). All ten members of this new church signed the covenant. Since Screven's congregation transplanted to Charleston, South Carolina, before 1700, and became the first Baptist church in the South, they took with them what may have been an influential covenanting tradition.

If American Congregationalism was the predominant background factor in the formation of covenants of early New England Baptist churches, the influence of Elias Keach, an English Baptist, was central to Baptist covenantal developments in the Middle Colonies. Keach, son of the famous London pastor Benjamin Keach, came to Philadelphia in the late 1680s. In 1688 he and others formed a Baptist church at Pennepeck, Pennsylvania, which became the mother congregation in the Middle Colonies for Baptists. He also assisted in forming three churches in New Jersey at Middletown (1688), Piscataway (1689), and Cohansey (1690). Therefore, his influence in the Middle Colonies widened.

Keach returned to England in 1692. In 1697 he and his father published separate materials containing the common covenant of their two churches (covenant 6). Benjamin published *The Glory of a True Church, and Its Discipline Display'd,* and Elias *The Glory and Ornament of a True Gospel-Constituted Church.* The latter writing (including its covenant) became popular in America where Elias had worked. Morgan Edwards, the first Baptist historian in America, wrote in 1770 that he had seen a book by Elias Keach "containing a confession of faith, a church covenant, treatise of discipline, &c."[9]

The Keach covenant apparently became the most widely used covenant in the Middle Colonies. The Welsh Tract Church, formed in 1701 as the first Baptist church in Delaware, was largely responsible for the spread of this covenant, even though it did not adopt it until 1710. Upon the advice of a council, which included members of the Welsh Tract Church, the Middletown Church adopted and signed the Keach covenant in 1712 to help quell a disruption in the church's fellowship. Examples of other New Jersey churches which later adopted the Keach covenant or a revision of it included those at Cape May (1712), Scotch Plains (1747), and Shrewsbury (1774). The Keach covenant even penetrated into New England for the 1727 covenant of the Newport Church in Rhode Island was clearly based upon it (covenant 19). The Keach covenant also made some inroads into the Southern Colonies, but this will be discussed later.

Baptists in the Middle Colonies, following typical Baptist diversity, also used covenants other than the Keach covenant. Two Seventh Day Baptist churches in New Jersey, for example, used a common document as the basis of their organization. These were the Piscataway Church, formed in 1705, and the Cohansey (later Shiloh) Church, formed in 1737. The document used by these churches (covenant 18) was primarily a confession of faith, but it ended with a covenantal thrust. Still a different covenant from the Middle Colonies was that adopted in 1738 by the Tulpohokin Church in Berks County, Pennsylvania (covenant 21).

Baptists in the Middle Colonies took their church covenants seriously. In New Jersey "The seriousness of obligations involved in becoming a church member was signified in the covenant which a new church adopted at its formation. While church members were not expected to be perfect, they were expected to do their best to be faithful to their covenant obligations."[10] The minutes of the Welsh Tract Church in Delaware show that Richard Seary was excluded from the congregation in 1720 for being "a covenant breaker in regard to the church covenant" and that the same judgment was laid upon Mary Rees in 1723 and Martha David in 1732.[11]

The actual process of constituting a church and adopting a covenant, as reflected in the 1712 proceedings of the Cape May Church in New Jersey, involved setting aside a day for prayer and fasting and inviting the pastor and elders of a neighboring church to assist. The visiting pastor first explained the nature of a true Baptist church and then asked questions about the willingness of the Baptists at Cape May to accept a covenant. They answered affirmatively, and the covenant was read and signed by each member. They were then pronounced a church.[12]

Many Baptist churches in the Southern Colonies also used covenants. The first Baptist church in the South had literally transplanted itself, under the leadership of William Screven, from Kittery, Maine, to Charleston, South Carolina, in the late 1600s. While in Kittery, the church did use a covenant (covenant 17); and it may have continued its covenantal patterns after moving to Charleston. But information is not clear, since the records of the Charleston Church were destroyed in 1752. Of interest, however, is that the Ashley River Church, which had been a branch of the Charleston Church, constituted itself with a covenant in 1736.

At least some General (Arminian) Baptists also used covenants. In 1742 fifty-seven people organized a General Baptist church at Chestnut Ridge, Maryland, by adopting a covenant (covenant 22). This statement was somewhat unique in that it was a "politico-ecclesiastical document"[13] in which the covenanters pledged, among other things, to defend Protestantism, King George, and the laws of Maryland, and to oppose Rome and the Pope.

Several South Carolina Baptist churches used revisions of the 1697 covenant of Elias Keach (covenant 6) in the 1700s and early 1800s. In 1737 some members of the Welsh Tract Church in Delaware, which used the Keach covenant, moved to Pee Dee River, South Carolina, and organized the Welsh Neck Church in early 1738. The church's minutes do not tell when the church adopted a slightly modified edition of the Keach covenant, but a copy of it appears in the August 1760 minutes. At least three other churches in the vicinity of the Pee Dee River accepted the Welsh Neck covenant: the Cashaway Church (1767), the Turkey Creek Church (1785), and the Salem Church (1812). Among other revisions, this last church added an article in which members vowed to be "truly Christian" toward Negro servants by urging them to attend worship, by refusing to treat them cruelly, by giving them a day of rest on Sunday, and by encouraging literate slaves to teach their illiterate companions how to read.[14]

Separate Baptists and the Covenant Idea

The Great Awakening, which flourished in New England in the early 1740s, divided the Congregationalists into two groups: the Old Lights, who opposed revivalism and favored the state-church concept, and the New Lights, who stressed revivalism and religious liberty. The Separates agreed broadly with the doctrines of Baptists, but some Separates refused to give up their preference for infant baptism. Large numbers of Separates who accepted believer's baptism became Baptists and were termed Separate Baptists. Entire churches often exchanged their status as Separates for that of Baptists. Significant increases occurred among the Baptists in New England because of the steady movement out of the ranks of Separates. Further, many Separate Baptists moved to the South, set up their headquarters in North Carolina, and experienced further growth there.

Isaac Backus, noted advocate of religious freedom and the separation of church and state, was one of the most important converts to the Separate Baptists in New England. In typical fashion Backus progressed through the stages of being a Congregationalist, a Separate, and a Separate Baptist. His experiences illustrate how Congregationalist covenants influenced Baptist covenants in New England.

Backus joined the First Congregational Church of Norwich, Connecticut, in 1742 but soon left it. This church had a covenant, and Backus even acknowledged its general soundness; but he felt that his own personal growth in grace required that he separate from the church. He gradually adopted New Light views and became associated with some Separates in Titicut, Massachusetts. These Separates wanted to form a church and asked Backus to prepare a confession of faith and a church covenant. He did write these documents, and sixteen persons signed them in early 1748 and constituted a Separate church. Backus became pastor and was ordained that same year.

Baptist beliefs soon entered the Titicut Church, and Backus accepted believer's baptism and was immersed in 1751. In 1756 six Baptists, including Backus, renounced their status as Separates and constituted the Middleborough (Massachusetts) Separate Baptist Church. A confession and covenant written by Backus were crucial to the organizing process (covenant 23). Backus recorded that he read aloud the documents he had drawn up and that each member of the new church signed them. In a letter to his mother, Backus emphasized the solemnity characterizing the covenanting process. He pointed out that he and five others did "solemnly and renewedly sign covenant together; I trust, with some real freedom and sense of divine things."[15]

Even the confession of faith prepared by Backus for use in forming the

Middleborough church reflected a covenantal interest in defining the church: "We believe that a visible Church of Christ is a number of his saints & people by mutual acquaintance & communion voluntarily and understandingly covenanting & embodying together for the carrying on the Worship & Service of God."[16]

Later, in commenting on the nature and purpose of a church covenant, Backus claimed that mutual obligations and privileges were basic to the concept of a covenant. A genuine covenant should demand that church members give themselves up both to God and fellow church members. Backus believed that a person could be brought into a covenantal relationship only through voluntary consent, that a covenant could never bind a person or a church to act in opposition to the will of God, and that a covenant could never exempt anyone from the duties central to God's will.[17]

The Backus covenant had wide influence throughout New England. Many churches and associations used the covenant or variations of it. Two Massachusetts churches which used it were those at Sandisfield (1779) and at Avon (1780). The New London Church in New Hampshire approved the covenant in 1788. In the late 1700s the Danville (New Hampshire) Baptist Association adopted this covenant as a guide for its churches. In 1805 the Bowdoinham Association in Maine printed a separate four-page insert in its minutes containing its statement of faith and the Backus covenant. The insert even suggested ways to use the documents: "These *Articles* and *Covenant* are printed in a small page that they may be taken from the Minutes, and put into a Bible or Hymn Book."[18] The Danville Association in Vermont adopted the covenant in 1825. The 1826 circular letter of the Eastern Maine Baptist Association noted that the association had printed its covenant in its minutes at least two times in recent years and then described the contents and meaning of the covenant, which was clearly a revision of the Backus covenant. The Hancock Association in Maine printed an abbreviated version of this covenant in its 1851 minutes.

The Backus covenant also moved outside of New England. For example, the Eleventh Baptist Church of Philadelphia adopted it in 1838. And between 1832 and 1878 numerous Baptist associations in Atlantic Canada and in Ontario printed the covenant as a model for their churches, but that story will be told in chapter 5.

The Separate Baptists in New England used church covenants widely and took them seriously, and they used many covenants other than the

Backus covenant. For example, the Separate Baptist churches in the following places adopted a variety of covenants: Harwich (1749) and Westfield (1784), Massachusetts; Stratfield (1751), Connecticut; Berwick (1768), Maine; and Shaftsbury (1768), Wallingford (1780), and Bennington (1783), Vermont.

Beginning in 1755 Separate Baptists in the South grew rapidly. Their church covenants tended to be complex in structure, strict in requirements, doctrinal in thrust, and Calvinistic in theology. Two covenants, those of the Grassy Creek Church in North Carolina (covenant 24) and of the Kiokee Church in Georgia (covenant 25), were especially significant because of their use in churches founded by Shubal Stearns and Daniel Marshall, the two men largely responsible for the rise of Separate Baptists in the South.

Stearns became a Separate Baptist in Tolland, Connecticut, in 1751 and headed south in 1754 to help organize new churches. Marshall, of Windsor, Connecticut, also became a Separate Baptist in 1751. In 1754 he moved to Virginia, after serving as a missionary to the Mohawk Indians in Pennsylvania, and joined efforts with Stearns, his brother-in-law. Stearns and Marshall soon traveled to Sandy Creek, North Carolina, and formed the first Separate Baptist church in the South in 1755. This church became the headquarters for Separate Baptist expansion into the South. Morgan Edwards referred to this church as "the mother of all the Separate-baptists" and claimed in 1772 that "it, in 17 years, is become mother, grand-mother, and great Grandmother to 42 churches, from which sprang 125 ministers."[19]

No information is available on the use of a covenant in the early years of the Sandy Creek Church. However, Robert I. Devin concluded that Stearns and Marshall constituted the Grassy Creek Church in 1757 and that Stearns apparently wrote the church's covenant, but George W. Paschal contested Stearns' alleged authorship because of the Calvinistic elements in the covenant, claiming that most Separate Baptist church covenants "during Stearns' lifetime . . . were free from Calvinism."[20] Stearns died in 1771.

Evidence, however, suggests that Calvinistic emphases soon entered Separate Baptist covenants. For example, John Taylor, a Regular Baptist minister who claimed to be seventy years old when he wrote *A History of Ten Baptist Churches* (1823), stated that when he was about seventeen, which would have been about 1770, he had witnessed the baptizing of over fifty people by Samuel Harris, a noted Separate Baptist, at Harper's

Ferry, Virginia. A church covenant was read in this baptismal setting, and Taylor wrote that he "happened to be near when their Church Covenant was read—I remember concluding no man on earth could comply with it." Taylor then summarized his view about the theological character of Separate Baptist covenants in general: "The separates had no public Confession of Faith, but were generally constituted of a Church Covenant, which to the best of my recollection, was truly Calvenistic [sic]."[21]

Further, the Kiokee Church, organized by Daniel Marshall in the early 1770s as the first Separate Baptist church in Georgia, stressed in the first article of its covenant a belief in "the great doctrine of Election," "particular redemption," and "the saints' absolute final perseverance [sic] in Grace" (covenant 25).

Some churches with Separate Baptist origins eventually denied the validity of churches labeling themselves as Separate Baptist or Regular Baptist and began to fellowship with other Baptists. One such church was the Meherrin Church in Lunenburg County, Virginia. Constituted in 1772 as a Separate Baptist congregation, this church officially broke down its bars to communion with the Regular Baptists in 1774. Then in 1779 the church adopted a covenant (covenant 26) which like many covenants of its era held high expectations for church members' conduct, contained multiple articles, and acknowledged that the members who adopted the covenant also signed it.

Covenants Among the Particular (Regular) Baptists

Particular Baptists (also known as Regular Baptists) held to Calvinistic emphases. They became the predominant strain of Baptists in early America, especially after forming the highly influential Philadelphia Baptist Association in 1707 as the first Baptist association in America. The confession of faith adopted by this association in 1742 became the most widely used confession among Baptists in America in the 1700s. Even the significant Charleston Association, formed in South Carolina in 1751 as the first Baptist association in the South, held strongly to Calvinistic doctrinal tendencies.

The acceptance of covenantal vows was integral to the founding of most new Particular and Regular Baptist churches in the post-Great Awakening period, and a larger percentage of these churches may have used covenants than did those of the Separate Baptists. At least, more of their covenants seem to be extant. Viewing covenants as guidelines for

Christian conduct, these Baptists took covenanting seriously and constituted their churches believing that initial covenantal commitments
should continue indefinitely. Infractions of one's pledges frequently led
to church discipline.

A detailed description of the process of organizing a church into a
covenantal relationship appears in the earliest records of the First Baptist
Church of Warren, Rhode Island. Constituted in 1764, the church's service of organization included an introductory sermon, a short dismission,
prayers by three ministers, and the presentation, reading, and signing of
the church's covenant. "Then those persons who had signed the covenant were asked . . . whether they, in the presence of that assembly, received that as their covenant and plan of union in a church relation,
which question was answered by them all in the affirmative, standing up
. . . ."[22] Next the church called a pastor, and the events of the day were
concluded with a sermon reminding the pastor and members of their
respective duties.

Three major statements on Baptist church discipline sponsored by key
Baptist associations in the 1700s provided theological rationale for using
church covenants and exerted a dynamic impact upon church life both
within and outside the associations. The close relationship established
between discipline and covenants in these statements reflected a pattern
that existed throughout early Baptist life in America.

The first statement, a lengthy document on church discipline printed
along with the 1742 Confession of Faith of the Philadelphia Baptist Association, observed that the orderly constituting of a church required
baptized believers to be "willing in the fear of God to take the laws of
Christ upon them, and do by one mutual consent give themselves to the
Lord, and to one another in the Lord . . . solemnly submitting to the
government of Christ in his Church, and being united, they are to be
declared a Gospel Church of Jesus Christ."[23] Then in commenting on
the duties of church members, the statement indicated that "all church
members, therefore, are under the strictest obligations to do and observe
whatsoever Christ enjoineth on them, as mutual duties towards one another."[24] Even though the word *covenant* did not appear here, the covenantal concept permeated these associational views of the nature of a
church and of church members' responsibilities.

The Philadelphia Association's treatise on church discipline also included a section on "The Manifold Duties of Christians, Especially to the
Household of Faith." Supported by Scriptures, the seven duties listed

included: (1) "Love unfeigned and without dissimulation, for all their things ought to be done in love"; (2) "To labour to keep the unity of the spirit in the bond of peace"; (3) "Endeavour for the edification and spiritual benefit of the whole body, that they all may grow up to be a holy temple in and for the Lord"; (4) "That they all watch over one another for good"; (5) "That they do pray with and for one another"; (6) "That they neglect not the assembling of themselves together, for the celebrating of divine worship, and so promote one another's spiritual benefit"; and (7) "That they use all means to keep the house of God in due order and cleanness, walking inoffensive towards one another, and all others, with conscientious diligence, and so unanimously to contend for the faith and truth once delivered to the saints, in the purity thereof, according to the holy scripture."[25] Although this outline of duties was not a church covenant, it served as a guideline for preparing many local covenants.[26] Its author, Benjamin Griffin, acknowledged his reliance upon Elias Keach and others.

The second statement, published in 1774 by the Charleston Baptist Association, employed covenantal language in defining a church and in describing how a church is formed. To begin with, "A particular gospel church consists of a company of saints, incorporated by a special covenant into one distinct body and meeting together in one place for the enjoyment of fellowship with each other and with Christ their Head in all his institutions to their mutual edification and the glory of God through the Spirit . . . ."[27] Then after the applicants for membership in a church about to be formed are satisfied that they all meet acceptable qualifications, "they should give up themselves to the Lord and to one another by the will of God (2 Cor. 8:5) by subscribing a written covenant consistent with the Word of God (Isa. 44:5), thereby binding and obliging themselves to be the Lord's, to walk in all his commands and ordinances, and in all respects to behave toward each other as brethren, agreeable to the spiritual relation into which they now enter."[28] Since the Charleston Association was a powerful force in the South, these covenantal encouragements undoubtedly led many new churches to prepare, sign, and adhere to church covenants.

The third statement, prepared for the Philadelphia Baptist Association by Samuel Jones and initially printed in 1798, was justified on the basis that the association's earlier treatise of church discipline (1743) was "materially defective." The statement referred to the covenanting process as "an act of mutual confederation" and then described a suggested procedure for constituting a new church. Elements included fasting; a sermon; interrogation of candidates for membership by a minister regarding their qualifications, their purpose in joining together, and their obedience to biblical requirements for membership; assent to a church covenant; the reading and signing of the covenant; an official pronouncement that they were a "regular gospel church"; the sharing of the "right hand of fellowship"; a suitable concluding address; and a benediction. Prayers and singing were to take place at appropriate places throughout the service.[29]

This 1798 Philadelphia Association statement even printed a model covenant for Baptists to consider using as they formed new churches (covenant 31). Since the Philadelphia statement on discipline has been described as "the first Baptist church manual printed in America," and since the covenant printed in it has been called "the first universal covenant,"[30] both must have achieved wide circulation and usage. For example, two Kentucky churches adopted this covenant in 1801 and 1828.[31] "With the publication of Jones' 'official' covenant, the idea of covenant as a locally styled uniquely congregational compact was diminished,"[32] but a wide variety of covenants still prevailed. Not until the mid-1800s would widespread congregational acceptance of "official" covenants published in church manuals and other places begin to work seriously against the traditional pattern of each church writing its own covenant.

Besides statements of discipline, other writings of Particular and Regular Baptists in the late 1700s and early 1800s provided helpful information on the nature and role of covenants. Individual writings of Morgan Edwards and David Thomas and a joint writing of Lemuel Burkitt and Jesse Read focused directly on the topic.

Morgan Edwards published his *The Customs of Primitive Churches* in 1774. Although apparently intended to serve as a manual for the polity and practices of the churches in the Philadelphia Association, the association never gave its official approval to the work. Still, Edwards' comments about church covenants were similar to the observations of other Calvinistic Baptist leaders of his era.

Edwards began by injecting the covenant idea into his description of the model way to constitute a church. His suggested procedures included the need for the minister to "interrogate them [the candidates for membership] in such a manner that the answers shall amount to a covenant or instrument of confederation." The new members then signed a written covenant and were pronounced a church.[33] Edwards printed a narrative of the proceedings of the constituting of an unnamed Baptist church from 1732, including the covenant used by the church (covenant 20).

Edwards continued by indicating the significance of a covenant, by identifying four key aspects of a covenantal relationship, and by discussing the signing of a covenant. "A covenant," he stated, "is the formal cause of a church: so that without a covenant, expressed or implied, a visible church there cannot be." The four aspects of a covenant included a willingness to be the Lord's people, an agreement to be subject to one another in the Lord, a commitment to obey the commandments of Christ, and a pledge to respect church officers. Edwards believed that each person who joined a church after its formation should sign the church's covenant and that an excommunicated person allowed back into church membership should re-sign the covenant.[34]

David Thomas, a Regular Baptist leader in Virginia, believed, like Morgan Edwards, that a covenant was essential for a church. In 1774 he listed five elements which he considered necessary to the being of a Baptist church: a certain number of persons, at least two or three; a profession of faith on the part of each member; proper baptism, namely, believer's baptism by immersion in the name of the Trinity; submission to the imposition of hands; and joining together in a mutual covenant. He defined a covenant as "nothing else but a mutual promise, or engagement to live together as brethren; and help one another to their utmost, to serve GOD; to uphold his truth; and promote the interest of his kingdom in the place where they dwell."[35] Thomas believed that a covenant should be signed. Thomas clearly had a lofty conception of the role of a covenant in church life, and many other Regular Baptists shared his view.

Lemuel Burkitt and Jesse Read, Baptist pastors in North Carolina, published a history of the Kehukee Baptist Association in that state in 1803. This association consisted of Regular Baptists until 1788 when they united with the Separate Baptists in the Sandy Creek Association and became known as United Baptists. Burkitt and Read wrote that the Regular Baptists in the Kehukee Association had customarily employed covenants in forming new churches.[36] They even printed a "specimen" covenant used by many Regular Baptists (covenant 33). This covenant was important and has had a long history because, according to a 1979 publication which reprinted it, some Primitive Baptist churches in Tennessee, North Carolina, and Alabama continue to use the covenant in constituting new churches and as a guide for discipline and practice.[37]

Burkitt and Read described the normal pattern by which churches in the Kehukee Association were constituted. They stressed fasting, the presence of an assisting minister, an examination of the candidates' qualifications, and questions about the intention of the candidates to live disciplined lives. These questions having been answered in the affirmative, "a covenant is produced . . . and being read, consented to, and subscribed, the ministers pronounce them a church."[38]

With the spread of Calvinistic Baptists in North Carolina, many of the General (Arminian) Baptists in that state in the late 1700s began to adopt the theology of the Regular Baptists. This transformation involved three important changes for the General Baptists: They gave more attention to a regenerate church membership, they accepted a stricter pattern of church discipline, and they assigned much more value to church covenants.[39]

The Covenant Concept in Frontier Churches

The early frontier comprised the territory between the Allegheny Mountains and the Mississippi River from the end of the American Revolution to 1830. "The covenant idea provided a powerful moral imperative for Christian conduct on the frontier."[40] Frontier Baptists tied church covenants and discipline closely together. Covenants often included disciplinary contents, and discipline was rigidly administered for failure to live up to covenantal expectations and commitments. Excellent examples of early frontier Baptist covenants still exist (covenants 28, 29, and 30), including the original 1783 covenant of the Cherokee Creek Church (covenant 28), the oldest continuing Baptist church in Tennessee.

Frontier Baptists sometimes covenanted in wilderness places which were filled with potential danger. A case in point related to the charter members of the Severn's Valley Church, organized in 1781 as the first Baptist church in Kentucky. The pre-1787 minutes of this church were eventually destroyed, along with any possible mention of a covenant used in constituting the congregation. In 1844, however, a church clerk wrote into the minutes that when the church was formed on June 18, 1781, with fifteen members "under a green sugar tree," those were "perilous times when the little band of Christians surrounded by an unbroken forest infested by savages gave themselves to God & to one another in Church Covenant."[41]

Most frontier Baptist churches distinguished clearly between church covenants and confessions of faith, but some did not. Instead, these latter churches gave to the constitutive document of their congregations the title "covenant," but in reality the articles comprising the covenant focused on doctrine rather than conduct. Perhaps the reason why some frontier Baptists did not make this distinction was that they considered the doctrinal assertions of a particular congregation to be the proper substance of a covenant. Possibly they assumed that proper conduct would issue from faithful adherence to a confession of faith. Therefore, there was no need for a separate document dealing with guidelines for practicing one's faith. This occasional tendency to make covenants equivalent to confessions highlighted the theological dimension of frontier covenants.

While most frontier churches seemed to write their own covenants, sometimes a particular form of covenant (usually revised by each church to meet its individual needs) gained widespread usage. To illustrate, the following Kentucky churches used a common covenant: Buck Creek (1799), New Salem (1801), Shelbyville (1819), Sharon (1825), and Taylorsville (1828).[42] Structurally, frontier covenants tended to range in length from about 100 to 500 words.

Frontier Baptists maintained an extremely tight relationship between church covenants and discipline. The untamed character of frontier life led the churches to employ special taming devices, such as strict disciplinary procedures. Discipline resulted from failing to live up to one's covenantal promises. In the Mays Lick Church in Kentucky, the covenant was read frequently, and "it was insisted upon and emphasized by strict discipline that every member should strive to conform his life to his covenant." And in this church, following a typical pattern of most frontier churches, discipline was administered rigidly and impartially for a large variety of offenses. Disciplinary matters became primary agenda items for monthly covenant meetings.[43]

The rules of decorum of the Sharon Baptist Church, organized in Concord, Kentucky in 1825, also showed the bond between frontier covenants and discipline. The rules required the church clerk to read the covenant at the opening of every covenant meeting, which occurred on the third Saturday of every month. The rules then continued: "Whereas we have entered into a Solom Covenant to & with each other & Knowing our own frailties we think it very necessary as well as Scriptural to appoint faithful Bretherin whose duty it Shall be to take notice of all delinquency in the Members in their Relative duties & have power to reprove admonish & advise such as may appear in a state of declension & report any such matter to the Church when they may think it necessary."[44]

Because of the emphasis placed upon discipline for covenantal violations, church covenants attained an authority in frontier churches which
they seemingly had never before possessed among Baptists in America.
The importance assigned to covenants generally transcended that given
to confessions of faith and rules of decorum. Whenever a church member
departed from a doctrinal agreement or a rule of practice, his return to
his original covenantal vows or his persistence in his error of doctrine or
practice determined his disciplinary fate.

General Covenantal Trends

Several features characterized the Baptist approach to using church
covenants in America in the pre-1830 period. For one thing, the prevail-
ing practice was for each church to write its own covenant. Most covenants were local documents and gained little, if any, popularity beyond
the individual congregations which designed them. At times, however,
model covenants did emerge and were adopted by multiple churches and
occasionally even by associations. Examples were the 1756 covenant of
Isaac Backus, the 1697 covenant of Elias Keach, the 1798 covenant prepared by Samuel Jones for the Philadelphia Association, and the Regular
Baptist covenant printed in 1803 by Lemuel Burkitt and Jesse Read.

Still another model covenant appeared in two forms in the 1806 publication of Peter Philanthropos Roots (1765-1828) entitled *A Confession of
Faith and Church Covenant*. One edition appeared in prose (covenant
34A) and the other in verse (covenant 34B). The two versions of this
covenant had a unique purpose because Roots, a Baptist missionary from
New York, prepared them, as the subtitle for the publication indicated,
"especially for the assistance of Christians in our new settlements, who
wish to unite together in church-state."[45] As an itinerant missionary, he
preached in seventeen states and in parts of Canada[46] (his influence on
covenants in Canada will be discussed in ch. 5), so there is a strong possibility that some new mission churches in the states used his covenant.

Despite limited efforts to standardize certain covenants, no single covenant or group of covenants predominated among Baptists in America in
the pre-1830 period. Churches used a large variety of covenants. This
pattern reflected a commitment to local church autonomy, but it also
showed the diversity of Baptist life. Covenantal diversity ranged from the
simple and concise covenant written and used by Benjamin Randall in
organizing the first Free Will Baptist church in America in New Dur-

ham, New Hampshire, in 1780 (covenant 27), to the comprehensive and lengthy covenant adopted in 1798 by the Lower Banister (United Baptist) Church in Pittsylvania County, Virginia (covenant 32), to a continuing flow of Seventh Day Baptist covenants in the late 1790s and early 1800s.[47]

A second trend included tendencies related to the contents of covenants. Baptists repeatedly insisted that they attempted to base their covenants on biblical teachings. Peter P. Roots ended the 1806 verse edition of his covenant with a typical Baptist sentiment regarding the subjects included in covenants:

> New rules we do no mean to make,
> The Bible rules we only take,
> And shew by this our script'ral creed,
> In Bible truth we are agreed.[48]

A church in Ulysses, New York voted in 1817 to accept the twelfth chapter of Romans as its covenant.[49]

Baptists in America prior to the 1830s tended to construct their covenants around the same four general topics which seventeenth-century English Baptists had used: church fellowship, church discipline, worship and personal devotion, and pastoral and lay care. With an amazing consistency, Baptists included a similar statement about the essence of covenanting, which centered on giving themselves up to God and one another, in practically all of their covenants.

Baptists generally distinguished between covenants and confessions of faith. Covenants dealt primarily with conduct and confessions with doctrine. But Baptists also interrelated the two, for covenants usually contained some doctrinal content, and confessions often cited the value of covenants in defining the church. Frontier Baptists sometimes gave the title "covenant" to their confessions of faith, apparently believing that doctrinal affirmations were the proper substance of covenants and that right conduct would grow out of a faithful attachment to confessional statements.

Many churches added new kinds of material to their covenants. The governing principle behind the inclusion of new concepts seems to have been a desire to respond more effectively to changes in local cultural, social, economic, religious, and related conditions. Church members sought to conduct themselves and practice their faith with integrity by keeping themselves in ethical tension with their fluctuating environ-

ments. Thus, they adapted their covenants to their unique settings and
situations in order to deal more adequately with particular social issues
that affected the communities in which their churches were located. At
times, churches also included in their covenants items relating to parliamentary procedure and "rules of decorum."

Frontier Baptists went to great lengths in their covenants, almost to
the point of legalism, to identify specifics relating to conduct and the
practice of their faith. Because they viewed their covenants and statements of discipline as sources of social and moral stability, their covenants often included detailed lists of evils to avoid. For example, the 1797
covenant of the Dumplin Creek Church in Tennessee included the following pledge: "We promise . . . to renounce all evil words and actions,
foolish talking, jesting, cursing, lying, malacious anger, extortion and
fraud of every kind, covetousness, drunkness and keeping evil company
and to abstain from sinful whispering, back biting, all wilful hypocrisy
and dishonesty, all excess or superfluity to the gratification of pride and
also resist from gaming, wagering, singing of carnal songs and all Carnal
myrth, fidling, dancing and vain recreation . . . ."[50] By filling their covenants with such specifics, frontier churches may at times have neglected
some of the more permanent and comprehensive principles of the New
Testament relating to Christian conduct.

A third trend centered on using covenants in a variety of settings. Baptists tended to use covenants in constituting new churches, in accepting
new members into congregations, and occasionally in baptisms. After the
Great Awakening covenants began to be used extensively in Saturday
covenant meetings, especially among the frontier Baptists. Three main
purposes of the meetings, which usually took place on the Saturday prior
to the Sunday when a church celebrated the Lord's Supper, were to engage in covenantal renewal, to prepare for the Lord's Supper, and to deal
with disciplinary matters relating to covenantal infractions.

A fourth trend focused on the relationship between church covenants
and church renewal. Churches using covenants often experienced renewal and revival. A good illustration relates to the first Free Will Baptist
church in America formed in New Durham, New Hampshire, under the
leadership of Benjamin Randall in 1780. In the act of constituting itself,
this church used a covenant which Randall had written (covenant 27).
Initial progress occurred in the church's life, but by 1791 decline set in.
"Quite a majority of the members had become so lukewarm and indiffer-
ent about the duties of religion, that they wholly neglected their church

meetings; and many of them had become a public reproach to the cause."[51] Thus, the church decided to "re-embody" around a new covenant. Some members questioned the procedure of adopting a new covenant only eleven years after the first, but a tremendous revival took place. Within three months, sixty-seven new members were added to the church. And the covenantal experiences of this church also stimulated Free Will Baptist growth in other places in New England.[52]

A fifth trend among Baptists in America prior to the 1830s was that they took covenanting seriously. Several kinds of evidence show the significance which these Baptists attached to covenantal concepts and practices. For one thing, they tended to sign their covenants. This practice enhanced the level of commitment which church members gave to their covenantal pledges. By penning their names to the dotted line of mutual agreements, church members also voluntarily placed themselves within the disciplinary expectations of responsible congregational life. The 1771 covenant of the Potomac (Hartwood) Church in Stafford County, Virginia, made clear "that none are to be admitted into the church but such as are willing and do sign this covenant."[53] Pre-Great Awakening Baptist churches tended to allow only male members to sign covenants, while post-Great Awakening covenants often included the signatures of male and female members. Factors lying behind the change may have been both a growing awareness of the importance of women in church life and the emphasis on freedom and human rights that characterized the era of the American Revolution.

Another evidence was the tight-knit relationship which Baptists established between church covenants and discipline. Violations of covenantal vows normally resulted in disciplinary action, and this action was sometimes harsh. Preservation of the integrity of the church seemed to lie at the heart of disciplinary motives. In untamed and violent frontier regions, discipline sought to protect a healthy sense of biblical morality. However, because frontier discipline tended to be highly corrective and reformative in its application, the therapeutic values of preventive and nurturing discipline sometimes seemed to take second place.

Still a further evidence was direct comments in church minutes, covenants, associational writings, and other places urging Baptists to implement their covenants as fully as possible. To illustrate, the 1826 circular letter of the Eastern Maine Baptist Association focused on the covenant idea. After observing that the acceptance of a covenant "certainly means something," it pointed out that, among other things, it meant that "We should not only profess good things but strive to do them." Then with more encouragement to achieve consistency between faith and action, the letter stated: "We should engage in the spirit and practice of the covenant; not for once only, but for all our lives. We should watch, pray and strive to persevere in every good word and work till death. We should turn the covenant into a prayer, and endeavor to reflect daily on the great wickedness of vowing without suitable impressions of our deep obligations to live a life answerable to our profession."[54]

Conclusion

Regional tendencies characterized Baptist covenantal developments in America prior to the Great Awakening. In New England, where churches regularly used covenants from the 1660s onward, churches tended to write their own individual covenants and often relied heavily upon Congregationalist influence both for the idea and the expression of the documents. In the Middle Colonies, where covenants began to flourish shortly after 1700, the influence of Elias Keach led a large number of churches to adopt the covenant which he and his father, Benjamin, had used in their churches in England. In the Southern Colonies, where covenants did not generally become a part of Baptist life until the early decades of the 1700s, several churches accepted the Keach covenant, but most wrote their own.

Separate Baptists in New England evidently used covenants extensively; those in the South may not have used them quite as widely. Separate Baptist leaders, such as Isaac Backus, Shubal Stearns, and Daniel Marshall, helped found churches that used covenants. Congregationalist influence lay behind many Separate Baptist covenants. And in the South, such covenants tended to be complex in structure, strict in requirements, Calvinistic in theology, and more heavily doctrinal than most previous Baptist covenants. Particular and Regular Baptists employed covenants extensively and stressed their importance in defining a church, exercising church discipline, and constituting new churches. Frontier Baptists tended to write individual covenants, established a rigid bond between covenants and discipline, assigned more authority to covenants than Baptists had typically done, sponsored monthly covenant meetings more frequently than previous Baptists, and occasionally labeled as covenants statements that were actually confessions of faith.

Five major covenantal trends emerged among Baptists in America prior to 1830. First, most churches wrote their own covenants, although some model covenants did appear. Second, heavily influenced by British Baptists and American Congregationalists, Baptists sought to construct their covenants upon a biblical basis; designed the contents of their covenants around church fellowship, church discipline, worship and personal devotion, and pastoral and lay care; included doctrinal elements in their covenants; and added their own unique elements as needed. Third, churches used covenants in a variety of settings, such as constituting new churches, receiving and baptizing new members, and conducting monthly covenant meetings. Fourth, the use of covenants often resulted in church renewal. Fifth, Baptists took covenants seriously as reflected in the fact that they generally signed them, related them to church discipline, and frequently urged their use.

In his excellent study of church covenants among early Virginia Baptists, William L. Lumpkin reached three conclusions that can actually be applied to the larger scope of Baptist covenants throughout early America. First, as local documents expressing congregational consensus regarding desired patterns of church and individual life, covenants varied widely in form, expression, and content. Further, there was no concerted effort to formulate a uniform covenant for all Baptist churches. Second, as "instruments of church discipline," covenants "gave definiteness to the standards of conduct of the church." They never hardened into creedal laws nor took the place of the Bible, but they did assist multitudes of Baptists to understand and practice the way of life advocated by their churches. Third, they helped Baptists aim for balance between theological and practical matters. They "helped prevent preoccupation with doctrinal speculations and abstract theological argument and called Christians to the practice of their faith in terms of effective churchmanship and genuine citizenship."[55]

4

Baptist Church Covenants
in America Since 1833

This chapter will treat four major concerns. First, the rise, growth, influence, and predominance of the covenantal tradition initiated by the New Hampshire Baptist Convention in 1833 will be considered. Second, miscellaneous covenantal developments outside this tradition will receive attention. Third, church covenant ideals expressed in Baptist church manuals and other publications will be assessed. And fourth, discussion of a general decline in covenantal usage and significance among Baptists, which began in the late 1800s and continued well into the 1900s, will precede an examination of the factors behind and expressions of what appears to be a recent renewal of interest in covenants among Southern Baptists.

Readers will note several new trends in the covenantal life of Baptists in America. The 1830s and 1840s revealed a new level of interest in covenants by state conventions, especially in New England. Local associations in New England in the 1830s-1850s also expanded their concern for covenants. New England Baptists generally exerted a major influence on covenantal developments among Baptists throughout the United States. Compared to earlier Baptist life in America, perhaps the single most important covenantal trend from the 1830s to the 1990s has been the increased standardization of the covenants used by Baptists. Even though many churches throughout the period continued to write their own covenants, the proliferating publication of model covenants in a broad range of Baptist materials, such as church manuals, ministers' manuals, hymnals, church minute books, encyclopedias, study guides, curriculum pieces, pocket cards, hymnal inserts, wall charts, and baptismal certificates, led to widespread covenantal uniformity. And among the available model covenants published, the most amazing development of all is that the 1853 covenant of J. Newton Brown (see covenant 41 in ch. 6) became and remains the most widely used covenant among Baptists both in America and in some other countries.

Covenants in the New Hampshire Tradition

In the early 1830s the New Hampshire Baptist Convention initiated what became the first major movement toward a uniform covenant among Baptist churches in America. In a major study of the history of Baptist church covenants, Champlin Burrage claimed in 1904 that "the majority of Baptist church covenants in use in America to-day are based more or less on that connected with the New Hampshire Declaration of Faith,"[1] jointly published in 1833. This claim is probably as true at the end of the twentieth century as it was at the beginning.

The New Hampshire Convention's declaration of faith and church covenant were printed together throughout the 1800s. By 1883 at least seven editions of these documents on doctrine and conduct had been published in New Hampshire alone.[2] Since the New Hampshire confession of faith became the most widely used declaration among Baptists in America, and even served as the basis for the 1925 statement of faith adopted by the Southern Baptist Convention, it was inevitable that the covenant attached to it would also receive widespread acceptance. Several versions of the New Hampshire covenant were prepared in the nineteenth century.

The 1833 covenant of the New Hampshire Baptist Convention.—Because of the significance of the 1833 covenant adopted by the board of the New Hampshire Baptist Convention, the story of its development needs to be told. The New Hampshire Convention resolved on June 24, 1830, that a committee comprised of N. W. Williams, William Taylor, and I. Person should prepare and present at the next annual meeting "such a Declaration of Faith and Practice together with a Covenant, as may be thought agreeable to and consistent with the views of all our churches in this state."[3] This committee reported to the convention on June 22, 1831, that, although they had achieved some progress, "peculiar circumstances" had prevented their completing the assignment. The committee was abolished at the request of its members, and Person was appointed to complete the work and report to the board of the convention when convenient.[4]

Person presented his completed documents to the convention board on June 26, 1832 (covenant 35). The board then referred the documents to a

committee comprised of Baron Stow, J. Newton Brown, Jonathan Going, and I. Person.[5] In the annual meeting of the New Hampshire Convention on June 29, 1832, this committee reported in favor of adopting,
with a few alterations, the documents prepared by Person. The convention discussed the report and then referred the documents "to the disposal of the Board."[6] Later that day, the convention referred the documents
to a smaller committee consisting of Baron Stow and J. Newton Brown.
These two men were to revise the documents further and present them at
a future meeting of the board.[7]

On October 10, 1832, Brown presented to the convention board a report on the documents which he and Stow had revised. After a discussion
of the various articles in the documents, the board adjourned. It recon-
vened on the next day, accepted the report of Brown and Stow, and discharged the committee. The board then resolved that Brown be asked to
prepare a copy of the documents, including the modifications suggested
by the board, and to present the copy at the next meeting of the board.
Finally, the board appointed William Gault, E. E. Cummings, and
Brown to inquire about the most practical means of printing and circulating the documents among the churches.[8]

Brown presented the final edition of the revised documents to the
board at its meeting on January 15, 1833. The board then resolved "that
the Declaration of Faith and Covenant prepared by Brethren Stow and
Brown, and now read before the board of this Convention, are entitled to
their unanimous approbation, and are by them cordially recommended
to the adoption of the churches."[9] The board then asked Daniel Chase,
who was present, to copyright the documents, print them in pamphlet
form on fine paper with blue covers, and make the pamphlets available to
churches and ministers in New Hampshire at the rate of $2.50 per one
hundred copies or at thirty-six cents a dozen. Chase agreed to these conditions.[10] The pamphlet appeared five days later (covenant 36).

Several factors contributed to the spread of this covenant throughout
New Hampshire, across the United States, and even into Canada. (Its
presence in Canada will be discussed in ch. 5.) The first was the widespread distribution among New Hampshire churches of the January 20,
1833, pamphlet containing the covenant. Entitled *A Short Summary and
Declaration of Faith of the Baptist Church in* [blank space for a church to
write in its location] *to Which Is Added the Church Covenant,* this pamphlet was originally released in at least two editions.[11] An advertisement
in each edition indicated that the documents in the pamphlet "were is-

sued under the sanction of the Convention." Little did the convention realize that it was initiating a trend toward uniformity in covenantal usage among Baptists in America that would gain enormous momentum by the mid-1800s.

A second factor was the influence of J. Newton Brown. He played a significant role in the final stages of the covenant's development, including making his own input into its content, preparing the final copy for approval by the board of the New Hampshire Convention, and assisting in arranging for its printing and distribution. Brown served as a prominent pastor of the Baptist church at Exeter (1829-39), and worked later as editorial secretary for the American Baptist Publication Society (1849-59), a position which made him a highly influential person in Baptist life.

One of Brown's major contributions was the production of the *Encyclopedia of Religious Knowledge* (1835), of which he served as editor. The article entitled "Baptists" included a copy of the New Hampshire covenant.[12] This encyclopedia was reprinted at least ten times between 1835 and 1870.[13] Almost 100,000 copies had been circulated by 1853.[14] Thus, the encyclopedia helped to circulate the covenant far and wide. To illustrate just how far, the 1853 minutes of the First Baptist Church of Albuquerque, New Mexico, reveal that this church adopted the New Hampshire covenant directly from Brown's encyclopedia.[15]

A third factor was the publication of the covenant in multiple editions of a major Baptist church manual.[16] At least five editions of William Crowell's *The Church Member's Manual* appeared between 1847 and 1873.[17] In the late 1840s Crowell was pastor of the First Baptist Church in Waterville, Maine. His publication established an important precedent in presenting the New Hampshire covenant, or revisions of it, as a model covenant in numerous Baptist church manuals of the 1800s and 1900s.

Illustrative evidence of the geographical spread of the New Hampshire covenant across the United States included its adoption in 1835 by the First Baptist Church of Owensboro, Kentucky; its adoption in 1856 by the Montevallo Baptist Church in Shelby County, Alabama; and its appearance in the 1862 minutes of the San Francisco (California) Baptist Association. The covenant even appeared as a model in a church manual published in 1880 for use by Regular Baptist churches.[18] The New Hampshire covenant experienced considerable popularity throughout the 1800s.

The 1846 covenant of the Maine Baptist Convention.—The Maine Baptist Convention was the second state convention, after New Hampshire, to prepare and adopt a covenant for use by its churches. Maine convention minutes show that on June 20, 1844, the convention created a committee to study the possibility "of uniform Articles of Faith for the State," presumably including a covenant, and that on June 16, 1846, the convention adopted some articles of faith and a church covenant (covenant 39) after carefully revising the documents prepared by the committee.[19] Although shorter, this Maine covenant bore many resemblances in wording to the 1833 New Hampshire covenant. The two documents likely belonged to the same family of covenants.

The adoption of a covenant by the Maine Baptist Convention led many Baptist associations in Maine to print this covenant in their minutes. For example, the Bowdoinham Association printed the covenant in 1848 (moving away from a revision of the 1756 Backus covenant which it had printed in 1805); the Hancock Association printed it in 1850 (reversing itself in 1851 by voting to print the covenant "originally adopted by the Churches of this Association"—a revision of the Backus covenant); and the Kennebec Association printed it in 1858 (moving away from an 1841 covenant—covenant 38—which it had "adopted and recommended to the churches"). Other Maine associations which printed it included the Penobscot (1849, 1850, 1851), the Lincoln (1851, 1852, 1853, 1854), the Waldo (1854), and the Washington (1858).[20] Undoubtedly, numerous Maine Baptist churches must have used this covenant as a result of heavy state convention and associational support for it.

The 1847 covenant of William Crowell.—Crowell's 1847 publication entitled *The Church Member's Manual* included the 1833 covenant of the New Hampshire Baptist Convention, but it also included a second shorter covenant (covenant 40). About the same length as the 1846 covenant of the Maine Baptist Convention, it had similarities in wording with both the New Hampshire and Maine covenants; therefore, its relationship to them seems clear. While the origins of the Crowell covenant are difficult to pinpoint, variations of it existed as early as the 1820s. For example, the Dudley Street Baptist Church in Boston had adopted a similar covenant in 1821, as had the Halifax Baptist Church in Nova Scotia in 1827 (covenant 65). Perhaps some of the predecessors of the Crowell covenant were available to the writers of the original 1833 New Hampshire covenant and of the Maine covenant and even influenced their choice of wording at points.

Because Crowell's church manual was published in several editions in the 1800s, his short covenant was used widely. Examples of Baptist churches which used it between 1857 and 1902 included the First Church in Cambridge, Massachusetts; the Bartlett Church in Shelby County, Tennessee; and the Coliseum Place Church in New Orleans, Louisiana.

The same covenant appeared with two additional articles in Crowell's 1849 manual entitled *The Church Member's Hand-book: A Guide to the Doctrines and Practice of Baptist Churches.* The new articles stated: "that we will earnestly endeavor to bring up such as may be under our care in the nurture and admonition of the Lord" and "that we will endeavor, by example and effort, to win souls to Christ."[21] This version of the covenant also gained broad acceptance because at least eight editions of Crowell's handbook were printed between 1849 and 1858.[22] As far away as Oregon, the Corvallis Baptist Association printed the covenant in its minutes in 1869. The Eutaw Place Church in Baltimore, Maryland, used the covenant in the 1880s, as did the Chestnut Street Church in Louisville, Kentucky, in the 1890s.

The 1853 covenant of J. Newton Brown.—In 1853, in his *The Baptist Church Manual,* J. Newton Brown published his personal revision of the 1833 covenant of the New Hampshire Baptist Convention (covenant 41). As editorial secretary of the American Baptist Publication Society, Brown exerted a massive influence upon the denomination. "His covenant as printed in the *Manual* became the standard for membership conduct in local churches," and "Brown was clearly a household word in local church life and doctrinal uniformity."[23] Further, "Due largely to its spirit of local church protectionism, Brown's 'Church Covenant' achieved what few standard expressions have done among Baptists: It is broadly accepted and has outlived its author."[24]

Brown thoroughly modified the wording, phraseology, and arrangement of the New Hampshire covenant. In addition, he added a Trinitarian emphasis to the first paragraph. He added two new causes: "to avoid all tattling, backbiting, and excessive anger; to abstain from the sale and use of intoxicating drinks as a beverage." He softened the section relating to church discipline. He added a new concluding paragraph stressing the need for a church member to join another church soon after leaving the one to which he currently belonged. And he took the last paragraph of the New Hampshire covenant and attached it to his revision as an appendage entitled "Prayer."

At least nine important factors accounted for the fact that Brown's revision became, and still is, the most prevalent covenant among Baptists in America. First, his covenant had the strong support of the American Baptist Publication Society. As the editorial secretary of this body between 1849 and 1859, Brown led it to publish and distribute his *The Baptist Church Manual.* Thirty-eight printings of this manual were made between 1853 and 1985 by the Publication Society and its successor, Judson Press.[25] The society and press have published other model covenants, but none has had the same impact as that of Brown.

Second, numerous Baptist church manuals and ministers' manuals have included Brown's covenant as a model or example, beginning with his own in 1853. At least nineteen manuals published between 1867 and 1988 included the covenant.[26] Considerable variation existed in the covenants used by Baptist churches in America before the mid-1800s, when church manuals began to appear in large numbers. One result of these manuals, however, was that churches tended to adopt the covenants published in them. The manuals "not only contributed to making covenanting a characteristic of Baptist churches, but also in fixing the form of the covenant,"[27] and Brown's form was primary. Some of the manuals changed parts of Brown's covenant, usually by omitting the clause on intoxicating drinks.

Third, Brown's covenant received the approval and sponsorship of many Landmark Baptists. Landmarkism, a Baptist movement which arose in Tennessee in the 1850s, placed a heavy emphasis on the local church, viewed Baptists as the only true expression of the Christian faith, and defended a successionist approach to Baptist history, meaning that Baptists could be found in every era of church history. This movement made a major impact on Baptist life in America, especially under the initial leadership of J. R. Graves, J. M. Pendleton, and A. C. Dayton. Pendleton led in promoting Brown's covenant when he included it in his *Church Manual* in 1867. In 1946 Judson Press reported that Northern Baptists had printed 150,000 copies of this manual.[28] Further, Broadman Press, operated by the Southern Baptist Sunday School Board, published a revised edition in 1966 entitled *Baptist Church Manual.* By early 1989 Broadman had distributed more than 69,000 copies.[29]

The impact of Pendleton's writing upon the adoption of Brown's covenant was widespread. Examples of Baptist churches which adopted the covenant and stated in their minutes or written histories that they had taken it directly from Pendleton's manual were the Olive Branch Church in Wayne City, Illinois (1900); the East Side Church in Paragould, Arkansas (1912); the First Church in Heavener, Oklahoma (1912); and the

First Southern Baptist Church in Salinas, California (1938). Further, a Texas Baptist leader claimed in the early 1900s that in Texas the churches in both the Baptist General Convention, composed of Southern Baptists, and the Baptist Missionary Association, composed of Landmark Baptists, "have very generally" adopted the covenant in Pendleton's manual.[30]

Other evidence of Landmark sponsorship of Brown's covenant has expressed itself in four publications of the Baptist Sunday School Committee of the Landmark American Baptist Association, located in Texarkana, Arkansas-Texas. These include Ben M. Bogard's *The Baptist Way-Book* (1945), which simply prints the covenant; I. K. Cross's *Church Covenant* (1955, revised 1972), a series of twenty-six outlines on the covenant for preaching and special studies; Albert Garner's *The Church Covenant* (1957), a series of thirteen studies on the covenant; and Roy M. Reed's *Christian Engagements: A Study of the Church Covenant* (1962), a lengthy exposition of Brown's covenant. In 1988 the Baptist Sunday School Committee also distributed a 5"x 8" card with Brown's covenant printed on it.

Fourth, various Baptist publishers, north and south, published record books in which churches could keep their membership rolls and the official minutes of their business meetings. Many of these record books preprinted Brown's covenant on an initial page. This undoubtedly led many churches to adopt the covenant. Three examples of these record books included the *Church Roll Alphabetically Arranged and Record Book* (1907, 1910), published by the Baptist Book Concern in Louisville; *The World Church Roll and Record Book Alphabetically Arranged* (1910), published by the American Baptist Publication Society in Philadelphia, Boston, Chicago, and St. Louis; and the *Convention Church Record With Declaration of Faith, Church Covenant, Rules of Order, Alphabetical List of Members, Blank Pages for Minutes and Other Features* (no date), published by the Southern Baptist Sunday School Board in Nashville. Everyone of these record books indicated that the covenant printed was taken from J. M. Pendleton's *Church Manual.*

Fifth, Brown's covenant made significant inroads into the Fundamentalist strain of Baptist life when the Baptist Bible Union of America adopted a revised version of the New Hampshire Confession of Faith in 1923 and printed it in pamphlet form along with Brown's covenant, except for the omission of the article on intoxicating drinks.[31] Since the New Hampshire Confession was "the keystone of the Fundamentalist reform program,"[32] it is not surprising that leaders of the Fundamental-ist movement put forward a covenant related to the New Hampshire tra-dition. When one considers that, along with the publication of the Lon-don Confession of 1644 and the formation of the Baptist Missionary Society, as Baptist historian William H. Brackney has posited, "The third watershed event in the making of Baptist identity was the establish-ment of the Baptist Bible Union in 1923,"[33] one gains increased perspec-tive on the surge of influence which that movement had in advancing Brown's covenant.

Sixth, a major form of sponsorship for the Brown covenant occurred in 1927 when the Southern Baptist Convention's Commission on Co-Operative Program recommended in its January meeting that churches across the convention observe March as Church Covenant Month. The motivation behind this recommendation was the desire to create "a deep-er, a more consistent and persistent, cultivation of the spiritual life of our churches" so that "we shall have no shortage of funds" to finance con-vention work. The commission's recommendation, which was published in the 1927 Southern Baptist Convention *Proceedings,*[34] referred to "the Church Covenant" with capital "C's" as if there were only one accept-able covenant. Such designations clearly meant the Brown covenant and equally clearly showed the stature which that covenant had gained in the denominational mind-set of Southern Baptists.

After acknowledging that "it is unfortunately and sadly true that a great host of our people have no intelligent appreciation of these obliga-tions [contained in the covenant] and that the Church Covenant occupies small place in their thinking," the commission recommended several spe-cific approaches for churches to take in making Church Covenant Month meaningful. Pastors were urged to observe one Sunday during the month as Church Covenant Day and to preach one or more sermons on the covenant during the month. Churches were encouraged to print the covenant in their bulletins, to read it publicly along with applicants for church membership, and to "make loving, sympathetic and persistent effort to impress upon all our people the fundamental Christian virtues and obligations contained in the Covenant."

In its 1927 report to the Southern Baptist Convention, the commission noted that Church Covenant Month had been "very generally observed throughout the bounds of the Convention," that denominational papers had printed it, that churches had placed it in their bulletins and read it publicly, and that pastors had preached on it, sometimes series of sermons. The net result of such achievements was that the Brown covenant gained enormous exposure and detailed attention. And the commission's assessment of usage was undoubtedly accurate. To illustrate, the Baptist state papers of North Carolina, South Carolina, Georgia, Illinois, Missouri, and New Mexico all promoted Church Covenant Month in either February or March 1927.[35] Four of these papers printed the Brown covenant in full, and two of them, South Carolina and Missouri, printed it on their front pages.

Suggestions given to churches in the six papers were to observe Church Covenant Month, to read the covenant, preach on it, "magnify" it, distribute it among church members, renew allegiance to it, "let it be lived up in the lives of the members," and order from the Sunday School Board small covenant cards "at fifty cents a hundred" and for $1.50 a large covenant chart "printed on cloth in letters which can be read across the room." Such widespread promotion of the Brown covenant as an integral part of a Church Covenant Month emphasis surely led scores of churches to adopt and stress this covenant. Actually, the covenant must have already been rather prevalent. The South Carolina paper observed, for example, that "you will find it [the Brown covenant] in the record books of almost all of our churches."

Seventh, although the Southern Baptist Convention has never officially adopted Brown's covenant, or any other covenant, the printing and wide circulation of Brown's covenant by the denomination's Sunday School Board have contributed to the fact that "most churches participating in the Southern Baptist Convention use this covenant."[36] The board has circulated Brown's covenant in millions of copies of several different types of publications, such as books, booklets, periodicals, curriculum studies, and tracts.[37] Of special importance was the board's printing of the covenant in the 1956 edition of the *Baptist Hymnal.* By early 1989 more than 6,507,000 copies of this hymnal had been distributed in such diverse forms as a pew edition, a pulpit edition, a loose-leaf edition, a sheets-only edition, and a miniature edition.[38] Because of its widespread use in the public worship of Southern Baptist churches, this hymnal, possibly more than any other single factor, helped make the Brown covenant the predominant covenant among Southern Baptists in the last half of the twentieth century.

The Board's *Baptist Book Store Catalog, 1988-89* included in its "Church Covenant Supplies" section a 3½" x 5½" church covenant card "for pocket or purse," a 6" x 4" pressure-sensitive church covenant insert which "may be affixed to inside front or inside back cover of new Baptist Hymnal" (the 1975 edition of this hymnal did not contain the Brown covenant, as had the 1956 edition), and a 35" x 55" church covenant wall chart. The Sunday School Board distributed covenant cards as early as 1924. At that time, some churches asked candidates for membership to read the covenants on these cards, since they would be expected to live up to their contents, and other churches even required candidates for membership to sign the cards.[39]

Eighth, the two largest black Baptist denominations in America have made extensive use of the Brown covenant, with a few modifications, in pastors' guides, hymnals, wall charts, cards, baptismal certificates, and other kinds of publications. The Sunday School Publishing Board of the National Baptist Convention, U.S.A., Inc., the largest black Baptist convention with more than 30,000 churches, has featured the Brown covenant in many publications. The only significant change in each case has been the addition of a final paragraph which reads like a prayer: "And now unto Him, who brought again from the dead, Our Lord Jesus, be Power and Glory forever. Amen."

Besides featuring this covenant in the much-used *The Baptist Standard Hymnal with Responsive Readings* (1924; reprinted 1985), edited by Mrs. A. M. Townsend, and in an undated "Certificate of Baptism," the Sunday School Publishing Board has printed it for sixty years in Lewis Garnett Jordan's popular *The Baptist Standard Church Directory and Busy Pastor's Guide* (1928; reprinted 1988). Identified as "a standard church polity directory and guide for pastors among National Baptists,"[40] this directory has recommended the Brown covenant for more than half a century "for adoption by all Baptist churches at the time of their organization" and has encouraged churches to read the covenant "at regular intervals, frequently enough to have the membership become familiar with its import."[41]

The second largest black Baptist convention in the United States is the National Baptist Convention of America with more than 12,000 churches. The Publication Board of this convention has given high visibility to a revised version of the Brown covenant in numerous publications. Among the more conspicuous changes typically made in the Brown covenant are (1) the addition within the paragraph on the church of the pledge "to give it [the church] a place in our affections, prayers and services above every organization of human origin"; (2) the addition to the end of the paragraph on the church of the sentence, "In case of difference of opinion in the church, we will strive to avoid a contentious spirit, and if we cannot unanimously agree, we will cheerfully recognize the right of the majority to govern"; (3) the addition to the paragraph on personal and family life of the vow "to study diligently the word of God," and the deletion from that same paragraph of the clauses, "to avoid all tattling, backbiting, and excessive anger; to abstain from the sale and use of intoxicating drinks as a beverage"; and (4) the addition near the end of the covenant of the promise "through life, amid evil report, and good report, to seek to live to the glory of God, who hath called us out of darkness into his marvelous light."[42]

One of the Publishing Board's most influential publications containing this version of the Brown covenant as a suggested model for use in churches has been R. H. Boyd's *Boyd's National Baptist Pastor's Guide and Parliamentary Rules.* The National Baptist Convention adopted this pastor's guide in 1900 as "a standard guide for churches," and the popularity of the guide led the Publishing Board to release the twenty-fifth edition in 1983.[43] The guide's preface to Brown's covenant states that "The following is a suitable church covenant to be adopted upon organization [of new churches]."[44] Through almost a century of influence, this ministers' manual has undoubtedly made a marked impact upon the use of Brown's covenant by many churches.

Other materials of the National Baptist Publishing Board which have contained the revised edition of Brown's covenant include R. H. Boyd's *What Baptists Believe and Practice* (13th edition; 1986), *The New National Baptist Hymnal* (1987), *Articles of Faith and Church Covenant* (undated booklet), a 17½" x 25" church covenant wall chart, and small church covenant cards. The presence of the covenant in such a variety of places illustrates its importance to the black Baptist tradition of the twentieth century. R. H. Boyd's *Boyd's National Baptist Sunday School Teacher's Class Book* (1987) used a version of Brown's covenant that was closer to the original 1853 edition in its wording.

Ninth, Swedish and German Baptist denominations in America have used Brown's covenant across a broad geographical spectrum. David Guston, archivist for the Baptist General Conference (Swedish), recently claimed that "We have the impression that most of our congregations include a church covenant in their constitution and by-laws."[45] He supplied copies of eleven covenants used by churches in the Baptist General Conference.[46] Ten of them were either exact replicas of Brown's covenant or some revision of it. Three Illinois churches used Brown's covenant without change: the Calvary Church in Evanston (1936), the Emerald Avenue Church in Chicago (1944), and the Evangel Church in Wheaton (1960).

Changes in the remaining seven covenants related primarily to Brown's two clauses, "to avoid all tattling, backbiting, and excessive anger; to abstain from the sale and use of intoxicating drinks as a beverage." Two churches deleted only the second clause relating to alcohol: the Bethlehem Church in Minneapolis, Minnesota (1946), and the Washington Avenue Church in Ludington, Michigan (1956). The Calvary Church in Roseville, Minnesota (1980), deleted both clauses. A Baptist General Conference church manual, *My Church: A Manual of Baptist Faith and Action* by Gordon G. Johnson (1957), and one church, the Immanuel Church in Waukegan, Illinois (1970), changed both clauses to read: "to avoid unkind words and unrighteous anger; to abstain from the use and the sale of intoxicating liquors as a beverage and from every form of evil." The Salem Church in New Brighton, Minnesota (1963), changed both clauses as follows: "to avoid unkind words and unrighteous anger; to abstain from the use and sale of mood-altering chemicals except as prescribed and deemed necessary by a physician, and from every form of evil." And the Elim Church in Beloit, Wisconsin (1969), changed both clauses to read: "to avoid unkind words and unrighteous anger; to abstain from the use and sale of tobacco and intoxicating liquors and from every form of evil." This last church also added the following new paragraph to the end of its covenant: "This covenant shall be read in the public service of the church at least quarterly and, with the constitution and by-laws, shall be presented to those contemplating church membership."

German Baptists in the North American Baptist Conference have also adopted on a wide scale either the Brown covenant or a revision of it. John Binder, executive director of the conference, supplied copies of covenants used by nine German Baptist churches in six states. Eight of these were based on the Brown covenant.[47] Two Minnesota churches used Brown's covenant without change: the Faith Church in Minneapolis (1960) and the Brook Park Church in Brooklyn Center (undated). And the 1969 covenant of the Sherwood Forest Church in Redmund, Washington, made only one change; it deleted Brown's clause on intoxicating drinks.

Five covenants contained changes in Brown's clause, "to religiously educate our children." Various readings included: "to educate our children in the Christian faith" (undated covenant of First Church, Chancellor, South Dakota); "to teach our children the Christian truths" (1971 covenant of Bethany Church, Milwaukee, Wisconsin); "to train our children in the fear and admonition of the Lord" (1975 covenant of Shakopee Church, Shakopee, Minnesota); "to train our children in the Christian faith" (1977 covenant of Sunrise Church, Fair Oaks, California); and "to diligently train our children in the way of the Lord by teaching them the Word of God and by our exemplary living" (1978 covenant of Century Church, Bismarck, North Dakota).

Four of these same covenants also made other changes relating to Brown's clause on intoxicating drinks. The Bethany Church and the Sunrise Church deleted it. The Shakopee Church changed it to read: "to remember that our bodies are the temple of the Holy Spirit and to abstain from those habits (1 Cor. 6:19-20) that enslave the body and mind." The Century Church changed both it and the clauses preceding and following it to read: "We believe that in order to live a holy life, we must surrender to God's will and trust Christ as our sanctification; allowing Him to do whatever may be necessary in our lives each day in purity, freedom, peace, and power for His Glory and the advancement of His kingdom."

Besides minor changes in the wording of Brown's covenant in several of these covenants, the only other covenant to include major changes was that of the Shakopee Church, which added two new elements to Brown's paragraph on the church: "to heed the Scriptural admonition, 'not forsaking the assembling of ourselves together,' at such time and place as the church may appoint for instruction, prayer, business or evangelizing" and "to give it [the church] a sacred pre-eminence over all institutions of human origin."

Some of the changes which Swedish and German Baptists have made in the Brown covenant illustrate an important principle in Baptist covenantal development, namely, the application of the autonomy of the local church in creatively adapting a covenant to meet the specific needs and intentions of an individual congregation. For example, both Swedish and German Baptists have struggled with Brown's clause on abstaining from intoxicating drinks. Their struggle has reflected the combined influence of their cultural backgrounds and their belief that Brown's covenant deals inadequately with matters of personal and social ethics. Thus, they have altered Brown's wording to make their covenants express more adequately the individual disciplines which they have considered more biblical in nature and to which they have been willing to commit themselves.

These nine factors, among possible others, have created enormous popularity for the Brown covenant. Additional evidence illustrates the wide geographical distribution achieved by this covenant. A widely used 1959 study book entitled *The Meaning of Church Membership,* published by the American Baptists, both included Brown's covenant in numerous printings and stated that this covenant "has been adopted by most Baptist churches."[48] Second, a 1973 survey on the use of church covenants among Southern Baptists received responses from 217 of 324 churches to whom questionnaires had been sent. These 217 returns came from churches in thirty-two state conventions, including Alaska and Hawaii, as well as from several states where conventions did not exist. Not surprisingly, the survey showed that eighty-nine percent of these churches used either officially or unofficially the covenant, or some variation of it, which Brown had published in 1853.[49] More recently, the Calvary Baptist Church in Anchorage, Alaska, used the covenant in the 1980s. And in 1988 the Halawa Heights Church in Honolulu, Hawaii, made Brown's covenant the basis for its own but completely reworded it (covenant 62).

Feeling that Brown's covenant has not focused sufficiently on moral issues other than intoxicating drinks, Baptists at times have made additions to it. For example, a West Virginia church adopted the covenant in 1867 with the following revisions: "to abstain from the sale and use of intoxicating liquors and drinks as a beverage; also, from cards, theaters, and dancing, believing they detract from our spiritual growth."[50] Further, in 1970 the Southern Baptist Convention requested the Sunday School Board to "study for revision the church covenant appearing in the *Baptist Hymnal* and elsewhere to include a statement of abstinence of illegally dispensed drugs, pornography, and other evil products which can be bought and used."[51] Some later printings of Brown's covenant in various Sunday School Board products, such as covenant cards and wall charts, have not included these changes. Certain others have included new emphases on drugs and pornography. Printings of the covenant in *Developing a Church Covenant* (1971) and in the *Broadman Church Manual* (1973) added these words: "to use our influence to combat the abuse of drugs and the spread of pornography." Another Sunday School Board product, hymnal inserts, initially printed in 1976 for insertion in the 1975 edition of the *Baptist Hymnal,* which did not contain Brown's covenant, as had the 1956 edition, made the following additions to Brown's covenant: "to abstain from the sale of, and use of, destructive drugs or intoxicating drinks as a beverage; to shun pornography."

Other changes, which probably reflect theological considerations, have occurred in the first paragraph of Brown's covenant in different printings of small covenant cards distributed by the Sunday School Board. Some printings present the covenant exactly as Brown published it. Others substitute the word *Spirit* for *Ghost* and delete the word *angels.*

The 1859 revision of Edward T. Hiscox.—In addition to the 1833 covenant of the New Hampshire Baptist Convention, the 1846 covenant of the Maine Baptist Convention, the 1847 covenant of William Crowell, and the 1853 covenant of J. Newton Brown, one other major covenant appeared in the New Hampshire tradition in the 1800s. In 1859 Edward T. Hiscox, pastor of the Stanton Street Baptist Church in New York City, who formerly served as pastor in New England, where he had been born and educated, published *The Baptist Church Directory.* This important church manual contained his revision of the New Hampshire covenant (covenant 43).

Hiscox remained closer to the content of the New Hampshire covenant than J. Newton Brown did. His first, fourth, fifth, and eighth paragraphs had virtually the same content as the original. His second paragraph combined into an abbreviated form the second and sixth paragraphs of the original. His third and sixth paragraphs were essentially the same as the third paragraph in the original. His seventh paragraph, "That, we will, in all conditions, even till death, strive to live to the glory of him, who hath called us out of darkness into his marvellous light," was the only significant addition for which there was no precedent in the original. Hiscox revised the original primarily by shortening it, rearranging its contents, and altering its wording. Unlike Brown, Hiscox omitted any reference to intoxicating drinks.

Hiscox's revision never achieved the popularity of Brown's covenant, but it did attain wide acceptance. By 1894 about 60,000 copies of *The Baptist Church Directory* had been distributed.[52] This and other church manuals which he wrote or which bore his name have been primarily responsible for its circulation. His other manuals containing the covenant included: *The Star Book on Baptist Church Polity* (1874; by 1880, 30,000 copies had been printed); *The New Directory for Baptist Churches* (1894; reprinted as recently as 1970); *The Standard Manual for Baptist Churches* (1890; by 1949, 150,000 copies had been printed); *The Hiscox Guide for Baptist Churches* (1964); and *The Hiscox Standard Baptist Manual* (1965).[53] Many of these manuals, as well as other materials containing the Hiscox covenant, were published by the American Baptist

Publication Society and its successor, Judson Press. So these publication operations had a significant role in promoting both the Brown and Hiscox covenants. Major Baptist presses in the South have not generally given Hiscox the same attention as they have Brown.

Hiscox's covenant also appeared in writings other than his own,[54] and Baptist churches have used it in many states and time periods. Examples include the Second Church of Liberty, Missouri (1860s); the First Church of Texarkana, Texas (1870s); the First Colored Church in Savannah, Georgia (1880s); the First Church of Suffolk, Virginia (1890s); the Second Church of Florence, South Carolina (first decade of 1900s); the Beaucoup Church of Pinckneyville, Illinois (1910s); and the Island Home Church of Knoxville, Tennessee (1960s). Interestingly, although the Texarkana Church adopted the Hiscox covenant in 1877, it adopted three successively different covenants by 1917, at which time the Brown covenant finally won out.[55]

A unique variation of the Hiscox covenant, which also included elements of other covenants in the New Hampshire tradition, appeared in an 1871 hymnbook entitled *The Baptist Praise Book: For Congregational Singing* (covenant 45). Since this hymnbook was prepared by such renowned Baptists as Richard Fuller, Thomas Armitage, and Basil Manly, Jr., the covenant in it likely gained some recognition.

Miscellaneous Church Covenants

Although this chapter has focused on major covenants within the New Hampshire Baptist tradition, Baptists in America since 1833 have used hundreds of other covenants as well. Some of these covenants may have had slight kinship with the New Hampshire covenantal tradition, based on occasional similarities in wording and/or content; but most have been radical departures from that tradition. Many of these covenants experienced only limited usage, but some achieved a certain popularity among small Baptist groups. Besides appearing in local church records, these covenants have also been printed in such sources as pamphlets, booklets, denominational handbooks, church and ministers' manuals, church histories and anniversary brochures, encyclopedias, hymnbooks, and periodicals. A description of sample covenants found in these kinds of materials follows.

Two examples of covenants developed within the context of local Baptist associations, both in New England, existed in the 1830s and 1840s. In 1836 the Old Colony Association in Massachusetts appointed a committee of three men to prepare some articles of faith and a covenant "for the general use of the Association" and to present them at the next annual meeting. The committee presented its proposed documents to the association in 1837, and the association seemed to approve them. A problem arose, however, when someone suggested that recommending these items to the churches "might have the appearance of dictation to the churches." Therefore, the committee was discharged, and the subject was discontinued indefinitely.[56] Thus, a fear of intruding into the autonomy of local churches through recommending model articles and a covenant to them led the association to take such action.

The committee which had prepared the articles and covenant did not let the matter rest, however. In 1838 the three men published a pamphlet entitled *A Summary of Christian Belief and Church Covenant* which included the documents they had presented to the association.[57] The title page included the words "Adopted by the Baptist Church in" followed by a blank space in which a church using the articles and covenant could write in its location. Obviously, the covenant in this publication (covenant 37) was intentionally designed to serve as a model for churches, and it was one of many Baptist church covenants, both before and after its time, printed by individuals without the endorsement of any specific church, association, or other Baptist body.

Then in 1841 the Kennebec Association in Maine, which had appointed a committee the previous year to revise its articles of faith and covenant, adopted a covenant and recommended it to the churches (covenant 38). Unlike the Old Colony Association in Massachusetts, this association did not hesitate to place a model covenant before its churches. Seventeen years later, in 1858, the Kennebec Association printed in its minutes the covenant "recommended by the Baptist State Convention [in Maine] of 1846" (covenant 39). This action shows how a smaller Baptist body acceded to the influence of a larger one in recommending a model covenant, even when the smaller body had taken the initiative to write its own.[58]

Typical covenants printed in denominational handbooks, encyclopedias, church manuals, and church minutes represented the covenantal life of such diverse Baptist groups as the Free Will Baptists in the 1850s and 1880s (covenants 42 and 48), the Swedish Baptists in the 1870s (covenant 46), the Seventh Day Baptists in the 1920s and 1970s (covenants 50 and 58), the Primitive Baptists in the 1940's (covenant 51), the General Baptists in the 1940's and 1960's (covenant 52), and the German Baptists in the 1980s (covenant 61). These covenants illustrate both the pervasive nature of written covenants in the broad spectrum of Baptist life and an underlying urge toward covenantal diversity, even though covenants in the New Hampshire tradition dominated covenantal patterns.

The tendency for individuals to write unique covenants has been an important feature of the Baptist covenantal landscape. Three pre-1890 examples of such covenants deserve attention. First, in 1868, the Citadel Square Baptist Church in Charleston, South Carolina, adopted a covenant (covenant 44). The church's minutes for that year indicated that the covenant had been prepared by Richard Furman and that it had been "incorporated into the Constitution of so many Baptist churches of our land."[59] Furman (1755-1825) had been one of the leading Baptist pastors in the South, had served as first president of the Triennial Convention (the first national convention of Baptists in America), had helped found and served as the first president of the first Baptist state convention (in South Carolina), and had sponsored significant educational efforts among Baptists. Although Furman's authorship of the covenant is difficult to verify, the covenant clearly was used in other places. For example, the First Baptist Church of Livingston, Alabama, adopted it in 1871.[60]

Two distinctive features of this covenant were its pledges relating to ecumenical relations and Christian citizenship. "We promise . . . to conduct ourselves with uprightness and integrity, and in a peaceful and friendly manner, towards mankind in general, and towards Christians of all descriptions in particular; and also to pay a conscientious regard to civil government, and give it our support as an ordinance of God." This point about openness towards other Christians was important because it countered the negative attitude toward other denominations which often characterized the Landmark movement that had begun to permeate the South in the 1850s.

A second important covenant written by an individual appeared in William Cathcart's 1881 *The Baptist Encyclopaedia* (covenant 47). The outstanding feature of this covenant is its lengthy article on church discipline. While many covenants in earlier Baptist life had often established explicit connections with church discipline, many others had not. Therefore, Cathcart may have highlighted discipline in his covenant as an attempt to reinvigorate what he viewed to be an ideal relationship between the two concepts. When he prepared his encyclopedia, Cathcart was both pastor of the Second Baptist Church of Philadelphia and president of the American Baptist Historical Society.

A third individually written covenant appeared in church record books available from at least two different publishers in the 1880s and 1890s. By 1886 one such record book had been published by Graves, Mahaffy and Company of Memphis. The covenant printed in front of this book was "undoubtedly a product of the indefatigable J. R. Graves,"[61] noted leader of the Landmark movement in Baptist life. A second publisher, Charles T. Dearing of Louisville, also printed the covenant in the 1895 *Church Book and Alphabetically Arranged Record Book* (covenant 49). One church which used the former record book and in 1886 adopted the covenant printed in it was the First Baptist Church of Texarkana, Texas. The Oak Ridge Baptist Church in Lincoln County, Missouri, began using the latter record book in 1896.

More recently, several Southern Baptist writers have sought to move beyond covenants in the New Hampshire tradition and to add momentum to covenantal renewal in local church life by preparing their own innovative covenantal statements. Included among these are the 1969 covenant of Franklin M. Segler's *The Broadman Minister's Manual* (covenant 53); the 1969 covenant of R. Lofton Hudson in *Home Missions* (covenant 54); the 1969 covenant of Gerald Phillips in the *Illinois Baptist* (covenant 55); the 1971 covenant of James E. Fitch and John G. Mitchell in *Developing a Church Covenant: An Expression of Personal Commitment* (covenant 56)—this covenant gained even wider circulation through its printing in Howard B. Foshee's 1973 *Broadman Church Manual*;[62] and the 1983 covenant by Chevis F. Horne in *The Baptist Program* (covenant 60).

These recent Southern Baptist covenants possessed certain key characteristics. For one thing, they stressed the nurturing aspects of Christian relationships and the need to remove superficiality from those relationships. As Hudson put it, "We commit ourselves to accepting one another in all of our uniqueness, without respect to race or class, in our estrangements and separation and loneliness." Further, he continued, "We commit ourselves to our families, to those closest to us. We will try to peel off our pretenses and our facades and be frank, open, honest, and sincere. We hope to do more than guess at one another." Phillips wrote, "I commit myself to try to live before all men a life free of pretense and hypocrisy, a life that is frank, open, honest and sincere." And in describing the nurturing of the Christian fellowship, Horne stated, "We shall love, accept, affirm, and pray for one another. There will be no cheap person among us and no friendless person in our midst. We want the doors of our church to be as wide as the love of Christ."

Second, the covenants accented the need for church members to become involved in ministry. One pledge in Hudson's covenant stated, "We commit ourselves to getting with as many of the world's needs as we can focus on and find time and energy for." Fitch and Mitchell's covenant included the promise, "Because we are members of Christ's body, the church, I covenant with you to share life and service with you, with all its joys and sorrows." And Horne led covenanters to vow, "With the benediction on Sunday, we shall not leave the church within these sacred walls. We shall be the church in the world! We shall go, all of us, into the world as ministers of Christ. We shall speak the reconciling word and do the reconciling deed."

Third, the covenants advanced beyond J. Newton Brown's isolated reference to one moral issue—abstaining from the sale and use of alcoholic beverages—to a much broader application of the principles of Christian ethics. Segler's covenant did not mention alcohol or any specific moral issue; instead, it led church members to pledge "to follow Christian principles of morality in our daily living." Fitch and Mitchell's covenant included an agreement "to apply our faith in all aspects of our lives." Horne inserted into his covenant vows that "We shall reach across barriers, keep open communication, and care for people the way Christ has cared for us. We shall seek economic justice so that the good life will be within the reach of everyone. We shall try to overcome racial prejudice and all conditions that demean and cheapen human life. We shall abstain from the use of drugs while being concerned about those who are the victims of drugs."

In addition to recent covenants prepared by individuals, many churches have also prepared covenants reflecting contemporary emphases. Two examples are the 1972 covenant of The Baptist Church of the Covenant in Birmingham, Alabama (covenant 57) and the 1976 covenant of the First Baptist Church of Decatur, Georgia (covenant 59). Emphases of one or both covenants included commitments to worship, stewardship, participation in ministry and missions, nurturing the fellowship of believers, and applying Christian ethics to all dimensions of life. The covenant of the Birmingham church included a series of far-reaching pledges: "I am committed to an interracial, intercultural, and international church. I am committed to an innovative church—one that is warmly evangelical and socially concerned. I will strive mightily to assist the church to be a faithful people of God."

Church Covenant Ideals

In addition to writing and promoting specific covenants, Baptists have also attempted to describe their covenantal ideals. Typical discussions of covenants have focused on four aspects of the Baptist covenantal vision: (1) the nature of a covenant, (2) the role of a covenant in defining and constituting a church, (3) the relationship between a covenant and church discipline, and (4) special church covenant meetings. An assessment of these four areas offers useful insights into the theology, ecclesiology, and practicality of the Baptist covenantal experience.

The nature of a covenant.—Baptists have written numerous definitions of a church covenant. Ten representative definitions from the twentieth century, and mainly from Southern Baptist writings, have variously described a covenant as a document used "to summarize the membership objectives or, in other words, to express the united aims of the body"; as "a frank recognition of the obligations, both spiritual and material, which are assumed by each believer when he enters upon church membership and which continually rest upon him thereafter"; as "a statement of obligations voluntarily assumed when joining a Baptist church"; as "a short, concrete, practical rule of church membership conduct"; as "a statement of some principles by which he [a church member] promises to live"; as "a statement that, when accepted, binds the members of a church to high and holy living"; as "a statement of agreement among members of a Baptist church regarding their conduct"; as "primarily a guideline to Christian thought and living"; as "a voluntary commitment of church members to give mutual care and support to one another and to work together in the ministry of the church"; and as "a definition of the shared responsibilities of church members."[63]

Perhaps a more complete definition would define a church covenant as a series of written pledges based on the Bible which church members voluntarily make to God and to one another regarding their basic moral and spiritual commitments and the practice of their faith. Such a definition gives a more balanced stress to the theological character and biblical basis of a covenant; to the meaning of a covenant in responsible church membership; and to the application of a covenant to Christian conduct, ethics, relationships, mutual obligations, and discipleship. These emphases are important because many definitions, surprisingly, have reflected little awareness of the biblical and theological dimensions of covenanting. Some definitions have described little more than social contracts because they contain little reference to God, the Bible, or the church.

The Baptist covenantal ideal has insisted that a responsible covenant does not try to add to the Bible; instead, it reflects Scripture. It condenses and accents key biblical principles relating to the conduct of church members. The ideal has further stressed that a covenant should not be confused with a creed, even in situations where churches have either requested or made optional the signing of a covenant as an indication of commitment and, in some instances, as a requirement for entrance into membership. Practically, however, many Baptists have avoided signing covenants both out of concern that this could have creedal implications, especially since most covenants do contain some doctrinal content, and also out of a fear that such signing could work against the voluntary nature of the covenanting process. Even though Crowell could write in his 1847 church manual that most churches had a covenant "which every candidate for membership is expected to sign,"[64] the signing of covenants has not been a predominant pattern in Baptist life in the 1900s. That decline has been part of the overall decline in covenantal practices to be discussed later in this chapter.

Baptist writers have addressed at great length the ideal contents of a church covenant. Some have preferred that a covenant should enumerate specific pledges designed to meet the unique needs and situation of the church which writes it. Others have viewed an ideal covenant as one which presents permanent duties that are rooted in the New Testament and applicable to contemporary life. One recent Baptist manual urged that only these matters which have "universal validity for Christians" should be included in a covenant. "Trifling things and customs based upon peculiar cultural conditions ought not to be included in its obligations."[65] Many writers have discouraged using a covenant as a legal document and have declared that a covenant's strength does not lie in a legalistic attachment to its wording but in a reliance upon the biblical principles which stand behind the wording.

Covenantal applications in defining and organizing a church.—Baptists have largely agreed that the covenant idea is essential to definitions of the church, that a covenant should exercise a vital role in the act of constituting a new church, and that each church has complete freedom to design its own covenant.

Many important Baptist confessions of faith have tended to make the covenant concept an integral part of their definitions of the church. The highly influential New Hampshire Baptist Confession of 1833, which was reprinted in numerous writings in the 1800s, stated that a church is "a congregation of baptized believers, associated by covenant in the faith and fellowship of the Gospel."[66] This same emphasis, and practically the same wording, continued in doctrinal statements adopted by the Fundamentalist Baptist Bible Union of America in 1923 and by the Southern Baptist Convention in 1925 and 1963.

Many church and ministers' manuals have also inserted the covenant idea into their definitions of a church.[67] In 1847 William Crowell described a church as "a company of baptized believers, voluntarily associated in a sacred covenant to obey and execute the commands of Christ." In 1867 J. M. Pendleton claimed that a church is "a congregation of Christ's baptized disciples, united in the belief of what he has said, and covenanting to do what he has commanded." A 1928 manual designed for black Baptist pastors defined a church as "a company of regenerate persons, baptized by immersion on a profession of faith in Christ; united in covenant." In 1972 a manual of procedures for Seventh Day Baptist churches observed that "a solemn agreement, entered into by a number of people before God, is the basic foundation of the local church. To be without a covenant is to be without a church." Therefore, it continued, "it is essential that care can be taken to make the covenant a meaningful assertion of individual and corporate responsibility to which members may conscientiously subscribe."

Baptist church manuals have repeatedly urged the case of a church covenant in the act of constituting a new church. A recent manual helpfully placed a covenant in its proper context through describing three stages by which a church comes into being. First, a group of Baptists become a church "essential" when they formally express in a covenant their intention to be a church. Second, they become a church "completed" after adopting a constitution and electing officers. Third, they become a church "recognized" after admission into a Baptist association.[68] Many Baptists have typically and unflinchingly insisted, as did William Crowell, that in the act of forming a new church, "none but the spiritually regenerated should be admitted" into the covenanted community.[69]

Although Baptists have published numerous significant model covenants which have achieved broad usage in churches, writers at times have sounded out a major point of clarification: in the act of constituting itself, no church is under authoritative obligation to use a covenant which comes from an outside source. Davis C. Woolley, second executive director of the Historical Commission of the Southern Baptist Convention, made this point explicit in 1968 when referring to the role of J. Newton Brown's covenant among Southern Baptists: "Because the Broadman Press or the Convention Press [or any other press] publishes the Church Covenant and circulates it as 'The Church Covenant' doesn't mean that it is an authority for every Baptist church. It becomes an authority when a Baptist church votes to accept it as its Covenant."[70] The covenantal heritage of Baptists has long contended that every church has complete freedom as an autonomous congregation of believers to write its own covenant, and many churches have maximized covenantal impact in their congregational life by taking advantage of this opportunity.

Church covenants and church discipline.—Baptists have tended to view covenants and discipline along with believer's baptism as basic practices for establishing and maintaining a regenerate church membership. Churches have often viewed the biblical contents of covenants as the basis for applying discipline (both preventive and corrective) and have often disciplined members for violating their covenantal vows. Both a disciplinary application of covenants and a covenantal application of discipline have characterized an unlimited number of documents from Baptist heritage.

Examples of the ties established between the two practices come from circular letters of three New England Baptist associations of the 1840s and 1850s.[71] The Meredith Association in New Hampshire listed situations in which it believed the use of church discipline would be appropriate, one of which was "the omission of certain Christian duties by which covenant obligations are violated." After claiming that a church "must be composed of *saints*, united in covenant as a Gospel candlestick, to hold up its light to the world," the Kennebec Association in Maine asserted that such a church "must maintain the *discipline* of the house of God" and that "The duty of keeping the church pure, holy, active and efficient, by means of scriptural discipline, belongs not to bishops and councils, nor to pastors and deacons, but to all its members." And the Washington Association, also in Maine, addressed the duty of church members to provide financial support for their ministers and then concluded: "To neglect this is a violation of covenant obligations and subjects you to be disciplined by the church, as for any other break of covenant, neglect of duty, or violation of the principles of honesty and common justice."

Besides strong associational support for linking covenants and discipline, Baptist church manuals, especially of the 1800s and early 1900s, stood rather solidly behind the need to relate the two practices. Some manuals associated covenants mainly with corrective discipline. Crowell's feeling was typical: "a church has the right to require of all its members a punctual performance of all the duties prescribed in the church covenant and in the Word of God, and to call them to account for neglect or violation."[72] The net result was that covenants often came to be identified with the negative and legalistic side of discipline. Punishment for covenantal violations sometimes received more attention than did a positive stress on the redemptive possibilities inherent in meaningful covenanting. Despite this, however, some other manual writers did assign to covenants a significant role in preventive and nurturing discipline.[73]

What is the ideal relationship between the New Testament and church covenants in applying discipline? A pastor's guide for black Baptists addressed this issue in 1900: "When a member falls into immorality or departs from the faith of the church, or otherwise violates or neglects church covenanted obligations, it is the right as well as the duty of the church to place him under discipline and deal with him according to the laws Christ has given in the New Testament."[74] William Hendricks, a noted Southern Baptist theologian, made a valuable point about the relationship between church discipline and the biblical authority underlying a covenant when he said that "church discipline is not to be decided by the articles of the Covenant, but by the biblical principles which may be expressed in the Covenant. To use the Church Covenant as a measuring rod for church discipline is to short circuit biblical authority."[75]

Church covenant meetings.—Special monthly church covenant meetings flourished among Baptists in the 1800s. Major purposes of the meetings, which usually took place on the Thursday, Friday, or Saturday preceding the Sunday on which a church celebrated the Lord's Supper, were to prepare members for participation in the Supper, to remind them of their covenantal obligations, to provide an opportunity for them to share meaningful spiritual experiences of the previous month, and to make possible regular renewal of covenantal pledges. In some places Baptists also used these meetings to conduct church business, including disciplinary proceedings. Implying that such meetings had declined in the twentieth century, an important Baptist church manual of the early 1960s observed that "the recovery of such a practice today could help to impress upon us the significance of our covenant obligations and prepare us for a more meaningful participation of the Lord's Supper."[76]

Covenant meetings were widespread, as were complaints that many Baptists neglected their duty to attend the meetings regularly. The 1846 circular letter of the Milford Baptist Association in New Hampshire claimed that "it is the uniform practice of all [churches], to have a monthly meeting for the church, called a *covenant* or conference meeting" but expressed a concern that while church members were under solemn obligation "to attend the covenant meetings as punctually as possible," many of them were "living in constant violation" of their covenantal vows.[77] Noting in 1857 that "as is too generally the case, the prayer and conference and covenant meetings are neglected," Francis Wayland, president of Brown University, cited as two reasons for the neglect the fact that ministers too often did not pay any attention to them and that, when they did conduct such meetings, ministers monopolized the time, preventing laymen from participating.[78] Despite the failure of some covenanted Baptists to attend such meetings, Edward T. Hiscox, the famous writer of Baptist church manuals, stated in 1859 that "in most churches, once each month, a Covenant meeting is held."[79]

Two publications in the 1890s gave extensive information on Baptist covenant meetings. One was Hiscox's *The New Directory for Baptist Churches*. The other was Augustine Carman's monograph, *The Covenant and the Covenant Meeting*, probably the most detailed Baptist treatment of covenant meetings. The prevalence of covenant meetings appeared in the results of a survey which Carman made in the late 1890s of Baptist leaders in various parts of America. He discovered that, although Baptists in the South did not generally use such meetings, the meetings were a common feature of churches in other sections of the country. (Actually, many churches in the South did hold such meetings, so Carman's survey must have been extremely limited.) His survey showed that covenant meetings flourished in such geographically diverse Baptist churches as the Calvary Church in New York City, the First Church in Chicago, the Calvary Church in Washington, D.C., the Ruggles Street Church in Boston, the Woodward Avenue Church in Detroit, the First Church in Indianapolis, and the First Church in San Francisco.[80]

In trying to convey the importance which he attached to the covenant meeting, Hiscox stated that if a church member could attend only two church services in a month, he should give first priority to the Lord's

Supper and second to the covenant meeting.[81] Carman basically concurred in describing the covenant meeting as "the heart of the devotional life of a Baptist church." Carman cited several biblical verses as the basis for covenant meetings, such as 1 Corinthians 11:28, Galatians 6:2, and Ephesians 5:21.[82]

Carman presented ten suggestions which he believed would make a covenant service effective:[83] (1) The service should be different from the prayer meeting where exposition of Scripture is prominent and only a few participate. (2) The meeting should be understood to be the family or fellowship meeting of the church. (3) It should be a time for introspection and the sharing of personal experiences, both positive and negative. (4) Everyone should be encouraged to participate, but no one should be forced to do so. (5) The room should be taken by sections with each person who wishes participating. At the end of each section, the stanza of a hymn may be sung without books or accompaniment. (6) Thursday or Friday evenings are good times for covenant meetings, since this prevents interference with Wednesday prayer meetings. (7) It is good to stress different clauses in the church's covenant in successive meetings. (8) The entire covenant should be read at each meeting. (9) Printed copies of the covenant should be given to all members and especially to each new member. A covenant chart might be placed on a conspicuous wall in the meeting room where church members can study it and be reminded of its contents. (10) Pastors can have sermons on the covenant to complement the attention given to it in covenant meetings.

Hiscox claimed that although churches in cities, towns, and villages held covenant meetings on weeknights, churches in frontier districts and on sparsely settled land usually held their covenant meetings more conveniently on Saturday afternoons, at which time they also transacted church business. Further, in many places the covenant meeting took the place of prayer meeting for that week.[84] Covenant meetings traveled with Baptists all the way to the Pacific Ocean. For example, Baptists in Oregon generally accepted such meetings in the latter half of the 1800s.[85] And even in the twentieth century, pastors' guides prepared for the two largest black Baptist bodies in America in the early 1900s and reprinted in the 1980s, have encouraged the use of covenant meetings.[86] So regardless of the time, place, or race of the Baptists using them, covenant meetings have tended to provide Baptists with a regular means by which to reaffirm the covenantal character of their congregational life.

Generally, covenant meetings have experienced a virtual demise in much Baptist life in the twentieth century. In addition to falling victim to a growing lack of interest in using covenants, the causes of which will be discussed in the next section of this chapter, covenant meetings have also declined because of the multiplication of other kinds of meetings in church life, some of which have absorbed at least a few original values of covenant meetings. Recognizing the loss of such meetings in helping church members to prepare for participation in the Lord's Supper, some Baptists, black and white, have sought to recover part of the intent of the meetings by urging the reading of a church's covenant during the Supper.[87]

Decline and Renewal of Covenantal Emphasis

Intense emphasis upon Baptist church covenants declined at the end of the 1800s and well into the 1900s. Only in recent years have Baptists, especially Southern Baptists, renewed their interest in the covenant concept. After presenting evidences of the decline along with suggested reasons as to why it happened, the following material will also describe the evidences and causes of a recent renewal in writing about and using covenants.

Awareness of covenantal decline.—Two major writings on Baptist church covenants published close to the turn of the twentieth century agreed that covenantal neglect was both a reality and a problem. Carman asserted in 1898 that there was a real danger inherent "in a modern tendency to neglect the covenant and the obligations which it is intended to express," and Burrage wrote in 1904 that "the covenant idea has ceased almost entirely to have for us the great significance it had for the early New England colonists."[88]

Although Southern California Baptists used covenant meetings widely in the latter half of the 1800s, these meetings were far less common by 1900. In New Jersey the signing of covenants and the use of discipline for violating covenantal obligations were "practically ended before World War I." The editor of the Baptist state newspaper for North Carolina observed in 1923 that "a vast majority of the members of our churches have never seen the covenant of the church, or heard it read."[89] And even as recently as 1963, the writers of an important Baptist church manual concluded that "Few people know the significance of the covenant idea in the history of their churches, and little attempt is made to impress upon them the significance of their words when they read this document together."[90]

Reasons for covenantal decline.—Several factors contributed to the decline in covenantal emphasis. Perhaps the most significant was the unexpected and paradoxical effect resulting from the widespread printing of model and uniform covenants, especially J. Newton Brown's covenant, in church manuals and other publications. Prior to the middle of the 1800s, a high percentage of churches seemed to write their own individual covenants, although model covenants did exist during that period. However, after the surge in publishing church manuals after 1850, churches tended simply to adopt uniform covenants printed in them and in other sources.

The net result of churches' adopting external covenants from printed sources was that the value of church covenants deteriorated for many Baptists. Churches found it easier and more convenient to accept a covenant already prepared than to engage in the discipline required to write their own. Baptist presses and publications which have sponsored model covenants have apparently contributed to the weakening of congregational discipline by making it unnecessary for churches to think through, struggle with, and write down covenantal responsibilities to which they are willing to commit themselves.

A second possible reason for decline was a reaction to the seemingly legalistic application of covenants. Many Baptists responded negatively to the covenantal implications behind such opinions as "it is the duty of every member of the church to perform faithfully the letter and spirit of its covenant," and that "Baptists are pledged to observe the laws of the Church Covenant."[91] Since church discipline was often exacted with a heavy hand, and because much discipline was applied to "covenantal violators," many Baptists may have rejected the covenant idea believing that it lacked a positive and redemptive thrust.

Third, the decline may have been related to a general secularizing process that affected American religion beginning in the late 1800s. The lowering of standards of conduct in public and private life as a result of the Civil War, the tremendous increase in the wealth of the United States from about 1880 onwards, and the rapid growth of cities in the 1880s may all have contributed to covenantal depreciation.[92] The increase of secularization in the 1900s has no doubt continued to impact the use of covenants among Baptists.

Fourth, weaknesses attached to the prevalent Brown covenant have led many to question its continuing value. Hendricks viewed the covenant as outdated in much of its wording and content. He expressed concern about the covenant's focusing on intoxicating drinks while leaving out any reference to other ethical matters, such as drugs, pornography, labor, politics, and race. He claimed that it would be better for a covenant to present general biblical principles applying to human conduct than to list individual sins. R. Lofton Hudson agreed, attacking the covenant for its "museumish words" and its failure to speak to contemporary social issues and concluding that Brown's covenant "does not speak to our times."[93] Therefore, many Baptists have come to view Brown's 1853 covenant as irrelevant to the needs of modern Baptist life.

Fifth, because Baptist publications have broadly sponsored Brown's covenant, it has achieved a high level of alleged "official" authority in Baptist views of church polity. While such authority is unwarranted, many Baptists have continued to use the covenant though it has lost much of its value for their churches. Many Southern Baptists have believed, for example, that Brown's covenant is the official covenant of the Southern Baptist Convention. To the contrary, this Convention has never adopted the Brown covenant nor any other covenant for local churches. That would have been a serious infraction upon local church autonomy.

Sixth, Baptists have experienced a decline in covenanting because of their frequent failure to take seriously the doctrine of the church expressed in their major confessions of faith. Such confessions as the 1925 and 1963 doctrinal statements of the Southern Baptist Convention have clearly identified covenanting as integral to the nature of the church. Thus, many Southern Baptists have created a dilemma for themselves in neglecting covenants. In order to achieve consistency between faith and action, doctrine and conduct, they have faced the challenge of either eliminating a covenantal emphasis from their doctrine of the church and abandoning covenants or of taking seriously the covenantal commitments which are inherent in their views of what church ought to be. Some churches have chosen neither option but have simply decided to let the issue ride. In the meantime, the quality of responsible church membership has suffered.

Last, covenanting has declined as many Baptists, especially Southern Baptists, have focused increased amounts of programming upon numerical growth in church life, often at the expense of an essential stress on cultivating a truly regenerated membership. Among the factors contributing to this problem have been the impact of corporate growth and business models upon the life of the church; the growing tendency to measure most of a pastor's success upon how many new people join the church; high-level emphasis upon Sunday School as the "growth arm" of the church, with an accompanying decline in emphasis upon discipleship training programs; the application of some stewardship programs which practically view new church members as sources of revenue to support church budgets, rather than as persons needing training in the faith; and the adoption of church membership admission standards which make it easy for almost anyone to join, standards which place very few expectations upon applicants. Uninformed about expectations for church membership and knowing that virtually no accountability would be placed upon them for the ways they approached it, literally millions of Baptists have chosen to become nonresident church members, and millions more have become inactive resident members.

Evidences of covenantal renewal.—Since the 1960s, Southern Baptists have begun to place renewed stress upon the values of church covenants. Although this resurgence of interest has expressed itself primarily in publications, and has not attained broad implementation in local churches, evidence does suggest that a growing number of churches are either using covenants in an effective way or are considering covenantal concepts more seriously.

The late Davis C. Woolley, executive secretary-treasurer of the Historical Commission of the Southern Baptist Convention from 1959 to 1971, had a fascination for the history of Baptist church covenants. During his tenure he received numerous letters asking about the origin, development, nature, authority, and general significance of the J. Newton Brown covenant.[94]

Another key indication of a renewed interest in covenants lies in the fact that individual Baptists since the late 1960s have begun to write creative covenants for churches to consider (see, for example, covenants 53, 54, 55, 56, 60). Even more significant is that some churches have begun to write and implement their own personalized covenants (see, for example, covenants 57, 59, 62). In the early 1970s, The Baptist Church of the Covenant in Birmingham, Alabama, required each new member to sign a "Membership Covenant" (covenant 57) after conversations with the membership committee and pastor which occurred during a waiting period of about three months between a person's application for membership and being voted into membership. And in the late 1980s the Grace Baptist Church in Dumfries, Virginia, wrote into its "Articles of Cooperation" the expectation that each applicant for church membership would sign the church's "Covenant of Membership" after receiving believer's baptism by immersion and completing new member training and basic discipleship training. Further, the document continued, "Membership shall be renewable annually by signing the Covenant of Membership each January."[95] Churches have varied their patterns of covenantal implementation.

Causes of covenantal renewal.—Several factors led many Southern Baptists to renew their interest in church covenants. A preliminary boost to covenantal resurgence took place in 1956 when the Southern Baptist Sunday School Board published the *Baptist Hymnal*, which included Brown's covenant. That same year the Board also published an article and a lesson on Brown's covenant.[96] The article described the biblical basis for covenanting and the contents of Brown's covenant and presented a challenge to use this covenant. The lesson followed the same pattern but gave more attention to reasons why a church should have a covenant.

Southern Baptists' participation in the "church renewal movement," which began its ascendancy on the American religious scene in the early 1960s, also stimulated their interest in covenants. The covenant idea fit well within the context of renewal. To illustrate, one important writing in the church renewal movement in American Christianity was Elizabeth O'Connor's *Call to Commitment* (1963). The chapter entitled "Approach to Integrity of Church Membership" presented the covenant, or "the present minimum discipline," of the Church of the Saviour in Washington, D.C. An example of the influence of church renewal writings upon Baptist life was a 1973 comment made by Robert H. Zbinden, pastor of the Wesley Heights Baptist Church in Columbus, Ohio, when describing factors that prompted his church to write its own covenant: "My own personal convictions [about covenants] have grown over the past decade as I have read much in the area of church renewal."[97] And Baptist professors, such as Findley B. Edge at The Southern Baptist Theological Seminary in Louisville, Kentucky, were teaching courses in church renewal to hundreds of students in the 1960s and 1970s.

Beginning in the early 1960s various Southern Baptist publications began to reflect an intensified interest in the covenant idea. At least two key articles appeared in *The Baptist Program*, a publication of the Southern Baptist Executive Committee sent monthly to all Southern Baptist pastors, denominational leaders, and others. The titles of the articles expressed dissatisfaction with the J. Newton Brown covenant: "The Church Covenant: Is It Accurate? Is It Adequate?" (1961) and "Is It Time for a New Church Covenant?" (1983).[98] Written by William L. Hendricks, the former article discussed misuses of a covenant, such as treating it as a legal document and suggested modifications in the wording and content of Brown's covenant. The latter article, written by Chevis F. Horne, a retired pastor, described the biblical idea of covenant, sketched the history and theology of Baptist church covenants, attributed much covenantal apathy to the fact that many churches were using the out-of-date J. Newton Brown covenant, urged Southern Baptists to write their own covenants and give increased attention to them, and included a new covenant to illustrate the kinds of content a church could consider for its own covenant (covenant 60).

Horne's ideas about covenants and his covenant were exceptionally innovative and contained a prophetic ring. After commenting that "One of the most urgent needs of Southern Baptist churches is to give serious attention again to covenant" and to use "fresh and new covenants again," he stated forthrightly: "A covenant should come from the current life of a Baptist church and is most effective when written by the local church." Further, Baptist churches should "rewrite their covenants in each generation. Only in this way can the church be where the people are, articulating their faith and commitments, and speaking to their world." He insisted that an authentic covenant should have three dimensions: a theological basis in "God's mighty and saving action"; a concern for the inward life of the church by encouraging it to have a biblical faith, a Christlike character, and a sustaining, nurturing, and maturing fellowship; and a concern for the outward life of the church, making certain that it is free from the bondage of locking itself "behind sacred walls" during "sacred hours." Because the world is such a dangerous place with many destructive forces, as the environmental crisis and the possibility of nuclear war, "A church covenant should help a church address these and other issues and do something about them."[99]

In 1961 the Sunday School Board invited Earl Waldrup, a Florida pastor and former Board employee, to serve as a consultant in the Training Union Department "with the specific responsibility of developing and projecting a new church member orientation program."[100] Waldrup's acceptance of this position turned out to be what was probably the most important factor in creating and maintaining a renewed covenantal interest among Southern Baptists in the 1960s. Immediately, he began to design and write covenantal materials in the context of new church member orientation. For example, in 1963 and 1964 he published articles in *The Baptist Training Union Magazine* in which he gave the covenant idea a prominent role in new church member orientation.

Waldrup's contributions in 1965 and 1966 were extremely important. In that year the Sunday School Board's Convention Press published his important *New Church Member Orientation Manual* (revised 1970). This study course book clearly viewed the covenant concept as central to new-member orientation; stressed the need for new members to understand the nature of the covenantal relationship; identified sermons, a church's educational program, an emphasis on renewal, and the living of disciplined lives as means of strengthening covenantal relationships within a church; and concluded that a thorough study of a church's covenant should be an integral part of new member orientation. Also in 1965 a series of six Training Union lessons by Waldrup appeared in *Baptist Adults*. Focusing on "The Meaning of Church Membership," each lesson highlighted covenantal relationships. Further, in the same year, the Board published four booklets with accompanying teachers' guides, all designed by Waldrup for various age groups in new member orientation classes: *Promises to Keep*, *Belonging*, *A New Commitment*, and *In Covenant* (all revised 1970). Each booklet printed J. Newton Brown's covenant, contained a chapter which attempted to identify a church covenant, showed the potential significance of a covenant, and described the contents of Brown's covenant. Then in 1966, Waldrup published three more articles on covenantal relationships in *The Baptist Training Union Magazine*.

Miscellaneous other Sunday School Board publications in the 1960s-1980s also included covenantal emphases. Examples include:

(1) The 1964 Broadman Press publication of J. Winston Pearce's *My Church Covenant*, an exposition of J. Newton Brown's covenant which received wide circulation in the Broadman Readers' Plan;

(2) The 1967 publication in *Adults Training for Action* of a crucial series of five curriculum lessons in the unit "Improving the Church Covenant" which described the biblical background of covenanting, discussed mutual duties of the church and its members, interpreted the meaning of the articles in Brown's covenant, and suggested ways to implement covenantal commitments;

(3) The publication between June 1968, and December 1972, of at least twenty-four articles[101] by several writers in the new church member ori-

entation sections of *The Baptist Training Union Magazine* and its successor, *Church Training*, which mentioned the importance of the church covenant in training new members (eleven of the articles were written by Forrest H. Watkins, who served as consultant for the two periodicals in the area of new member orientation);

(4) The 1971 booklet by James E. Fitch and John G. Mitchell entitled *Developing a Church Covenant: An Expression of Personal Commitment* which described the nature of the covenantal experience, presented eleven guidelines for preparing a church covenant, discussed the biblical and historical background of covenanting, and printed three sample covenants, including an original one (covenant 56);

(5) The 1973 publication of Howard B. Foshee's *Broadman Church Manual* which included a chapter on church covenants that gave guidelines for writing a covenant and presented three sample covenants, along with a brief historical sketch of each; and

(6) The publication of articles in three periodicals of the Board's Church Administration Department. Writing in *Church Administration* (October 1973), James E. Fitch described reasons why covenants where being neglected, gave guidelines for writing a covenant, and suggested the use of a covenant in worship, as a hymnal insert, and at the time new members join a church. Writing in *Proclaim* (July-September 1976), Cooper Waters offered suggestions for preaching from Brown's covenant and presented a brief bibliography on church covenants. Writing in *Search* (Fall 1985), Bill J. Leonard addressed "The Use of Church Covenants in Southern Baptist History," which concluded with four prophetic implications of the role of church covenants for Southern Baptist life:

> First, each congregation should recognize that it is gathered around a covenant. The people of God are a covenant people bound by response of God's grace and a commitment to follow God's will. The absence of a written covenant does not negate the church's covenantal relationships.
>
> Second, as doctrinal disputes become increasingly prominent in Southern Baptist life, churches may be tempted to judge Christians more by right belief than by right conduct. Indeed, obsession with various styles of "orthodoxy" may obscure certain ethical imperatives of the gospel. Faith and ethics are inseparable. Confessions of faith and covenants of commitment provide a proper balance for the church's belief and practice.

Third, Southern Baptists should construct covenants as one aspect of the ministry of discipleship. New converts must be instructed in the commitment required by the gospel. They must know the "cost of discipleship" beyond the "cheap grace" of easy belief and shallow faith.

Fourth, each congregation should compose a covenant appropriate to its life and witness. While using segments of earlier covenants, it should reflect the specific identity and concerns of that gathered community of faith. In so doing, believers, old and new, may better recognize that they belong to a family with a past, a present to be experienced, and a future to be anticipated. Let us affirm such a covenant and, by God's grace, live it.[102]

Miscellaneous influences on the renewal of covenanting included such items as the Southern Baptist Home Mission Board's 1969 publication of R. Lofton Hudson's attack on J. Newton Brown's covenant, concluding that it "does not speak to our times,"[103] along with Hudson's suggested new covenant (covenant 54); the adoption by the 1970 Southern Baptist Convention of Nevi Townsend's motion that "the Sunday School Board study for revision the church covenant appearing in the *Baptist Hymnal* and elsewhere to include a statement of abstinence of illegally dispensed drugs, pornography, and other evil products which can be bought and used";[104] and articles appearing in state Baptist newspapers, such as that of Gerald Phillips in the *Illinois Baptist* (June 25, 1969) in which he presented his own proposed new covenant (covenant 55).

In addition the author has written eleven items on church covenants: a 1973 Ph.D. dissertation at The Southern Baptist Theological Seminary entitled "The Origin, Development, and Use of Church Covenants in Baptist History"; a chapter in his 1978 book, *A Community of Believers: Making Church Membership More Meaningful*; an essay in *Repent and Believe: The Baptist Experience in Maritime Canada*; an article in *The Canadian Baptist* (April 1983); three articles in Southern Baptist Sunday School Board publications (*Church Training*, September 1973; *Search*, Fall 1974; *Equipping Youth*, October-December 1986); a five-session study unit in the Sunday School Board's 1977 Convention Press book *Living in Covenant*, a curriculum piece for leaders of Vacation Bible School for adults; two articles in the Southern Baptist Historical Commission's journal *Baptist History and Heritage* (January 1974, and April 1980); and a 1989 Historical Commission pamphlet entitled "Responsible Church Membership." These writings typically presented the biblical and historical backgrounds of covenanting and offered suggested guidelines for writing and implementing church covenants.

Conclusion

This chapter has discussed three distinct covenantal trends in Baptist life in America since 1833. First, for most of the nineteenth century, covenanting was a basic and significant feature of Baptist life. After the 1850s, uniform covenants became prevalent, and J. Newton Brown's covenant became the most popular of all. Second, at the end of the 1800s and continuing well into the 1900s, covenantal usage apparently entered a period of decline. Fewer and fewer churches wrote their own covenants as Brown's covenant, and other model covenants, were published in untold millions of pieces of literature. Third, an explicit renewal of covenantal interest has emerged since the early 1960s, at least among Southern Baptists. Increasing numbers of writers have expressed discontent with Brown's covenant and have urged churches to write their own, even to the point of offering suggested guidelines to follow in preparing individualized covenants.

Throughout the period covered by this chapter, Baptists have stated forcefully and repeatedly that the covenant idea is essential to the nature, definition, and constitution of a church. Baptists have wrestled with an obvious gap between their doctrine of a regenerate church membership (with its heavy covenantal thrust) and their frequent failure to implement effective covenantal practices. The recent resurgence of interest in covenants may reflect efforts by Baptists to take more seriously their views of responsible church membership and to make their doctrine of the church more viable in today's world.

Perhaps Archibald C. Cree, Georgia Baptist state convention leader, best expressed the Baptist covenantal ideal of the 1800s and 1900s, even if the ideal was not reached at times, when he stated in 1927 that "In proportion as we perform the practical duties to which we are committed in our church covenants, in that measure will we see our churches vitalized and militant and the cause of Christ advanced unto the uttermost." Put another way, "Via the church covenant is one clear way to advance the kingdom of our Lord."[105]

5
Covenants in Canada and Selected Other Countries

Most discussions of Baptist church covenants focus on their use in England and the United States. But Baptists in many other parts of the world use covenants, and their story needs to be told, too. Perhaps the following sketch of international covenantal developments among Baptists in selected countries can open the subject on a broader scale, identify basic trends, and stimulate more in-depth research by other writers into various facets of the topic. Baptist covenants in Canada (especially in the Maritime Provinces) will receive special attention, but representative covenantal thrusts in several other countries will be described in an abbreviated way. In defense of a basic New Testament conviction, many Baptists (though not all) throughout the world have attempted to safeguard a regenerate church membership against the onslaught of secularism, and it is within this context that they have introduced covenants into the practice of their faith.

Baptist Church Covenants in Canada

Jarold K. Zeman, noted Canadian Baptist church historian, has observed that "Covenants played a central role in Canadian Baptist life until the early twentieth century."[1] That acknowledgment and the reality behind it reflected a parallel with a covenantal development among Baptists in the United States, for the centrality of covenants among Baptists in America also began to decline at the turn of the 1900s. A basic reason why Canadian and American Baptist covenantal patterns have generally followed this and other parallel tracks in the 1800s and 1900s is that Canadian Baptists have derived many of their prominent model covenants and covenantal practices from American sources. At the same time, however, Canadian Baptists have initiated some distinctively unique covenants. Formative nineteenth-century developments occupy most of the following discussion, although the treatment of covenants in the western provinces of Canada will focus on the 1950s-1980s.

Covenants in the maritime provinces.—Several major covenantal traditions arose among the Maritime Baptists (who lived in the provinces of New Brunswick, Nova Scotia, and Prince Edward Island) in the one-hundred-year period beginning in 1778 with the rise of the First Horton Baptist Church in Nova Scotia, now the Wolfville United Baptist Church and Canada's oldest continuing Baptist church. Covenants were a vital part of Maritime Baptist life in this period and appeared in the minutes of churches, associations, and conferences, as well as in other sources. While covenants were diverse in form and content, the basic pattern was for churches to adopt model (uniform) covenants recommended by associations and conferences, rather than to write individual and personalized covenants. Many of these covenants were either exact reprints or derivatives of covenants prepared by Baptists in the United States.

The most widespread and influential covenant used by Maritime Baptists was prepared by Isaac Backus, renowned advocate of religious liberty, for use in constituting the Middleborough (Massachusetts) Separate Baptist Church on January 16, 1756 (covenant 23 in ch. 6). The Maritime version included minor variations in wording, spelling, and punctuation; it also added an enlarged statement on church discipline: "reproving, rebuking, and admonishing one another for good as occasion may require; and if we at any time know that any of the members of the church are guilty of immoral conduct, that we will not expose them by tattling it to others, but will faithfully labour with them, according to the direction of our Lord: *Mat. 18, 15-17,* that sin may be put away from among us, and that iniquity may not be harboured in the church."[2]

This covenant appeared repeatedly in the minutes of various Baptist associations: New Brunswick (1832-33, 1841), Western New Brunswick (1848, 1850, 1852, 1855, 1857, 1859, 1862, 1864-65, 1867-73, 1875-76, 1878), Eastern New Brunswick (1849, 1853, 1855, 1859, 1862-64, 1867-73, 1875-76, 1878), and the African Association of Nova Scotia (1869).

Although Nova Scotia associations, other than the African, apparently did not print this covenant in their minutes, they did sponsor it at times. The covenant appeared, for example, in a brief undated leaflet entitled "A Declaration of the Faith, Practice, and Covenant of the Churches of Christ, Composing the Nova Scotia Baptist Association," which was bound with the 1850 minutes of that association.

Further, in 1854, only a few years after the Nova Scotia Association divided into three associations, the minutes of the Eastern Nova Scotia Association indicated that "the Western Association has requested the cooperation of the Central and Eastern Associations in the re-publishing of the Articles and Covenant mutually adopted, with such slight verbal corrections of the last edition as may be requisite."[3] The Eastern Association then resolved, in acceding to the request, that the corrections be made, that they be submitted to the associations the next year for evaluation, and that churches wanting copies of the revision should send money to help cover printing expenses.[4] In 1855 the revised covenant, which with minor variations was still close to the Backus covenant, was printed in a leaflet entitled "A Declaration of the Faith, Practice, & Covenant of the Churches of Christ Composing the Nova Scotia Baptist Associations."[5]

The Prince Edward Island Association, whose first meeting occurred in 1868, included no direct reference to covenants in their minutes through 1878. However, an article in the association's 1869 constitution stated that "The religious sentiments of this body are such, in general, as are held by the Associated Baptists of Nova Scotia and New Brunswick."[6] Further, the churches forming the Prince Edward Island Association had formerly been related to the Eastern Nova Scotia Association. These two factors at least suggest the possibility that some of the churches in the Prince Edward Island Association could have used the same covenant generally used by other Maritime associations.

Exactly how Backus's covenant made its way to the Maritimes is not known. Numerous possibilities exist, for many early Maritime Baptist leaders came from Massachusetts. Two examples will suffice. First, Ebenezer Moulton, who had served as pastor of the Brimfield (Massachusetts) Baptist Church since 1741, lived and preached in Nova Scotia from 1761 to 1771, when he returned to Brimfield. He participated in the initial covenanting of the Horton Church about 1765 (this church later disbanded and was reconstituted in 1778). Moulton had known Backus and had personally influenced him to change from a Separate Congregationalist to a Baptist.[7]

Second, about 1763 some Baptists who had formed themselves into a church at Swansea, Massachusetts, moved the entire church to Sackville, New Brunswick. Backus was personally acquainted with Nathaniel Round who was ordained as a Baptist minister in Rehoboth, Massachusetts, in 1768 and then moved to Sackville to work with the church already there.[8] Although the Sackville Church eventually discontinued in its original form, either Round or some other New England Baptist leader could have brought Backus's covenant to the Maritimes.

Besides the Backus covenant, another covenant which entered Maritime Baptist life had been prepared by the New Light Congregationalists and clearly showed the impact of the New Lights upon the Baptists. In 1778 the Cornwallis (Nova Scotia) New Light Church printed a covenant in its minutes.[9] This church became a Baptist church in 1807. In 1800 the Old Canning Baptist Church in Queens County, New Brunswick, approved the same covenant (covenant 63). Further, the Horton Church in Nova Scotia used this covenant at least as early as 1807.[10] (The Horton Church minutes show that this church renewed covenant from 1778 onward, but the covenant used before 1807 is apparently not known. The first few pages of the original minutes for 1778, which may have included the earliest covenant, are missing.)

This covenant also appeared in an early "Church Covenant" document of the First Baptist Church of Yarmouth, Nova Scotia. Although the date is not given, the handwriting and paper seem to match the handwritten "Articles and Discipline" of this church, dated August 1814. Most important, this covenant had the sponsorship of the first Maritime Baptist association. Contained in the undated handwritten document of the Nova Scotia and New Brunswick Association entitled "The Church Covenant," this covenant was probably adopted by the association prior to 1810, since the extant minutes of the association after that year make no reference to a specific covenant being adopted.

Another important covenantal tradition existed among the Free Baptists, who possessed Arminian tendencies, favored open communion, and opposed associations. In 1855 the Free Christian Baptist General Conference of New Brunswick printed a covenant in its minutes (covenant 67) with the suggestion that it "be adopted in all cases at organization [of new churches], with such additions as may be deemed necessary." Further, the covenant was to "be read at every monthly Conference Meeting, and as much oftener as may be practicable."[11] In 1863 the General Conference voted to print 1,000 copies of this covenant, along with some other documents, and to arrange for their sale.[12] The covenant appeared again in the 1864 minutes, and a revised edition was printed both in the 1868 minutes and in the *Free Christian Baptist Handbook* (1873).[13]

The Free Baptist Conference of Nova Scotia adopted a covenant at its 1866 meeting and printed it in the minutes for that year with the indication that it should "be read in Church Conference at least once in three months."[14] Further printings of the covenant occurred in the 1877 minutes and in an undated pamphlet (with no publication data) entitled "A Treatise on the Faith of the Free Baptists of Nova Scotia." The covenant was an obvious variation of the one approved by the Free Christian Baptist General Conference of New Brunswick.

The exact origin of the related covenants used by the Free Baptists of New Brunswick and Nova Scotia is not known. Two points are clear, however. First, the Free Will Baptists, who had been founded by Benjamin Randall in the formation of a church at New Durham, New Hampshire in 1780 did use covenants (covenant 27). Second, one of the primary developers of Free Baptist work in Nova Scotia was Asa McGray, who had been ordained by the Free Will Baptists in New England in 1814 before moving to Windsor, Nova Scotia, in 1816.[15] The covenant concept could easily have entered the Free Baptist life of the Maritimes from New England through some person such as McGray. And the Maritime Baptist associations could have influenced the Free Baptist conferences regarding covenants.

Maritime Baptists also used covenants related to the New Hampshire Baptist tradition (discussed in ch. 4). The covenant adopted by the New Hampshire Baptist Convention (covenant 36) made limited headway in the Maritimes in the 1800s, but it did gain some exposure. In 1874 the Western New Brunswick Association, which had regularly printed the Isaac Backus covenant since 1848, printed instead the New Hampshire covenant. Then in 1875 the association began printing the Backus covenant again for several successive years. In a slightly modified form, the New Hampshire covenant also appeared in the 1881 minutes of the African Baptist Association of Nova Scotia.[16]

J. Newton Brown's 1853 revision of the 1833 New Hampshire covenant (covenant 41), which eventually became the most widely used covenant in the United States, also began to make some inroads into Maritime Baptist life in the 1870s and 1880s. A manual of the beliefs and practices of the Baptists of Prince Edward Island, published in 1878, printed Brown's covenant as a model. Further, the Southern New Brunswick Association, which held its first meeting in 1880, included Brown's covenant in its 1884 minutes. To illustrate the apparent influence of this association's suggested covenant, the Brussels Street Baptist Church in Saint John, New Brunswick, printed a handbook in 1895 which contained the Brown covenant. A good indication of the eventual impact of Brown's covenant is that it received convention-wide support when a modification of it appeared as a model in the 1923 *Handbook of the United Baptist Convention of the Maritime Provinces.* [17]

Another covenant related to the New Hampshire tradition and even preceding it was the 1827 covenant of the First Baptist Church of Halifax, Nova Scotia (covenant 65). The Cornwallis Church in Nova Scotia adopted this same covenant in 1849. The origin of the covenant apparently lay in New England, for a slight variation of it had been adopted by the Dudley Street Baptist Church in Boston in 1821. [18] Interestingly, the Halifax covenant had similarities to the 1833 New Hampshire covenant, the 1846 covenant of the Maine Baptist Convention, and especially to the 1847 short covenant published by William Crowell (covenants 36, 39, 40). Thus, the Halifax covenant, apparently influenced by New England Baptists, lay in the background of the development of the most significant covenantal tradition in America.

Miscellaneous other covenants also emerged in Maritime Baptist life. Unique covenants arose at times, such as the 1833 "Meetinghouse Covenant" of the Baptists in Digby and Clements, Nova Scotia, who formed themselves in 1837 into the Digby Joggins Church. Designed to consolidate the Baptists of Digby and Clements around the common task of constructing a building in which to worship, this covenant called for "a Calvinistic meetinghouse" which would "be kept in repair by a tax upon the pews" and which designated special seating areas for blacks. [19] More recently, in 1945, the Primitive Baptist Conference of New Brunswick, Maine, and Nova Scotia printed a distinctive covenant along with the conference's constitution and by-laws (covenant 68).

Maritime Baptists in the 1800s viewed covenanting as integral to the nature of the church. Various associational statements of faith made this amply clear. [20] Maritime Baptists closely related church covenants and church discipline; used covenants in such settings as forming new churches, baptism, the Lord's Supper, receiving new members, and in special covenant renewal meetings; and typically signed new covenants. Churches used covenant meetings, which tended to be held monthly on the Friday or Saturday before the Sunday on which the Lord's Supper was celebrated, to renew covenantal pledges, prepare for the Lord's Supper, share personal testimonies, qualify persons who had applied for baptism, conduct church business, and administer discipline. [21]

To conclude, covenanting was fundamental to the first one hundred years of Maritime Baptist life. Churches, associations, and conferences of various Baptist groups included the covenant idea in their definitions of the church, employed many different covenants, and used covenants in various settings. An illustration of the significance assigned to covenants appeared in the 1862 minutes of the Horton (Nova Scotia) Church: "It would certainly be advisable for each member of the church, in unison with every other, to renew their covenant with God and with each other, not as a matter of form, but to let the covenant be solemnly read in the meeting. Let all present deliberately rise, and signify their assent thereto. It is a document which, if fully carried out, would answer all our requirements."[22]

In the 1900s covenants have not held the central place among Maritime Baptists that they occupied in much of the 1800s. Philip G. A. Griffin-Allwood, a Maritime Baptist minister and historian, recently noted the important status given to covenants by Maritime Baptists in the nineteenth century and hinted at the twentieth-century decline. And his observation that "Morality standards in Baptist church life are expressed in the church covenants"[23] suggests the potential values inherent in a meaningful recovery of responsible covenanting.

Covenants in Ontario and the western provinces of Canada.—Ontario was an important center for Canadian Baptist developments in the 1800s. (Known as Ontario since 1867, previous names for the same geographical area included Upper Canada, 1800-1840, and Canada West, 1840-1867.) Ontario Baptists in the early 1800s tended to use covenants in forming their churches. Most of these covenants had their sources among Baptists in America. American Baptist missionaries and associations exerted a heavy influence on covenantal patterns among Ontario Baptists. Baptist associations in Ontario and surrounding areas often took an aggressive role in printing and promoting various covenants. Churches began to hold special covenant meetings early in the 1800s. "If not the centre or heart of Baptist faith, the keeping of the covenant [for these early Canadian churches] was the implication and visible manifestation of it."[24]

One of the earliest covenants used by Ontario Baptists, dating from the first decade of the 1800s (covenant 64), was used by many churches, such as those in Charlotteville (Vittoria), Townsend (Boston), Oxford, Malahide, and Port Colbourne. Dating at least as early as 1805, this covenant was written by Lemuel Covell, pastor of the First Baptist Church of Pittstown, New York, and a missionary from the Shaftsbury Association in

New York, who helped organize some of the early Ontario churches.[25]

Another early covenant, which apparently gained even wider usage, was that written by Peter Philanthropos Roots (1765-1828), a Baptist missionary from New York, and published in Utica, New York, in 1806. His covenant appeared in prose and verse editions (covenants 34A and 34B), but churches and at least one association tended to adopt the prose edition. Baptized into the First Baptist Church of Boston, Massachusetts, in the early 1790s, Roots was soon ordained as an evangelist. Serving as a Baptist missionary for most of the rest of his life, he traveled and preached in seventeen states.[26] In addition, he visited Ontario on several occasions, beginning in 1804.[27]

Roots' 1806 publication, *A Confession of Faith and Church Covenant,* included a statement on the title page that he had prepared it "especially for the assistance of Christians in our new settlements, who wish to unite together in church-state." Several pieces of evidence show that some Ontario Baptists did choose to use the prose edition of Roots' covenant, even though some versions of it contained minor variations from the original. First, Roots' 1806 work was republished in Canada as *The Calvinistick Baptist Confession of Faith . . . Also, the Church Covenant* (St. Catharines: Hiram Leavenworth, 1826). Second, examples of Ontario churches which used the covenant included the Clinton (Beamsville) Church (1807) and the Cramahe Church (pre-1820).[28] Third, the Western Association of Regular Baptist Churches in Upper Canada printed the covenant in 1832.[29] Fourth, the Welland Church published the covenant in 1856 in its *Articles of Faith and Practice of the Regular Baptist Church in Welland.* The introduction, stating that the articles were used by all the Regular Baptist churches in Canada and the United States, was an obvious exaggeration, but likely indicated that the articles had gained considerable popularity.[30]

Associational sponsorship of covenants by Ontario Baptists grew as the 1800s advanced. Most of the covenants were based on models from the United States, although some were probably unique to Canada. In 1829 the Johnstown Association printed a covenant which it had borrowed from the Danville Association in Vermont.[31] This was the same covenant which the famous Isaac Backus had prepared in Massachusetts in 1756 for use in forming the Middleborough Baptist Church (covenant 23). Then in 1844 the Amherstburg Association, a black association comprised of churches on both sides of the Canadian/American border (presently the Windsor/Detroit area), also adopted the Backus covenant, though with significant changes.[32]

Other Ontario associations also presented model covenants. Both the Long Point Association (1843) and the Grand River Association (1854) used the same covenant (covenant 66). Perhaps the former association prepared this unique covenant, since any earlier source for it is not known. Then, in 1865, the Western Association printed the covenant which the New Hampshire Baptist Convention had adopted in 1833. By this time other associations also began to adopt the New Hampshire covenant.[33]

Several Baptist groups reside in the provinces of western Canada. A brief look at covenants used since the 1950s by just two representative groups, the North American Baptist Conference (German Baptist) and the Canadian Convention of Southern Baptists, shows a widespread use of the 1853 J. Newton Brown covenant (covenant 41). Among the German Baptists in Alberta, two churches, Central Church in Edmonton (1957) and Grace Church in Calgary (1974), used the Brown covenant with virtually no change, while the Community Church of Red Deer (1980s) used its own revised edition of Brown's.[34]

Among the Southern Baptists in British Columbia, examples of churches in the 1980s using the Brown covenant or a revision of it included the Faith Church in Penticton and the Towers and Gladstone Churches, in Vancouver. The two Vancouver churches deleted Brown's emphasis on abstaining from the sale and use of intoxicating beverages, and the Penticton Church changed the wording to "abstain from the sale or use of drugs nonmedically, intoxicants as beverages, and other intemperances which are, or may become socially acceptable or even fashionable."[35]

Illustrations of Southern Baptist churches in the western provinces in the 1980s using apparently original covenants included the New Covenant Church in Winnipeg, Manitoba (covenant 69), the Faith Church in Calgary, Alberta (covenant 70, which is a progressive restatement of Brown's 1853 covenant), and the Discovery Church in Regina, Saskatchewan. This last covenant was unique in several ways: its use of the personal pronoun "I" before each pledge; its vow to attend Bible study and worship weekly "except when working, sick, on holidays, too old, or providentially hindered"; and its commitments not to "commit immorality, engage in homosexual relationships, or continue in a common-law marriage, or relationship."[36]

Covenants in Selected Other Countries

Examination of sample covenants used by Baptists in selected countries around the world reveals at least three clear trends. First, Baptists have used covenants in widely diverse areas of the globe. Illustrations include covenants used in Jamaica (1796), France (1879), China (1895), Australia (1948), Republic of Cameroon (1954), New Zealand (1962), South Africa (1960s), Sweden (1974), and Russia (1985)—see covenants 71-79. While some of these covenants likely resulted from British or American influence, all had their own wording and some were probably original to Baptists in those countries. Second, uniform covenants produced by Baptists in America, especially the 1853 covenant of J. Newton Brown and the 1859 covenant of Edward T. Hiscox, made a significant impact in many countries. And third, Baptists in some countries have apparently chosen not to use covenants. Each of these trends will now be discussed.

Unique covenants.—One of the oldest of the covenants found outside England, Wales, the United States, and Canada was that written by George Liele, a black Baptist, and printed in 1796 for use by early Baptists in Jamaica. A slave born in Virginia, Liele was converted in Georgia about 1780. Baptized by a Baptist minister, he began Christian work among slaves and assisted in forming the first Baptist church in Savannah. Befriended by a certain Colonel Kirkland, the two moved to Kingston, Jamaica, in 1783. There Liele helped form a Baptist church late in that year. In describing the covenant which he drew up for the church, Liele wrote that the church read it monthly "on sacrament meetings."[37]

Some of the unique features of the Liele covenant (covenant 71) included its support for river baptism, foot washing, and anointing the sick with oil; its prohibition against church members going to the law with one another, swearing, eating blood or meat offered to idols, wearing costly raiment, and allowing slaves to join the church without producing character references from their owners; a strong emphasis on church discipline (four articles related to this topic), including forbidding an excommunicated church member to be interred in the church's burial ground unless the person had been received back into membership prior to death; and its placing the covenant into a firm biblical context both by citing biblical references along with each of the twenty-one articles and by affirming in the last article: "We hold to all the other Commandments, Articles, Covenants, and Ordinances, recorded in the Holy Scriptures as are set forth by our Lord and Master Jesus Christ and His Apostles, which are not written in this Covenant, and to live to them as nigh as we possibly can, agreeable to the Word of God."

An example of a covenant sponsored by a major Baptist body in another country took place in 1879 when the Union of the Baptist Churches of France published a covenant (covenant 72) along with a confession of faith. W. J. McGlothlin, Baptist historian, claimed in 1911 that this covenant had initially appeared along with a French Baptist confession printed at Douai in 1848 and that "it reflects American opinion."[38] Although much of the covenant's content was similar to certain American covenants, the content had enough distinctive differences to view it as original with the French. The French Baptist Federation continues to use this covenant in a slightly revised form.[39]

An illustration of missionary influence upon the rise of a covenant in another country occurred in 1895 when Peyton Stephens, a Southern Baptist missionary to China, led the Hwe Ching Baptist Church to organize itself using a covenant (covenant 73). Showing how a covenant can be adapted to a specific cultural situation, this covenant focused one of its articles on opposition to idolatry: "That we will abstain from every form of idolatrous worship, whether directed to images or tablets or to Heaven & Earth, such as burning of paper and incense to the dead, or to demons, bowing to tablets or to the bodies of the dead, or such like worship; and that, so far as we are able to prevent it, we will not allow any such worship in our homes."

As in England, the United States, and Canada, Baptists in other places have, at times, printed uniform covenants in church handbooks or manuals with encouragement for churches to use them. A case in point was a covenant published as early as 1948 by the Home Mission Department of the Baptist Union of Victoria, Australia (covenant 74). According to Howard Crago, archivist for the union, one church which adopted it was the Heathmont Church, which presents the covenant to applicants for church membership and annually recites it on the church's anniversary. "We cannot trace its date, nor the name of its compiler. It was included in a handbook issued by the Home Mission Department of this Union and circulated for the guidance of new churches between 1948 and 1981. Churches were 'encouraged' to adopt it."[40]

Other examples of covenants appearing in a handbook or manual have occurred among Baptists in the Republic of Cameroon and in Sweden. According to Samson E. Khama, of the South West Province of the Republic of Cameroon, a covenant adopted in December 1954, "is found in the Cameroon Baptist Convention Hand Book, page 109"[41] (covenant 75). David Lagergren, of Stockholm, Sweden, has observed that "Baptists in Sweden don't use the word 'covenant' on the same occasions as you Americans do, as far as I understand. However, we have special models to be used when we form a new church. They are to be found in our pastors' manuals and are of fairly recent date."[42] (However, the documents he cited possess many similarities in content and function with church covenants.) One such document (treated as a covenant here) appeared in the 1955 *Manual for the Baptist Union of Sweden;* a slightly varied version appeared in the 1974 revised edition of the same manual (covenant 78).

Baptists in New Zealand have also used a covenant which achieved wide popularity. One church which used it in 1962 was the Mount Roskill Church in Auckland (covenant 76). Some churches still used this covenant in the late 1980s. According to Stan Edgar, secretary of the New Zealand Baptist Historical Society, "Covenants have been used fairly widely, and probably by most of the Baptist churches in New Zealand at some time or another."[43]

An example of a Baptist church in another country which prepared a covenant to meet special needs of its membership was the Rosebank Union Church in Johannesburg, South Africa (covenant 77). Desiring to establish a strong biblical basis for membership, the church designed its covenant in the early 1960s "to fulfil the function of ascertaining that prospective church members should consist only of those who are truly converted. It is a simple document but it does stress the only true basis for membership and it outlines the responsibilities of that membership."[44]

In 1985 the forty-third congress of the All-Union Council of Evangelical Christians-Baptists (AUCECB) met in Moscow and adopted a "Statement of Faith of Evangelical Christians-Baptists." Upon request, Alexei Bichkov, general secretary of AUCECB, arranged for the International Department of the Baptist Union of USSR to send a copy to the present writer. This valuable document (now housed in the Southern Baptist Historical Library and Archives in Nashville, Tennessee) urges "holy walking before God" in its section on sanctification. Then after identifying a church as being comprised of those "who have voluntarily united for common serving the Lord and meeting their spiritual needs," the document presents an important section titled "Church member obligations." Judging by its content and thrust, this section takes on the characteristics of a typical Baptist covenant, although it is not called one and although it is written in third person (covenant 79). This list of membership obligations may be part of the "oral confession" laid out as a prerequisite for becoming a member of a local church.[45] At any rate, Bichkov did affirm that AUCECB churches have a "Church Covenant" available to them,[46] and a possible source or perhaps a reflection of that covenant is the statement of "Church member obligations" adopted in 1985. At least, that is the statement which Bichkov provided when asked for a copy of the covenant(s) used by AUCECB churches.

   Uniform covenants adopted from American sources.—The 1853 covenant of J. Newton Brown (covenant 41) became popular in many countries outside the United States. Three major factors causing this to happen included publications of the American Baptist Publication Society in Philadelphia, publications of the Baptist Spanish Publishing House in El Paso, Texas, and the influence of Baptist missionaries from the United States.

   Edward C. Starr's *A Baptist Bibliography* indicates, without giving publication dates, that the American Baptist Publication Society released translations of Brown's *The Baptist Church Manual* (1853), which contained his covenant, in Spanish, Polish, and Italian. While these translated editions may have been designed for ethnic Baptist groups in America, some copies undoubtedly made their way into other countries through missionary efforts.

   Good evidence shows that the Baptist Spanish Publishing House has aided the spread of the Brown covenant into some Latin American countries. Letters written in 1987 and 1988 from Baptist leaders in three of these countries illustrate the point.

   First, Crea Ridenour, of the Colombian Baptist Convention, claimed that the Brown covenant "so far as I can determine [is] the only Church Covenant used in Colombian Baptist churches," with the possible exception of the English-speaking islands of San Andres and Providence. Further, the covenant used is the one "printed and promoted by the . . . Baptist Spanish Publishing House."[47]

   Second, Luis Magin Alvarez, of the National Baptist Convention of Venezuela, wrote that "After inquiring with some of our largest and oldest churches, I find that none of them have original Baptist covenants. What we have been using through the years in our churches is a covenant printed by the Baptist Spanish Publishing House in El Paso, Texas."[48]

And third, Kate Carter, Southern Baptist missionary to Chile, where her husband, William, has served as professor at the Baptist Theological Seminary in Santiago, noted that the covenant "translated by the Baptist Spanish Publishing House" is the only one they know to be used by Baptists in Chile. She also shared that her husband has written a series of four booklets designed for use by pastors in classes of new converts preparing for baptism. One of these booklets, "The Integration of Your New Life," published by the Evangelism Board of the Baptist Evangelical Convention of Chile, and used in many churches in the discipleship program ADVANCE 2000, prints and explains a slightly revised edition of the Brown covenant. (One variation in the covenant is its focus on abstaining from the sale and use of drugs, as well as of intoxicating drinks.) In their own church, Puente Alto Baptist, William Carter gives a copy of the covenant to each applicant for membership; after baptism, new members read the covenant as a group.[49]

Jimmie Ross, director of library services for the Baptist Spanish Publishing House, claimed that the Spanish translation of Brown's covenant "is the only one in use in Latin [American countries] and Spain as far as we have been able to determine."[50]

There is solid evidence of missionary influence on the spread of the Brown covenant in Haiti. Ivah T. Heneise, professor of church history at the Baptist Theological Seminary of Haiti, observed that the Brown covenant is used both by the churches of the Baptist Convention of Haiti and by the Conservative Baptist Churches of Haiti. Both Baptist groups print the covenant on baptismal certificates. He even ventured to say that "virtually all Baptist churches in Haiti subscribe to this covenant." He claimed also that A. G. Wood, pioneer missionary from the American Baptist Home Mission Society, beginning in 1923 introduced the covenant into Haiti. Further, an adaptation of the Brown covenant was translated into Haitian Creole in 1985 by Jules Casseus, president of the Baptist Theological Seminary of Haiti. Reflecting certain changes in content "in the light of the nature of the Haitian Church and its role in Haitian society," this covenant "is gaining in popularity," although "few Baptist churches here have as yet adopted it." One of the changes in the covenant is its emphasis on abstaining from the sale and use of tobacco, as well as of intoxicating drinks.[51]

Wallace Turnbull, of The Conservative Baptist Haiti Mission Society, Inc., commented on the baptismal certificate with the Brown covenant printed on it. He stated that "When I give the newly-baptized person the card to sign, I read it [the covenant] off to the assembly in Haitian Creole, as few would understand the official French perfectly."[52]

While most European Baptists apparently do not use covenants, exceptions include some churches affiliated with the European Baptist Convention (an English-speaking body formed in 1964 which supports and identifies itself with the Southern Baptist Convention, although it actively supports mission work in Europe). These churches use the Brown covenant.[53]

In addition to Brown's covenant, another covenant that made headway in other countries was that published in 1859 in Hiscox's *The Baptist Church Directory* (covenant 43). William Cathcart claimed in *The Baptist Encyclopaedia* (1881) that Hiscox's manual had been translated into six foreign languages and "is generally used by our foreign missionaries."[54] Starr's *A Baptist Bibliography* identifies translations into Burmese, French, Chinese, Telegu, Portuguese, and Japanese.

Representative countries without covenants.—Baptists in some countries have apparently chosen not to use covenants. Reasons may vary from lack of covenantal influence exercised by missionaries to a healthy skepticism about accepting any documents into one's faith which have even the slightest potential for creedalistic application. Regarding this latter point, G. Keith Parker, director for Europe for the Foreign Mission Board of the Southern Baptist Convention and former professor at the Baptist Theological Seminary in Ruschlikon, Switzerland, observed in 1987 that the use of church covenants "is not a common practice in continental Europe as far as I know." He then noted that "There is a greater issue at stake on continental Europe in terms of the tremendous sense of persecution and great difficulties that early Baptists had. They suffered at the hands of creedal arrangements and state church concepts."[55]

H. Wayne Pipkin, professor of church history at the Baptist Theological Seminary in Ruschlikon, wrote in 1988 that "As far as I am aware, there is no common practice of the use of church covenants among Baptists in Europe."[56] Letters received in 1987 and 1988 from Baptist leaders in Austria, the Federal Republic of Germany, Switzerland, Italy, the Netherlands, Denmark, and Finland stated unanimously that covenants have not been a feature of Baptist church life in their countries, except for rare exceptions.[57] In referring to Baptist life in Scotland, D. W. Bebbington, professor of history at the University of Stirling, claimed that "covenants are not customary among us," and Peter H. Barber, general secretary of the Baptist Union of Scotland, pointed out that "it has been a more common Scottish Baptist tradition for churches to work to a Constitution and Church Rules rather than to a Covenant."[58]

One illustration of a country outside of Europe where Baptists apparently do not use covenants is the African nation of Zimbabwe. R. Heaton, general secretary of the Baptist Union of Zimbabwe, wrote in 1987 that "It would appear that our churches do not follow the practice of using covenants."[59] Even though English and American Baptists have helped to shape the Baptist life of Zimbabwe, evidently they did not import their covenants and covenantal practices into Zimbabwe or else the Baptists of that country have not found them useful to their church life.

Conclusion

In reviewing the Canadian Baptist scene in recent years, three points stand out. First, the 1853 J. Newton Brown covenant has become widespread, just as it has in the United States. Two significant publications have printed this covenant as a model for churches. *A Manual for Worship and Service* (1976), published for Canadian Baptist churches by the Baptist Federation of Canada, printed a slightly modified version of Brown. Examples of changes included adding to the second paragraph a new pledge to assist the church in "its work against sin and injustice in the world" and rephrasing Brown's statement about refraining from the sale and use of alcoholic beverages to read "to practise temperance in all things." *What Canadian Baptists Believe* (1980), prepared by William H. Jones, editor of *The Canadian Baptist,* printed Brown's covenant but deleted two clauses: "to avoid all tattling, backbiting, and excessive anger; to abstain from the sale and use of intoxicating drinks as a beverage."[60]

Second, covenantal practices do not generally have the strength that they once had. To repeat Jarold K. Zeman's insightful summary, "Covenants played a central role in Canadian Baptist life until the early twentieth century."[61] In the 1800s, monthly covenant meetings, the reading of a covenant during the Lord's Supper and in the act of receiving new members, and using covenants as the basis for church discipline enhanced the values of the whole covenanting experience. However, "The neglect of covenantal commitments has no doubt been one of the main factors in the rising number of nonresident and inactive resident members. If uncorrected, it inevitably leads to the denial of the concept of 'the gathered church' (the believers' church)."[62]

Third, "in recent years, a number of congregations have returned to the use of covenant as a public commitment to responsible membership."[63] Evidence of this claim is that some churches are taking the initiative to write and implement their own covenants, even though a trend toward covenantal uniformity has gained major momentum in the twentieth century. Viewing the church covenant as "a statement of membership responsibility and accountability," some churches ask new members to make covenantal pledges, and at least once a year the churches read a covenant publicly and expect all members "to recommit themselves to the agreement of responsibility that is theirs in church membership."[64]

While Baptists in many parts of the world have drawn up their own unique covenants, others have tended to adopt uniform covenants whose origins lay among Baptists in the United States. Special factors affecting the appearance of the covenants of Brown and Hiscox in other countries have included missionary influence and the translation into foreign languages of church manuals containing their covenants. At times, covenants in other countries have received the sponsorship of national bodies (as in France) and gained publication in denominational handbooks and manuals (as in Australia, the Republic of Cameroon, and Sweden). In some countries (as in New Zealand) the use of covenants has became widespread in Baptist life. In other countries (as in China and Jamaica), covenants have included content designed to meet specific needs of certain cultural situations, such as slavery and idol worship. Special applications of covenants to the process of admitting persons into church membership and in baptismal settings have occurred in such countries as Chile and Haiti.

While Baptists in some countries have apparently chosen for various reasons not to use written church covenants, Baptists in all countries have entered into the inevitable covenantal relationships inherent in the New Testament concept of local church life. They have entered such relationships eager to put forward and maintain the Baptist conviction of a regenerate church membership. Though Baptists worldwide have found this biblical ideal difficult to achieve, whether using formal covenants or not, they have continued to place it squarely in the center of their views of the church. Therein lies hope for a quality Baptist future.

6

Covenants:
A Collection of Documents

Chapters 2-5 contain numerous cross-references to the texts of seventy-nine Baptist church covenants prepared between 1640 and 1988. In this chapter, these covenants appear chronologically in four sections. Section A presents thirteen covenants of Baptists in England and Wales, Section B forty-nine covenants of Baptists in the United States, Section C eight covenants of Baptists in Canada, and Section D nine covenants of Baptists in other countries.

Besides providing an international sampling of major and representative covenants, these primary-source documents demonstrate diversity and similarity in covenantal content, show the variety of sources in which covenants appear, enable the reader to verify the accuracy of historical development and interpretation offered in chapters 2-5, reveal the common tendency of many Baptists worldwide to write and adopt biblically based documents relating to their conduct (and to a lesser degree to their doctrine), help churches considering writing their own covenants to see the kinds of elements Baptists have included in their covenantal statements, and dispel the widely held opinion among some Baptists (especially Southern Baptists) that there is only one legitimate covenant in use in Baptist life, namely, that of J. Newton Brown.

Baptist sources for the covenants printed in this chapter include church and associational records and histories; proceedings of national bodies; letters and other manuscripts; pamphlets, booklets, and books on various phases of Baptist history; church and ministers' manuals, directories, and handbooks; hymnbooks; encyclopedias; periodicals; state newspapers; and a dissertation. Typical writers for the covenants are individuals and church, associational, and convention (or conference) committees.

The covenants range in length from less than seventy-five words to more than 1,500 words. Some covenants are simple in content and structure, others complex. Many appear in paragraph form, some are broken down into articles, and one even expresses itself in prose and verse editions (34A and 34B). The pledges of most covenants are phrased in the first person plural (we), but a few use the first person singular (I).

While a doctrinal thrust dominates a few covenants, most focus on conduct and spiritual disciplines. Some contain major sections on church discipline, others barely mention it. A few cover a broad range of social issues, most take a much more limited approach, often dealing merely with alcohol and/or one or two other concerns. Some contain very specific pledges, others are more generalized in overall thrust. Many include a strong biblical and theological basis for their contents; a few do not. Some attempt to be innovative and progressive in wording and content; most reflect traditional covenantal language and emphases.

Section A: Covenants of Baptists in England and Wales
(See ch. 2 for history and interpretation of this section.)

Covenant 1: 1640 Covenant of Broadmead Baptist Church, Bristol, England

1640. Soe that in the year of our for ever blessed Redeemer, the Lord Jesus (1640) one thousand six hundred and forty, those five persons, namely Goodman Atkins of Stapleton, Goodman Cole a Butcher of Lawford's Gate, Richard Moone a Farrier in Wine Street, and Mr. Bacon a young Minister, with Mrs. Hazzard, at Mrs. Hazzard's house, at the upper end of Broad Street in Bristol, *they Mett together,* and came to a holy Resolution to Separate from the Worship of the World and times they lived in, and that they would goe noe more to it, and with godly purpose of heart Joyned themselves together in the Lord; and only thus Covenanting, *That they would, in the Strength and assistance of the Lord, come forth of the world, and worship the Lord more purely, persevering therein to their end.*—Source: Edward Terrell, *The Records of a Church of Christ Meeting in Broadmead, Bristol, A.D. 1640 to A.D. 1688,* ed. Nathaniel Haycroft (London: J. Heaton & Son, 1865), 15.

Covenant 2: 1656 Covenant of the Baptist Church in Leominister, Herefordshire, England

The 25th of the 7th Month 1656 The Church of Christ meeting at

Brother Ioseph Patshalls House in Leominster was Constituted & the Persons undernamed did after Solemn Seeking of God by Prayer, give up themselves to the Lord, & to each other to Walk together in all the Ordinances of Iesus Christ according to his appointments, which was done in the presence of our Brother Daniell King & other Brethren.—Source: Champlin Burrage, *The Church Covenant Idea: Its Origin and Its Development* (Philadelphia: American Baptist Publication Society, 1904), 154.

Covenant 3: 1675 Covenant of Amersham
Six-Principle Baptist Church *(England)*

Artickells of Agreement which wee the Church of Christ Meeting at Amersham doe desier to bee walking vp to and keeping & according to the worde of god how can two walke together Except the bee Agreed

Furst to walk in and kepe pure all the prinsiples of the doctrine of Christ viz heb the 6: 1: 2 and not to haue Comunion at the Lords tabell with Any yt doe not keep them in purity Acording to the word or that shall Alow them selves so to doe

21y Not to haue Any Communion with those yt take ye Oath and doe not repent of it as A sin Against God Mathew the 5

31y Not to have Any Communion with thos that Marry out of the Lord . . .

41y Not to Rece any stranger in praying or preaching, with out the consente of the whole & A letter of recommendation from the Church hee belongs to or good testmony hee is of Life and Conuersation and of a good report

51y To Act in all differances that may or shall fall out in the Church as a Church Joyntly to Gether with thos Officers God shall bles vs with the Lord giuing the defined sentance by his word: and if Elder or Deacon or Elders or deacons shall A sume Any power or prerogative A boue the Church & Contrary to the words that thee Church shall Judg & the Lord by his word shall giue they defined sentance and if any diffarance fall out betwene Elder and Member or Deacon and Member & it bee brought orderly to the Church ye both shall stande by and the Church shall Judg Acording to Gods word

61y That if any Member of Any other Church or peopell shall for conueniency desier to sit down with us not to receue them till wee can be satisfied they Com orderly of and Are not vnder Any Eiuell being Charged by the Church they did belong too before

71y That noe member shall bringe A Charge to the Church Against ether officer or Member but what shall bee brought orderly Acording to gods word and if they doe through Ignorance not to receue it but to Admonish them to doe there dutyes furst one to the other Licke wise that no member receue any Evell Report one Against Another but if they know Any thinge of an Euell tendancy or sin itself Let them keepe it in there own brest tell they haue An Opertunity to doe ther duty Acording to Gods word that soe as James saith we may gaine a sole to God and hide a Multitude of sin

Thes Artickells ware sinned buy the Church who one the 12 day of the 12 month kept a day of fasting with prayer Commiting them selves to the Lorde and to Each other by the will of God: and the next day being Lords day sat down to gether as a Church of Christ in Number Nineteene.— Source: W. T. Whitley, ed., *The Church Books of Ford or Cuddington and Amersham in the County of Bucks* (London: Kingsgate Press, 1912), 202-3.

Covenant 4: 1681 Covenant of
Hitchin Baptist Church *(England)*

We who through the mercy of God, and our Lord Jesus Christ, have obtained grace to give ourselves to the Lord, and one to another by the will of God to have communion one with another as saints in our gospel fellowship. Do, before God our Father, and the Lord Jesus Christ, and the holy Angels, agree and promise, all of us (the Lord assisting) to walk together in this our gospel communion and fellowship, as a church of Jesus Christ in love to the Lord, and one to another, and endeavour to yield sincere and hearty obedience to the laws, ordinances and appointments of our Lord and Lawgiver in his church.

And also do agree and promise (the Lord assisting) to follow after the things which make for peace, and things whereby the one may edify another: that so loving and walking together in peace, the God of Love and Peace may be with us. Amen.—Source: Joseph Ivimey, *A History of the English Baptists* (London: Printed for the author, 1814), 2:195-96.

Covenant 5: 1686 Covenant of Pinners Hall
Seventh Day Baptist Church, London, England

This Congregation having been in a scattered & unsettled condition, & deprivation, & destitute of that spiritual sustenance which they sometime enjoyed from the ordinances of God, since they were deprived of their Faithfull & carefull pastor Mr. Francis Bampfield, first by his imprisonment & then by his death; yet continuing their assemblies for the exercise of Sabbath-worship still, which were frequented by the major part of the members of the society; they (at one of those meetings) agreed, solemnly to set apart the 14th day of the 8th moneth, 1686, for a day of fasting & prayer, to humble their souls before the Lord with confession of their sins whereby they had provoked him to withdraw & withold from them those means of grace with which he had formerly favoured them, & to beg sparing grace from him, if he would not lay their iniquities to their charge, nor remove their candle-stick out of its place; but that he would give them obedient & willing minds to serve him, & that he would reunite & reestablish them, & trust them again with the enjoyment of those precious ordinances which they had long wanted, and ardently thirsted for & likewise direct the means of obtaining of these great blessings.

This day was according to the appointment solemniz'd. . . . On the evening of the twenty fifth day of the eighth moneth, the Holy Supper was accordingly solemnized by them, when almost all the persons that had before given their consent to the foremention'd reunion, were present, & communicated together with much comfort & satisfaction.— Source: "An Historical Record of the Principal matters that have Occurred in the Church that was Formerly Gathered by Mr. Francis Bampfield (Deceas'd) upon & since their Reunion, taking date from (Vulg.) the 14th day of the Eighth Moneth in the year 1686" (photocopy of original document provided in a letter from Don A. Sanford, historian, Seventh Day Baptists of USA and Canada, Janesville, Wisconsin, December 23, 1987).

Covenant 6: 1697 Covenant of
Benjamin and Elias Keach *(England)*

We who desire to walk together in the Fear of the Lord, do, through the Assistance of his Holy Spirit, profess our deep and serious Humiliation for all our Transgressions. And we do also solemnly, in the Presence of God, of each other, in the Sense of our own Unworthiness, give up our selves to the Lord, in a Church state according to the Apostolical Constitution that he may be our God, and we may be his People, through the Everlasting Covenant of his Free grace, in which alone we hope to be accepted by him, through his blessed Son Jesus Christ, whom we take to be our High Priest, to justify and sanctify us, and our Prophet to teach us; and to subject to him as our Law-giver, and the King of Saints; and to conform to all his Holy Laws and Ordinances, for our growth, Establish ment, and Consolation; that we may be as a Holy Spouse unto him, and serve him in our Generation, and wait for his second Appearance, as our glorious Bridegroom.

Being fully satisfied in the way of Church-Communion, and the Truth of Grace in some good measure upon one anothers Spirits, we do sol emnly join ourselves together in a Holy Union and Fellowship, humbly submitting to the Discipline of the Gospel, and all Holy Duties required of a People in such a spiritual Relation.

1. We do promise and ingage to walk in all Holiness, Godliness, Hu mility, and Brotherly Love, as much as in us lieth to render our Commu nion delightful to God, comfortable to our selves, and lovely to the rest of the Lord's People.

2. We do promise to watch over each others Conversations, and not to suffer Sin upon one another, so far as God shall discover it to us, or any of us; and to stir up one another to Love and good Works; to warn, re buke, and admonish one another with Meekness, according to the Rules left to us of Christ in that Behalf.

3. We do promise in an especial manner to pray for one another, and for the Glory and Increase of this Church, and for the Presence of God in it, and the pouring forth of his Spirit on it, and his Protection over it to his Glory.

4. We do promise to bear one anothers Burdens, to cleave to one an other, and to have a Fellow-feeling with one another, in all Conditions both outward and inward, as God in his Providence shall cast any of us into.

5. We do promise to bear with one anothers Weakeness, Failings, and Infirmities, with much Tenderness, not discovering to any without the Church, nor any within, unless according to Christ's Rule, and the Order of the Gospel provided in that case.

6. We do promise to strive together for the Truths of the Gospel, and Purity of God's Ways and Ordinances, to avoid Causes, and Causers of Division, endeavouring to keep the Unity of the Spirit in the Bond of Peace; Ephes. 4. 3.

7. We do promise to meet together on Lord's Days, and at other times, as the Lord shall give us Opportunities, to serve and glorify God in the

way of his Worship, to edify one another, and to contrive the good of his Church.

8. We do promise according to our Ability (or as God shall bless us with the good things of this World) to Communicate to our Pastor or Minister, God having ordained that they that Preach the Gospel should live of the Gospel. (And now can any thing lay a greater obligation upon the Conscience, than this Covenant, what then is the Sin of such who violate it?)

These and all other Gospel-Duties we humbly submit unto, promising and purposing to perform, not in our own Strength, being conscious of our own Weakneess, but in the Power and Strength of the Blessed God, whose we are, and whom we desire to serve: To whom be Glory now and for evermore. Amen.—Sources: Benjamin Keach, *The Glory of a True Church, and Its Discipline Display'd* (London, n.p., 1697), 71-74; Elias Keach, *The Glory and Ornament of a True Gospel-Constituted Church* (London, n.p., 1697), 71-74.

Covenant 7: 1699 Covenant of Great Ellingham Baptist Church, Norfolk, England

We, a little handfull of the meanest, both of the Children of men and of the Children of God, being called by the grace of God, out of the Iron Furnace of the Land of Egypt, judge it our Duty to enquire by what methods we may glorify our Redeemer, in the highest Form the saints are capable of attaining to in this life. After a diligent enquiry into the mind of God in this great Concern; we are Satisfy'd by Holy Writ, that a Church state, is next to a state of grace, and in order to a state of glory, the most conducive to the Saints' happiness here below, & forasmuch as the Lord hath shewed us the form of his house and the fashion thereof, we Judge it our privilege as well as our Duty, to be waiting at the place of Wisdom's Doors; for it is better to be Doorkeeper in the house of the Lord, than to dwell in the Tents of Wickedness: besides we find the way which God chose to lead his people in, both in the Old Testament's days, and also in the primitive times of the Gosple: he had his Church, in the Wilderness then, and he hath his churches in the Wilderness now. And we Esteem it a more Honourable thing to Follow Christ in a more Solitary path, than to Enjoy the pleasures of Sin, which are but for a season.

We likewise find in holy Writ, that an Explicit covenanting with, and giving up ourselves to the Lord, and one another, is the formal cause of a

particular visible gosple Church. We likewise desiring to be Added to the
Lord, Do make a Sure Covenant, according to the Example of the
Church, in Nehemiah's time; who made a sure Covenant, and wrote it;
and we do hereby Engage our Selves, (as the Lord shall Assist us) to walk
with one another to the Glory of God, and the Edification of Each other
in love, for the bearing of one anothers burdens, for the strengthening of
one anothers faith, for the improving of each others gifts, and the watching over one anothers Souls: and we do hereby further engage ourselves
as the Lord shall Assist us, to keep close to the Ordinances of our Lord
Jesus Christ, as they are delivered to us in the holy Gosple, without any
mixture of human Inventions.

We do likewise Covenant & agree together to separate ourselves wholly from the worship of the world, and the Religion of the Times we are
fallen into, that we may (thro' the strength of Christ) keep our Garments
unspotted from the world. And we likewise engage our Selves to walk
circumspectly in Gods house, not forsaking the Assembling our Selves
together, but to Worship God in Publick, and so oft as may be in private
one with another. We also engage ourselves so far as we are, or shall be
Able, to keep up the Ministry of the Word, and Ordinances of Christ,
amongst our Selves; that our Souls may be Edify'd, and the Church mul-
tiplied, and encreased with the Encrease of God.

And this Covenant engagement of ours, we [word omitted at turn of
page] through the strength of Christ to pursue, so long as we can walk
together to the glory of God, and the comfort and Edification of our own
Souls. And this, so far as we have learned from the Word, is that Covenant which the son of the Stranger, and the Eunuch, viz. the Gentiles are
to take hold of, that they may have a Name and a place in Gods house,
and within his Walls, even a better name than of Sons, and of Daughters;
and this is imply'd in giving our Selves to the Lord, and therein to one
another by the will of God, thereby to be visibly Added to the Lord, and
one another.—Source: "Church Covenants," *The Baptist Quarterly* 7
(January 1935): 228-30. Used by permission.

Covenant 8: 1719-20 Covenant of Baptist Church at Bourton on the Water *(England)*

We whose Names are underwritten having been Members & much the
Major Part of a Church or Separate Congregation late under the Pastoral
Care of the Rev. Mr. Ioshua Head decd. is still desirous to walk together

in all the Ordinances of Iesus Christ, as much as may be, blameless, (seeing that Church by reason of different apprehensions of some of the Brethren about the Choice of a Pastour; hath been, in the presence, & by the Advice of some neighbouring Ministers, peaceably dissolv'd) do now freely & heartily give up our selves afresh to God the Father & his Only Son our Lord & Lawgiver; & to one another according to his Will. And so becoming a new Church or Sacred Society incorporated by the Gospel Charter, do now in the presence of God & those that are here Witnesses of our Order unanimously agree in the Name & fear of Christ

1st That we will, to the utmost of our Power, walk together in one Body, & as near as may be with one Mind, in all sweetness of Spirit, and saint like Love to each other, as highly becomes the Disciples of Christ

2dly That we will jointly contend, & strive together for the Faith & Purity of the Gospel, the truths of Iesus Christ, & the Order, Ordinances, Honour, Liberty, & Priviledges of this his Church against all Opposers

3dly That we will with all care, Diligence, & Conscience labour & study, to keep the Unity of the Spirit in the Bond of Peace, both in the Church in general, & in particular between one another

4thly That we will carefully avoid all Causes & Causers of Divisions as much as lyes in us, & shun those that are Seducers & false Preachers of Errours & Heresies

5thly That we will sympathize & have a fellow feeling (to our power) with one another in every Condition, & endeavour to bear each others Burthens, where we are joyfull or sorrowfull tempted or otherwise, that we may be mutual Helps to one another, & so answer the End of our near Relation

6thly That we will forbear, & bear with one anothers weaknesses & Infirmities in much Pity, Tenderness, Meekness, & Patience not daring to rip up the weakness of any to those without the Church, nor to those that are within, unless it be according to Christ's Rule & Gospel Order, endeavouring all we can for the Glory of the Gospel, & for the Credit of this Church willing to cover, & hide one anothers Slips & common failings that are not sinfull

7thly That we will, as our God shall enable us, cleave fast to each other to the utmost of our power; & that if perilous Times should come, & a Time of Persecution (which God for our nonproficiency may justly send) we will not dare to draw back from our holy profession, but will endeavour to strengthen one anothers hands, & encourage one another to Perseverance, let what will fall to our Lot

8thly We do promise to keep the Secrets of our Church entire without divulging them to any that are not Members of this particular Body, tho' they may be otherwise near & dear to us; for we believe the Church ought to be as a Garden enclosed & a fountain sealed

9thly Those of us that are or may be single persons do fully design never to enter into conjugal Bonds with any that are Unbelievers for we believe it to be a Sin to be unequally yoked, that it is contrary to the Rule of Christ, & the ready way to hinder our souls peace, growth, & eternal Wellfare

10thly That we will communicate to one another of the good Things of this Life, as God hath or may prosper us, so far as our Ability will suffer, or any of our Necessities shall be thought to require

11thly That we will endeavour to watch over one anothers conversation for Good, not for each others halting, yet so as not by any means to suffer sin to rest in the bosom of our Brother but to remove it by using all possible Means to bring the person to repentance & Reformation of Life; & that we will endeavour to provoke one another to Holiness, Love, & good Works

12thly We do all purpose constantly to attend the Meetings appointed by the Church, both on the Lord's days & other Days, nothing hindring except Distances, sickness, or the Works of Mercy & Necessity

13thly That We will make Conscience of praying for one anothers Wellfare at all times, but especially in Time of Distress, as Poverty, Sickness, Pain, Temptation, Desertion, or the like; & that we will pray for the Peace & Growth of the whole Church in general & for our Ministers & the success of their Ministry in an especial manner.

Signed at Bourton on the Water the 30th day of Ianuary 1719-20.— Source: Champlin Burrage, *The Church Covenant Idea: Its Origin and Its Development* (Philadelphia: American Baptist Publication Society, 1904), 161-63.

Covenant 9: 1770 Covenant of Baptist Church at Caerleon, Wales

In the name and fear of the Lord and according to the golden rule of his Word and the dictates of our own consciences, we will endeavour and it is our firm resolution to fulfil and live under the influence of the following articles, viz:

1. We believe there is one God and He has authority over all His crea-

tures; therefore it is the duty of all reasonable creatures to obey him in the whole of His revealed will.

2. In solemn and religious manner we give ourselves unto the Lord, bodies and souls, to be His in life or death; likewise our time and talents (as far as we think it our duty) to the glory of His name and the support of His interests.

3. We give ourselves to one another according to the will of God to be a part of the visible church of Christ here upon earth, accounting it to our privilege and greatest honour to establish a church to God in a place where it never was before.

4. We desire and it is our unfeigned intention, in the name of fear and strength of Jehovah, to strive together for the faith of the Gospel:—that is to say the doctrines of grace in their several branches, as far as we can see them in the Word of God and other useful books, particularly the confession of faith as it was published by our baptised brethren in the year 1689.

5. Moreover in the same strength we will endeavour to support and practise the ordinances of the Gospel in their apostolic purity, taking the Word of God as our chief rule in this and all other things.

6. Besides we earnestly desire and pray and firmly resolve to walk in love with one another as far as possible without offence towards those without, and in the practice of every other duty to God and man though it has not been mentioned here.

7. Desire we do and endeavour we will to spread and adorn the interest of the Lord and Saviour Jesus Christ, with fervent and constant prayers for the influence of His Spirit, and rich communications of His grace to assist us herein.

We do in the presence of the ever blessed Trinity, the angels of heaven and this congregation sincerely, uprightly and religiously give the right hand of fellowship to one another, and set our names to the above articles saying, SO HELP US GOD, AMEN.—Source: Covenant included in a letter from D. Hugh Matthews, tutor, South Wales Baptist College, Cardiff, South Glamorgan, Wales, February 19, 1988.

Covenant 10: 1780 Covenant of New Road Baptist Church, Oxford, England

We, whose names are hereunder written, usually assembling for Divine Worship at the Meeting House in St. Peter-le-Bailey, in the City of

Oxford, being Protestant Dissenters from the Church of England, receiving the Books of the Old and New Testament as the Word of God and the only infallible external rule of our religion, faith, and practice; having solemnly devoted ourselves first to the Lord, and professed to each other our repentance towards God, faith in the Lord Jesus Christ, and the hope of eternal life through His atoning Blood and sanctifying Spirit, to our mutual satisfaction:

Do hereby solemnly covenant and agree to receive one another in the peculiar fellowship, form, and order of the Church of Jesus Christ; mutually granting to each other an equal right and title to, and interest in, all the privileges and emoluments of this our sacred confederation, and promising conscientiously to perform all the respective duties thence arising.

And, particularly, we promise and oblige ourselves (nothing extraordinary preventing) to meet together at all appointed seasons at His Table in devout remembrance of His Sufferings and Death; and on the Lord's Days (Providence permitting) and on all other occasional opportunities, to attend the Public Worship of God in prayers and praises, and hearing His Holy Word.

And also promise to watch over and admonish one another, as occasion requires, in the spirit of Christian love and meekness, and to live and walk together in unity and peace and the fear of God, according to His Word.

We also further promise and declare, that we will, so far as we conscientiously can, consent to and obey all such rules and resolutions of good order and discipline as the majority of the Church shall agree upon and regularly appoint.

And whereas some of us do verily believe that the sprinkling of the infant children of believing parents in the Name of the Father, the Son, and the Holy Spirit, is true Christian Baptism; and others of us do believe that true Christian Baptism is that which is administered to adults upon the profession of their repentance, faith, and experience of the grace of God, by Immersion in the Name of the Sacred Three; yet, notwithstanding this difference of sentiment, we promise and agree to receive one another into the same affection and love; and for this, among other many reasons: because we can find no warrant in the Word of God to make such difference of sentiment any bar to Communion at the Lord's Table in particular, or to Church fellowship in general; and because the Lord Jesus receiving and owning them on both sides of the question, we think we ought to do so too.

We also further declare that we are willing and ready to admit to our Church fellowship and communion all that are desirous of it and will give us such an account of their Christian faith and hope as shall satisfy us that they are partakers of the saving grace of God, and that their conversation in the world is such as becomes the Gospel, notwithstanding any difference of opinion as to the subject and mode of Baptism; and also all such as are recommended to us from any of the Churches of different denominations on that head as sincere Christians in full communion with them.

We therefore denominate ourselves a Protestant Catholic Church of Christ, desirous to live in Christian peace and love with all men, and to hold the Communion of Saints with all Protestant Churches and such as love our Lord Jesus Christ in sincerity.

In testimony of these things, and in the sincerity of our hearts, we have, as in the presence of the Eternal God, and of our brethren in the Ministry now attending with us in our solemn meeting for this purpose and to assist us with their advice and prayers, set our respective names, this sixteenth day of November, in the year of Our Lord One Thousand Seven Hundred and Eighty.—Source: "The Church Covenant of 1780: The New Road Baptist Church, Oxford, England," *The Chronicle* 2 (April 1939): 81-82. Used by permission of The American Baptist Historical Society.

Covenant 11: 1790 Covenant of Baptist Church in Horse Fair, Stony Stratford, Bucks, England

We whose names are underwritten do now declare, that we embrace the word of God as our only guide in matters of religion, and acknowledge no other authority whatever as binding upon the conscience. Having, we hope, found mercy at the hands of God, in delivering us from the power of darkness, and translating us into the Kingdom of his dear Son, we think and feel ourselves bound to walk in obedience to his divine commands. On looking into the sacred scripture, we find it was common in the first ages of Christianity for such as professed repentance towards God and faith in our Lord Jesus Christ, voluntarily to unite together in Christian societies, called in the New Testament, Churches. Their ends in so doing were, to honour God and promote their own spiritual edification. Having searched the written word, we trust, with a degree of diligence, in order that we may know how to act, as well as what to believe, and sought unto God by prayer for divine direction, we heartily approve of, and mean to follow their example. With a view to this, we now solemnly, in the presence of the all-seeing and heart-searching God, do mutually covenant and agree, in manner and form following.

1. To maintain and hold fast the important and fundamental truths of revelation. These we apprehend to be such as respect the natural and moral character of Jehovah, and the various relations he stands in to his rational creatures; the original purity but present depravity of human nature; the total moral inability and yet absolute inexcusableness of man as a guilty sinner before God; the perpetuity of a divine law, and the equity of its awful sanction; the infinite dignity of the Son of God in his original character as a divine person, possessed of all the perfections of Deity, and his all-sufficiency for the office of Mediator between God and Man, in consequence of the union of the divine and human natures in one person; the acceptance of our persons with, and the enjoyment of all good from God, through his mediation; the proper divinity and blessed agency of the holy Spirit in our regeneration, sanctification, and consolation; in one word, that our full salvation, from its first cause to its final consummation, is a display of sovereign goodness accomplishing the gracious purposes of him, who worketh all things according to the counsel of his own will, and known unto whom is the end from the beginning.

2. To seek by all proper means the good of the church with which we stand connected. To this end we engage to attend regularly, as far as we have opportunity, all seasons of public worship, church meetings, and meetings of prayer appointed by the church. When we are absent we will be ready to give an account why we were so, if required. We will diligently watch for the appearances of God's work in our congregation; and if we see any setting their faces Zion-ward, we will endeavour to instruct and encourage; and having hopeful evidence of the reality of God's work upon their souls, will lay before them the privileges they have a right unto, and the duties they ought to be found in, of following Christ in his Ordinances and Institutions. If called to the painful work of executing the penalties of Christ upon the breakers of the laws of his house, we will endeavour to exercise it in the spirit of the gospel, without respect of persons. In all questions that shall be debated at our church meetings, the brethren shall speak but one at a time; and if a difference in sentiment should take place, we will endeavour in brotherly love to weigh the matter fully and deliberately, and then put it to the vote in order that it may

be determined by the majority. Also we engage that according to our ability, we will contribute our share towards defraying all necessary expenses attending the worship of God. We likewise promise to keep the secrets of the church, and not to expose its concerns to the world around.

3. To esteem our pastor highly in love for his work's sake. This we will endeavour to manifest by frequently and fervently praying for him; diligently attending on his ministry; encouraging his heart and strengthening his hands to the utmost of our power in the work of the Lord; freely consulting him as we have occasion and opportunity, respecting our spiritual affairs; treating him affectionately when present, and speaking respectfully of him when absent. As he is a man of like passions with others, we will endeavour to conceal and cover with a mantle of love, his weaknesses and imperfections; also to communicate unto him of our temporal good things, knowing that the Lord hath ordained that they that preach the gospel should live of the gospel.

4. To walk in love towards those with whom we stand connected in bonds of Christian fellowship. As the effect of this, we will pray much for one another. As we have opportunity, we will associate together for religious purposes. Those of us who are in more comfortable situations in life than some of our brethren, with regard to the good things of Providence, will administer as we have ability and see occasion, to their necessities. We will bear one another's burdens, sympathize with the afflicted in body and mind, so far as we know their case, under their trials; and as we see occasion, advise, caution, and encourage one another. We will watch over one another for good. We will studiously avoid giving or taking offences. Thus we will make it our study to fulfil the law of Christ.

5. To be particularly attentive to our station in life, and the peculiar duties incumbent on us in that situation. We who are husbands or wives will conscientiously discharge relative duties towards our respective yoke-fellows. We who are heads of families will maintain the daily worship of God in our houses, and endeavour to instruct those under our care, both by our words and actions. We who are children will be obedient to our parents in the Lord. We who are masters will [render] unto our servants that which is just and equal. We who are servants engage to be diligent and faithful, not acting with eye-service as men-pleasers, but with singleness of heart as unto God, knowing we have a Master in heaven. We will in our different places of abode, enquire what we can do for the good of the church to which we belong, and as far as we have ability, we will open or encourage the opening of a door wherever we can, for the

preaching of the word, remembering that we ought to be as the salt of the earth.

6. To walk in a way and manner becoming the gospel, before them that are without, that we may by well-doing put to silence the ignorance of gainsayers. We will practise the strictest honesty in our dealings, and faithfulness in fulfilling all our promises. It shall be our study to repre sent a fair picture of religion before the eyes of the world in the whole of our conduct and conversation. We will abstain from all vain amusements and diversions, by which time would be foolishly spent, money wasted, our minds carnalized, and we exposed to many dangerous temptations. We engage in a special manner to sanctify the Lord's Day. In fine it shall be our study to keep our garments unspotted by the flesh, and walk as becometh saints.

7. To receive such, and only such, into communion with us as in a judgment of charity we think are born again; have been baptized accord ing to the primitive mode of administering that ordinance, and profess their hearty approbation of, and subjection to, this our solemn Church Covenant.

These things, and whatever else may appear enjoined by the word of God, we promise in the strength of divine grace to observe and practise. But knowing our insufficiency for any thing that is spiritually good, in and of ourselves, we look up to him who giveth power to the faint, rejoic ing that in the Lord we have not only righteousness but strength. Hold thou us up, O Lord, and we shall be safe! Amen!

The above Covenant signed by us whose names follow, at our Church Meeting November 4th, 1790, and other convenient opportunities.—
Source: "The Church Covenant of the Particular Baptist Church, Meet ing in the Horse Fair, Stony Stratford, Bucks," *The Baptist Quarterly* 3 (January 1926): 41-44. Used by permission.

Covenant 12: 1790 Covenant of Baptist Association in Wales

It is proper that the members of a church should bind themselves to the Lord, and to each other, by covenant. We often find that the people of Israel entered into covenant, and bound themselves by vows, Deut. v. 27. and xxix. 10-12. Neh. x. 28. &c. And we have some reason to conclude, that under the New Testament, some engaged by covenant; for they are mentioned as *truce-breakers* under the form of godliness, 2 Tim. iii. 3. 5.

Reason and experience shew, that no society can be supported orderly, comfortably, and peaceably, without it. This covenant at least implies these things; (1) that the persons bind themselves to strive against sin, and for the faith; or in other words, to lay aside the service of Sin and Satan, and cleave to the Lord, his worship and service; and adhere to the people of God, the excellent of the earth, especially to those of the same fellowship, remembring the old commandment and the new is, *Love one another*; (2) that they are to watch over one another in love, to exhort each other; and if it be needful, to reprove and rebuke one another, but in the spirit of the Gospel, and according to the rule of God's word; (3) that he who is overtaken in any fault should receive reproof, rebuke, or advice, in humility, confessing his fault, and forsaking it; (4) that none should behave as busy bodies and tale-bearers, mentioning the business of the church to the people of the world; (5) that all should endeavour to keep their place in the church, not forsaking the assembling of themselves together, as the manner of some is; (6) that they should be willing and ready to contribute what may be necessary and meet for the support of the *cause of Christ*, and that according to what they have, and not to what they have not.—Source: "The Welsh Letter on Church Discipline," in John Rippon, *The Baptist Annual Register for 1790, 1791, 1792, and Part of 1793* (London: John Rippon, 1790s), 65-66.

Covenant 13: 1935 Covenant of
The Baptist Quarterly (England)

Recognizing that the Church was called into being by Jesus Christ to win men to His leadership and to train them in His ways, We agree that

Within this church to which we have united, we will by God's help maintain a brotherly spirit; will remember the spiritual need of the young and the weak, the material need of the poor and the sick; will attend public worship, and contribute regularly towards the expenses of the church; will plan for and support such forms of activity in Christ's cause, both locally, in concert with other churches, and overseas, as seem to suit the varying conditions:

In all our relations the same spirit is to be shown; thus within the family we will maintain devotion, and will so live and speak that our conduct may lead to Christ those who see us most intimately; in commerce and in public life we will be trustworthy, doing what is honest in all things, behaving to others as we wish them to behave to us; as God may open the way, we will try directly to enlist others into Christ's church:

And as it is only by God's guidance and help that we may learn and do His will, we will maintain our private fellowship with Him in prayer, expecting thus to gain ever a clearer view of His hopes for each of us and for this His church.—Source: "Church Covenants," *The Baptist Quarterly* 7 (January 1935): 234. Used by permission.

Section B: Covenants of Baptists in the United States
(See chs. 3 and 4 for history and interpretation of this section.)

Covenant 14: 1663 Covenant of Swansea Baptist Church, Rehoboth, Massachusetts

Swansey in New England. A true copy of the Holy Covenant the first founders of Swansey entered into at the first beginning, and all the members thereof for divers years.

Whereas, we poor creatures are, through the exceeding riches of God's infinite grace, mercifully snatched out of the kingdom of darkness, and by his infinite power translated into the kingdom of his dear Son, there to be partakers with all the saints of all those privileges which Christ by the shedding of his precious blood hath purchased for us, and that we do find our souls in some good measure wrought on by divine grace to desire to be conformable to Christ in all things, being also constrained by the matchless love and wonderful distinguishing mercies that we abundantly enjoy from his most free grace to serve him according to our utmost capacities, and that we also know that it is our most bounden duty to walk in visible communion with Christ and each other according to the prescript rule of his most Holy Word, and also that it is our undoubted right through Christ to enjoy all the privileges of God's house which our souls for a long time panted after, and finding no other way at present by the all-working providence of our only wise God and gracious Father to us opened for the enjoying of the same, we do therefore, after often and solemn seeking to the Lord for help and direction in the fear of his holy name, and with hands lifted up to Him, the most High God, humble and freely offer up ourselves this day a living sacrifice unto Him, who is our God in covenant through Christ our Lord and only Saviour, to walk together according to his revealed Word in the visible gospel relation both to Christ, our only Head, and to each other as fellow-members and brethren of the same household of faith.

And we do humble pray that through his strength we will henceforth endeavor to perform all our respective duties towards God and each other, and to practice all the ordinances of Christ according to what is or shall be revealed to us in our respective place, to exercise, practice and submit to the government of Christ in this his church, viz.: further protesting against all rending or dividing principles or practices from any of the people of God as being most abominable and loathsome to our souls and utterly inconsistent with that Christian charity which declares men to be Christ's disciples. Indeed, further declaring in that as union in Christ is the sole ground of our communion, each with other, so we are ready to accept of, receive to and hold communion with all such by judgment of charity we conceive to be fellow-members with us in our Head, Christ Jesus, though differing from us in such controversial points as are not absolutely and essentially necessary to salvation.

We also hope that though of ourselves we are altogether unworthy and unfit thus to offer up ourselves to God or to do Him a, or to expect any favor with, or mercy from Him, He will graciously accept of this our freewill offering in and through the merit and mediation of our dear Redeemer, and that he will employ and improve us in this service to his praise, to whom be all glory, honor, now and forever. Amen.—Source: Henry Melville King, *Rev. John Myles and the Founding of the First Baptist Church in Massachusetts* (Providence, R.I.: Preston & Rounds Co., 1905), 52-55.

Covenant 15: 1665 Covenant of First Baptist Church, Boston, Massachusetts

The 28 of the 3d Mo. 1665 in Charlestown [Boston], Massachusetts, the Church of Christ commonly (though falsely) called Anabaptists were gathered together and entered into fellowship & communion each with other; engaging to walk together in all the appointments of their Lord & Master the Lord Jesus Christ as far as he should be pleased to make known his mind & will unto them, by his word and spirit.—Source: *Minutes,* First Baptist Church, Charlestown (Boston), Massachusetts, March 1665.

Covenant 16: 1671 Covenant of Seventh Day Baptist Church, Newport, Rhode Island

After serious consideration and seeking God's face among ourselves

for the Lord to direct us in a right way for us and our children, so as
might be for God's glory and our souls' good, we . . . entered into covenant with the Lord and with one another, and gave up ourselves to God
and one to another, to walk together in all God's holy commandments
and holy ordinances according to what the Lord had discovered to us or
should discover to be his mind for us to be obedient unto; with sense
upon our hearts of great need to be watchful over one another, did promise so to do, and in edifying and building up one another in our most holy
faith; this 7th day of December, 1671.—Source: Isaac Backus, *A History
of New England, with Particular Reference to the Denomination of Christians Called Baptists*, ed. David Weston (Newton, Mass.: Backus Historical Society, 1871), 1:325, citing "Manuscript of John Comer."

Covenant 17: 1682 Covenant of Kittery Baptist Church, Kittery, Maine

Wee whose names are here unde[r]written doe solemnly & on good
Consideration god Assisting us by his grace give up our selves to the
Lord & to one another in Solom Covenant, wherein wee doe Covenant &
promise to walk with god & one with another In a dew and faithfull
observance of all his most holy & blessed Commandmtts Ordinances Institutions or Appointments, Revealed to us in his sacred word of the ould
& new Testament and according to the grace of god & light att present
through his grace given us, or here after he shall please to discover &
make knowne to us thro his holy Spiritt according to the same blessed
word all the Dayes of our lives and this will wee doe If the Lord graciously please to Assist us by his grace & Spiritt & to give us Divine wisdome
strength knowledg & understanding from Above to performe the same
without which we cann doe nothing John 15:4 2 Corinthians 3:5.—
Source: *Minutes*, First Baptist Church, Boston, Massachusetts, September 1682.

Covenant 18: 1705 Covenant of Piscataway Seventh Day Baptist Church, Piscataway, New Jersey

I. We believe that unto us there is but one God, the Father and one
Lord Jesus Christ, who is the mediator between God and mankind and
that the Holy Ghost is the Spirit of God.
II. We believe that all the Scriptures of the Old and New Testaments,
given by inspiration, are the word of God and are the rule of faith and

practice.

III. We believe that the ten commandments which were written on two tablets of stone by the finger of God, continue to be the rule of righteousness unto all men.

IV. We believe the six principles recorded in Hebrews, 6:1-2 to be the rule of faith and practice.

V. We believe that the Lord's Supper sought to be administered and received in all Christian churches.

VI. We believe that all Christian Churches ought to have church officers in them, as elders and deacons.

VII. We believe that all persons thus believing ought to be baptized in water, by dipping or plunging, after confession is made by them of their faith in the above said things.

VIII. We believe that a company of sincere persons, being found in the faith and practices of the above said things, may truly to be said to be the church of Christ.

IX. We give ourselves up unto the Lord and one another, to be guided and governed by one another according to the word of God.—Source: Typescript copy provided in a letter from Don A. Sanford, historian, Seventh Day Baptists of USA and Canada, Janesville, Wisconsin, December 23, 1987.

Covenant 19: 1727 Covenant of First Baptist Church, Newport, Rhode Island

We who desire to walk together in the fear of the lord do by the help and assistance of the holy ghost profess our deep Sense of Sin & humiliaztion therefor & do now Sollomly in the presence of the great god the Elect angels & one another having a Sense of our unworthyness Considered of our Selves & looking wholly and alone to the lord Jesus Christ for worth yness & Exceptance give up our Selves to the lord in a Church state that he may be our god and we his people through the Everlasting Covenant ofhis free grace desiring to Submitt to Jesus Christ as the King & head ofhis Church Imbracing him as the prophet priest & King of our Salvation & to conform to all his holy laws and ordinances for our groath Establishment & Consolation that we may be a holy Spouse unto him; being fully Satisfied in the way of Church Communion & of the truth of grace on Each others Soul in Some good measure we do now Sollomly In the Name and fear of god Joyn our Selves together in a holy union & fellowship humbly Submitting to the discipline of the gospel and all holy Duties which our Spiritual relation Enjoyns & requires we promise by the help of Divine grace without which we can do nothing to walk in all godlyness humility & brotherly love so that our Communion may be delightfull to god and Comfortable to our Selves & the rest of the lords people to watch over Each others Conversation & not Suffer Sin upon one another as god Shall discover it to us or any of us & to stir up Each other to love & good works & if any fall into Sin to warn and admonish them according to the Nature of the offence with a Spirit of Meekness as the gospel requires[.]

[W]e promise & Engage to pray with and for one another as god Shall Enable us from time to time for the glory of this Church that the presence of god may be in it & his spirit rest upon it & his protection over it that it may be Increased with the Increase of god we do promise to bear one anothers burthens weeknesses Short Comings and Infirmities & not to acquaint any without the garden of Christ of them but to observe the Rule of Christ in Such Cases we do promise to strive togather for the truth of the gospel & purity of gods ordinances and Endevour to pass a Christian construction upon these that in Sone lesser & Extra fundimental points difer from us Endevouring to keep the unity of the Spirit in the bond of peace with all that hold the Head Jesus Christ both their lord and ours and that we will not retain a pharisaical Spirit to withdraw in the time of Prayer, but will Joyne with all Such as in the ground of Charity are true beleivers & Churches of Jesus Christ[.]

[W]e promise to observe the publick worship of god on lords days & at other times, as god may afford oppertunity & strive what in us lies for Each others Edification Each and Every of these things, we humbly Submitt to in the Name & fear of god promising and Purposing to perform not in our own strength being conscious of our own Weekness; but in the power & strength of the blessed god whose redeemed ones we trust we are and whome we Sincearly desir to Serve To whome be glory in all the Churches now & Evermore Amen.

Signed by us In the Name and behalfe of the whole Church at a church meeting this 4th day of May in the Year 1727.—Source: Champlain Burrage, *The Church Covenant Idea: Its Origin and Its Development* (Philadelphia: American Baptist Publication Society, 1904), 190-91.

Covenant 20: 1732 Covenant of Unnamed Baptist Church
(Published by Morgan Edwards in 1774)

In the name of the Lord Jesus, we do voluntarily and jointly separate ourselves from the world; and voluntarily and jointly give ourselves to the Lord, who hath promised to receive such, and be to them a God; holding ourselves henceforth as his, and no longer our own. We do also voluntarily and mutually give ourselves one to another, and voluntarily and mutually receive one another in the Lord; meaning hereby to coalesce into one one body, jointly to exist and jointly to act by the bands and rules of the gospel; each esteeming himself henceforth as a member of a spiritual body; accountable to it, subject to its control, and no otherwise separable therefrom than by consent first had, or unreasonably refused.

We do further voluntarily and jointly vow to do all things whatsoever the Lord hath commanded, and be obedient, that he may be with us alway: particularly, to deny ourselves; take up the cross; follow Christ; keep the faith; assemble together every Lord's-day to worship; love as brethren; submit one to another in the Lord; and observe all rules prescribed to church members.

Finally, we do voluntarily and jointly engage to know, honour, maintain, and obey them that shall have the rule over us in the Lord. This is the covenant we now solemnly enter into in the fear of God. In testimony and ratification whereof each of us signs his name hereunto. So help us God.—Source: Morgan Edwards, *The Customs of Primitive Churches* (n.p., 1774), 9-10.

Covenant 21: 1738 Covenant of Tulpohokin
Baptist Church, Berks County, Pennsylvania

We, whose names are underwritten, (some members of the Great Valley church, some of the church of Montgomery,) being removed into another county, and so remote frome the said churches, that we could not attend the means of grace, nor perform the duties of our membership as we could wish to do; being met together, according to appointment, on this 19th day of August, 1738; and having, by fasting and prayer, made our supplication to God, and a sermon preached on the occasion; and having unanimously owned the Confession of faith, set forth by the elders of baptized churches in England, and approved by the above named churches; and having showed our approbation of one another's

principles and charitable judgment of each others' graces; and having
mutually agreed to give ourselves to God, and to one another by the will
of God; we covenant, as God shall help us, to maintain the worship of
God and the truth of the gospel, to the edification of our own souls and
the good of others; and to practice all gospel ordinances, according to the
mind of God, revealed in his word; to admonish, exhort, and watch over
one another in love, and also to reprove according to gospel rule; to keep
our own secret matters to ourselves, according to the practice of the
primitive gospel churches and the custom of our neighboring churches of
the same order.

In testimony whereof, we, in the sanctity of our hearts, and in the fear
of God, desiring to wait upon, and trust in his faithful promises in our
Lord and Redeemer Jesus Christ, for all blessings and graces, and the
gifts of his Holy Spirit, to enable us to do our duties, for the honour of
God and the ornament of the gospel of Jesus, have hereunto subscribed
our names the day and year above named.—Source, A. D. Gillette, ed.,
*Minutes of the Philadelphia Baptist Association from A.D. 1707, to A.D.
1807* (Philadelphia: American Baptist Publication Society, 1851), 23-24.

Covenant 22: 1742 Covenant of Chestnut Ridge Baptist Church, Chestnut Ridge, Maryland

We, the humble professors of the Gospel of Christ, baptized upon a
declaration of faith and repentance, believing the doctrine of general redemption (or the free grace of God extended to all mankind), do hereby
seriously, heartily and solemnly in the presence of the searcher of all
hearts and before the world, covenant, agree, bind, and settle ourselves
into a church, to hold, abide by and contend for the faith once delivered
to the saints, owned by the best reformed churches in England, Scotland
and elsewhere, especially as published and maintained in the forms or
confessions of the Baptists in England; differing in nothing from the articles of the church of England and Scotland except in infant baptism,
modes of church-government, the doctrine of reprobation and some
ceremonies.

We do also bind ourselves hereby to defend and live up to the protestant religion, and to abhor and oppose the whore of Rome, Pope and
Popery with all her anti-christian ways.

We do also engage with our lives and fortunes to defend the crown and
dignity of our gracious sovereign king George, to him and his issue forev-

er, and to obey all his laws, humble submitting ourselves to all in authority under him, and giving customs to whom custom, honour to whom honour, tribute to whom tribute is due. We do further declare that we are not against taking oaths, nor using arms in defence of our king and country when legally called thereto; and that we do approve and will obey the laws of this province.

And further, we do bind ourselves to follow the patterns of our brethren in England to maintain order, government and discipline in our church, especially that excellent directory of Rev. Francis Stanly entitled, THE GOSPEL'S HONOUR AND THE CHURCHES' ORNAMENT, dedicated to the churches in the counties of Lincoln; Nottingham and Cambridge.

We alos [also] engage that all persons upon joining our society shall yield consent to and subscribe this our solemn league and covenant. Subscribed by us whose names are under written, this 10th day of July 1742.—Source: Morgan Edwards, *Materials Towards a History of the Baptists in America* (Philadelphia: Thomas Dobson, 1792), 2:8-9.

Covenant 23: 1756 Covenant of Middleborough Baptist Church, Middleborough, Massachusetts *(Written by Isaac Backus)*

We do now in the presence of the great allseeing and most glorious God; and before Angels & Men give up our selves to the Lord Jehovah, Father, Son, & Holy Ghost, & account him this day to be our God, our Father, our Saviour and our Leader and receive him as our Portion for ever. We give up our selves unto the Lord Jesus Christ and adhere to him as the Head of his people in the Covenant of grace, & rely on him as our Prophet Priest and King to bring us to eternal blessedness. We acknowledge our everlasting & indispensable obligation to glorify our God by living a holy righteous & godly life in this present world, in all our several places & relations: and we do engage by the assistance of the divine Spirit to improve all our time & strength, talents and advantages for his glory & the good of our fellow men: promising by divine help to walk in our houses with a perfect heart and to train up those under our care in the ways of God.

And we also give up our selves to one another in Covenant, promising to act towards each other as Bretherin in Christ; watching over one another in the love of God; and to watch not only against them that are reckned more gross evils, but also against all foolish talking & jesting which is not convenient; vain disputeing about words & things which gendure strife; disregarding promises & not fulfilling of engagements; tatling and backbiteing; spending time idly at taverns or else where, and vain & unnecessary worldly conversation on Lords-days, and whatsoever else that is contrary to sound doctrine according to the glorious gospel of Christ.

Promising to hold communion together in the worship of God, & in the ordinances & discipline of his Church according as we are or shall be guided by the Spirit of God in his world; expecting that he will yet further & more gloriously open his word & the mysteries of his kingdom: flying to the blood of the everlasting Covenant for the pardon of our many errours and, praying that the Lord would prepare and strengthen us for every good work to do his will, working in us that which is well pleasing in his sight thro' Jesus Christ, to whome be glory for ever and ever. Amen.—Source: *Minutes*, Middleborough Baptist Church, Middleborough, Massachusetts, January 1756.

Covenant 24: 1757? Covenant of Grassy Creek Baptist Church, Grassy Creek, North, Carolina *(Possibly Written by Shubal Stearns)*

Holding believers' baptism; the laying on of hands; particular election of grace by the predestination of God in Christ; effectual calling by the Holy Ghost; free justification through the imputed righteousness of Christ; progressive sanctification through God's grace and truth; the final perseverance, or continuance of the saints in grace; the resurrection of these bodies after death, at that day which God has appointed to judge the quick and dead by Jesus Christ, by the power of God, and by the resurrection of Christ; and life everlasting. Amen.

1st. We do, as in the presence of the great and everlasting God, who knows the secrets of all hearts, and in the presence of angels and men, acknowledge ourselves to be under the most solemn covenant with the Lord, to live for him and no other. We take the only living and true God to be our God, one God in three persons, Father, Son and Holy Ghost.

2d. We receive the Holy Scriptures of the Old and New Testament to be the revealed mind and will of God, believing them to contain a perfect rule for our faith and practice, and promise through the assistance of the Holy Spirit, to make them the rule of our life and practice, in all church discipline, acknowledging ourselves by nature children of wrath, and our hope of mercy with God, to be only through the righteousness of Jesus Christ, apprehended by faith.

3dly. We do promise to bear with one another's infirmities and weaknesses, with much tenderness, not discovering them to any in the church, but by gospel rule and order, which is laid down in Matthew 18: 15,16,17.

4th. We do believe that God has ordained that they who preach the gospel shall live of the gospel; and we call heaven and earth to witness that we without the least reserve, give up ourselves, through the help and aiding grace of God's Spirit, our souls and bodies and all that we have to this one God, to be entirely at his disposal, both ourselves, our names and estates, as God shall see best for his own glory; and that we will faithfully do, by the help of God's Spirit, whatsoever our consciences, influenced by the word and Spirit of God, shall direct to be our duty, both to God and man; and we do, by the assistance of Divine grace, unitedly give up ourselves to one another in covenant, promising by the grace of God to act towards one another as brethren in Christ, watching over one another in the love of God, especially to watch against all jesting, light and foolish talking which are not convenient, (Eph. 5:4)—everything that does not become the followers of the holy Lamb of God; and that we will seek the good of each other, and the church universally, for God's glory; and hold communion together in the worship of God, in the ordinances and discipline of this church of God, according to Christ's visible kingdom, so far as the providence of God admits of the same: 'Not forsaking the assembling of ourselves together, as the manner of some is,' but submitting ourselves unto the discipline of the church, as a part of Christ's mystical body, according as we shall be guided by the word and Spirit of God, and by the help of Divine grace, still looking for more light from God, as contained in the Holy Scriptures, believing that there are greater mysteries to be unfolded and shine in the church, beyond what she has ever enjoyed: looking and waiting for the great power, and 'have dominion also from sea to sea, and from the river unto the ends of the earth.'

This Covenant we make with full and free consent of our minds, believing that through free and boundless grace, it is owned of God and ratified in heaven, before the throne of God and the Lamb. Amen. Even so, come, Lord Jesus. Amen, and amen.—Source: Robert I. Devin, *A History of Grassy Creek Baptist Church, from Its Foundation to 1880, with Biographical Sketches of Its Pastors and Ministers* (Raleigh, N.C.:

Edwards, Broughton & Co., 1880), 43-45.

Covenant 25: 1771? (Rev. 1826) Covenant of
Kiokee Baptist Church, Kiokee, Georgia

1. According to God's appointment in his word, we do hereby in his name and strength covenant and promise to keep up and defend all the articles of Faith, according to God's word, such as the great doctrine of Election, effectual Calling, particular redemption, Justification by the Imputed righteousness of Christ alone, sanctification by the spirit of God, Believers Baptism by Immersion, the saints absolute final perserverance in Grace, the resurrection of the dead, future rewards and punishments, &C., all according to scripture which we take as the rule of our faith & practice, with some other doctrines herein not mentioned, as are commanded & supported by that Blessed Book: denying the Arian, Socinian & Arminian errors, & every other principle contrary to the word of God. no(w) yet since we are exhorted to prove all things, order(ly) ministers of any denomination may when invited, preach in our meeting house.

2. We believe that believers should attend to the celebration of the Lords supper, and should any neglect or refuse to attend, they may be required to give a reason of their conduct, this article forbids any of our members from communing with any who do not practice believers baptism by Immersion.

3. We do promise by the grace of God helping us, to bear with each other as brethren, and to manifest love by not receiving evil reports against each other without undeniable evidences: not to speak railingly of one another, but according to Matthew 15th [18th] 15.16. 17th admonish each other with a prudent and Godly fear, not to look on sin with the least allowance in any of the brethren, we also promise to manifest love to each other by Godly encouragement, waiting for all opportunity to do all kind offices to each other, as become saints, such as bearing with the weak in love sympathising with the afflicted & tempted, administering both godly admonitions and all such relief to them as Christian charity demands, promising also each for him, or herself to submit to all such admonitions, exhortations & reproofs administered to us by any prudent member, or church.

4. We do also promise as much as in our power to give all due attendance to the publick worship of God on the Lord's days, & all other days,

as we may have opportunity, also on such days as are appointed to transact the business of the Church, and when met calmly & faithfully give our opinions, avoiding clamorous disputations & whispering during discussion, & to do all in our power to maintain peace & good order among us—and who ever fails attending our regular meetings, three times in succession without sending or rendering a sufficient excuse, the church shall appoint some person or persons to cite & require such delinquent person to attend, and should he or she neglect or refuse yet to attend, he shall be dealt with as a disorderly member and for the better observance of this rule, the clerk shall be required at the conclusion of each conference to note down, & call for such absentees who shall be required at the next conference to give the reason of absence, the minutes of the last conference shall be read at the commencement of the next when thought necessary.

5. We promise to contribute according to our abilities for the support of our minister, & poor of the flock, also for the Lords Table, & the keeping, opening, shutting & cleansing our M.house & spring; also to encourage prom(i)sing gifts in our own church, travelling ministers who are orderly & in fellowship in their own church & such other persons as shall appear conformable to the rule of love & charity—no disorderly minister shall preach in our meeting house, & if any suspicious stranger attempts it, the deacons & minister of this church is hereby privileged to examine & call on him for his license, or credentials, to be satisfied.

6. We promise to strive together for the faith once delivered to the saints, to avoid all just cause of offence either amongst ourselves, or those that are without, to keep good order in our families, not to go to law with each other, if avoidable, or which the church shall judge—

7. All persons desiring to become members of this church shall be received into our fellowship only by the unanimous agreement of this church present, and they shall be kept in only by unanimous consent—this regards the taking in or turning out of members,—

8. We promise to make use of our endeavors to adorn our holy profession with a holy life and Conversation that God in all things may be glorified through Jesus Christ our Lord, this and all other possible duties, we do humbly submit by promising to preform [sic] them, not in our own strength but in the power and strength of the everlasting and ever Blessed God, whose we are in him we desire to (serve). To whom be Glory and dominion for ever & ever. Am(en).—Source: James Donovan Mosteller, *A History of the Kiokee Baptist Church in Georgia* (Ann Arbor, Mich.:

Edwards Brothers, 1952), 267-69.

Covenant 26: 1779 Covenant of Meherrin
Baptist Church, Lunenburg County, Virginia

Whereas in the providence of God we a part of the Baptist Church of
Christ residing and being in Meherrin Virginia known by the name of
Meherrin Church are now settled upon the waters of the Yadkin, very
remote from the seat of constitution and it being inexpedient in the
present circumstance of affairs for us to join any neighboring church and
that we did not fully intend or expect when we removed having our former pastor or minister of Meherrin with us, and being privileged if we
thought expedient to imbody [sic] as a church; we therefore taking the
matter into our serious and deliberate consideration, with fasting and
prayer to God, believe it will be for the glory of God so to do. We therefore solemnly in the presence of God Covenant to and with each other
under an humble sense of our own unworthiness and give up ourselves to
the Lord and to each other in a Church State, according to the primitive
mode and custom of constitutions, praying that God may be with us and
enable us to conform to all his desired laws and ordinances, that we may
be a Spiritual House built up together by His Divine Grace, that we be
enabled to serve and glorify Him and at last be received into the man-
sions of eternal glory—

Article 1st. We agree solemnly in the presence of God to give up ourselves to God and to each other in a Spiritual union and fellowship, humbly submitting to the Gospel discipline and to engage in all Religious
duties required of the people to each other in such a Spiritual connection,
and to stir up each other to love and good works, to warn, reprove, rebuke, exhort and admonish each other in meekness, according as the various circumstances occur or require, and as the Word of God shall direct
in particular cases.

Article 2nd. We agree and do promise, God assisting, to strive together
for the faith of the Gospel and purity of godliness and endeavor to keep
the unity of the Spirit in the bond of peace and that we shall bear one
another's burdens, weaknesses and infirmities, with much tenderness,
and conduct ourselves in such cases as to divulging or secreting agreeable
to the plain rule given us in the 18th of Matthew 15. 16. and 17th verses.

Article 3rd. We agree and do promise, God assisting, to meet together
on the Lord's Day and at other times, as the Lord shall give opportunity

(agreeable to the divine injunction, Hebrews 24 and 25) to receive instruction from the Word preached, to comfort and edify each other, to promote Godliness and do service to the Church of Christ.

Article 4th. We agree and do promise, God assisting, to do all the good we possibly can to all men both in a spiritual and temporal sense, but especially to the Household of faith, agreeable to Galatians 6th and 10th, and that we will do all the duties required of us in God's word, to our own minister or succeeding minister, but God in his providence has or may later set over us to watch for our Souls.

Article 5th. Whereas there has been and as yet in many parts of the States of Virginia and North Carolina certain bars of communion kept up and maintained between what is called Regular and Separate Baptists, much to the grief and mortification of many pious people and very prejudicial to the interest and establishment of Christ's Kingdom, which bars were taken down in full church meeting in Meherrin Church in December, 1774, and a free and open Communion kept up with all orderly Baptists without distinction with regard to the terms Regular and Separate— we therefore agree not to restrict our communion to any people Baptized upon profession of their faith where we have sufficient ground to believe that gospel order and piety are maintained by and among them.

Article 6th. And lastly, Meherrin Church at the time of their constitution, January, 1772, did fully adopt and receive a confession of faith by the delegates and Ministers of upward of one hundred congregations in England and Wales met in London in July, 1689, and since adopted by the Philadelphia Baptist Association met in Philadelphia, September, 1742, and now well known by the name of the Philadelphia Confession of faith. We therefore do hereby testify that that is yet a brief summary of our faith and principles (with some few exceptions not essential to salvation or church communion). We therefore adopt it as good Human Composition in the general, which we agree to observe both in principle and Church Government as long as we shall believe it agreeable to God's Word—no longer, as we believe the Scriptures of the Old and New Testament is the Only Standard of Truth by which the Church is to conduct herself (whatever respect she may have to good human composition) for that we believe the church of Christ will now grow and make more discovery of light into the Glorious Treasure of God's Word while she continues her Militant State, and so consequently it would be presumption before God and forming Chains to fetter our consciences with to bind ourselves unalterably and unchangeably to any set of principles whatever, except what is written and contained in the Glorious unchangeable Word of God, which liveth and abideth forever. We pray for grace to enable us to understand and walk agreeable thereto.

The above is a true copy of the Covenant received and signed by the aforesaid members of the day and the year above written.—Source: William L. Lumpkin, "Early Virginia Baptist Church Covenants," *The Virginia Baptist Register* (1977) 776-78. Used by permission.

Covenant 27: 1780 Covenant of New Durham Baptist Church, New Durham, New Hampshire *(Written by Benjamin Randall)*

We do now declare that we have given ourselves to God: and do now agree to give ourselves to each other in love and fellowship; and do also agree to take the scriptures of truth for the rule of our faith and practice, respecting our duty toward God, our neighbors, and ourselves.

We do promise to practice all the commands in the New Testament of our Lord and Savior Jesus Christ, so far as they are now, or shall be made known to us by the light of the Holy Spirit of truth, without which, we are sensible, we cannot attain to the true knowledge thereof. We also promise to bear each other's burdens, and so fulfil the law of love, which is the law of Christ. We do further agree to give liberty for the improvement of the gifts of the brethren, and to keep up the worship of God, and not to forsake the assembling of ourselves together, as the manner of some is. We do likewise further agree not to receive any person into fellowship, except they give a satisfactory evidence of a change in life and heart; and also promise to submit to the order of the Gospel as above. Amen.—Source: John Buzzell, *The Life of Elder Benjamin Randal, Principally Taken from Documents Written by Himself* (Limerick: Hobbs, Woodman & Co., 1827), 83-84.

Covenant 28: 1783 Covenant of Cherokee Creek Baptist Church, Washington County, North Carolina *(Now Jonesboro, Tennessee)*

As the Professors of Christianity are so Divided their principles and practice that they cannot hold communion together and passing by the several classes of pedobaptists. There are Several Classes of Antepedobaptists, with which we Cannot agree. Namely, the Seven Day Baptists, the no Sabbath Baptists, and those that Dip three times in Baptism, with all of which we cannot agree; Therefore think it Expedient to covenant or Agree together in matters of faith and Order, yet So as not to Reject those Christians as only Differ from us in Contra esential matters: But as a distinct Society do Embody ourselves and the following Rules References and Articles to our Several Names are annex. Yet as we do not Look upon ourselves infalible we Still Look to be further taught by the word and Spirit of God into those Misteryes Contained in the Holy Scriptures.

The Solemn Covenant of the Baptist Church on Cherokee Creek and the waters Adjacent, in the County of Washington and State of North Carolina Entered into the first Saturday in September 1783. Holding Believers Baptism by immersion the Laying on of hands particular Election of Grace by the predestation of God in Christ, Effectual Calling by the Holy Ghost free justification by the Righteousness of Christ imputed to us and Apprehended by faith, progression Santification thro Gods Grace and truth, and final perseverence of the Saints in Grace and holiness, The Resurrection of the Body, and Life Everlasting; . . . and now we do in the presence of the great and Eternal God who knoweth the Secrets of all hearts unitedly. Give Ourselves to the Lord To be at his disposal, Taking this one God to be our God, One God and three Persons, and to one another in Covenant Promising by the Grace of God, to Act Towards Each other as brethren in Christ.

1st—To attend Our Respective meetings and Especially Church meetings unless Providentially hindered and the reason to be given to the Church if called for 2ndly—To hold communion together in the worship of God, in the Celebration of his ordinances 3dly—To bear with Each others Infirmities with tenderness, not to discover them Out of the Community where it may be Avoided, nor in the Community, But by the gospel Rule and order as we Shall be directed by the word and Spirit of God, 4thly—To bear Reproof and admonition from each other patiently, to reprove and admonish Each other Faithfully, yet tenderly in Christian Charity and Brotherly Love. 5thly—To live orderly in our families in Keeping up the worship of God, in being faith to Instruct to Admonish and to ceese from Vice According to our Several abilities and respective Opportunities. 6thly—To use Reasonable Industry for temporal Sustenance. 7thly—To be Liberal According to our Several Abilities in Communicating To the Support of the Worship of God in money 8thly—not to remove our abode out of the Bounds of this Church without informing and Consulting the Church.

9thly—Not to take any in Our particular membership that will not Sign this covenant, that Disputes may be avoided and Concord Maintained, And if any shall Preach Profess or practice Contrary to these Articles of this Covenant or principals refered To therein He She or they Shall be Liable to the Censure of the Church. And in Case of obstinate Continuance Shall be Excluded Our Communion, nevertheless when the Case Calls for it they May and Ought to Excommunicate instantly

And in testamony of our Sincerity and that we have No Reserve we have hereunto Set Our hands Amen.—Source: Typescript copy provided in a letter from Glenn A. Toomey, director of missions, Nolachucky Baptist Association, Morristown, Tennessee, February 8, 1988.

Covenant 29: 1785 Covenant of Bent Creek Baptist Church, Bent Creek, Tennessee

Since in these latter days of the world the professors of Christianity are so different in their principles and practices that they cannot generally hold communion together, but we do mutually consent and agree who to embody ourselves together as a religious society to worship God through faith in Jesus Christ depending on Him alone for the salvation of our souls in all its parts and the blessings and immunities of this life and of that which is to come as it is contained in the scriptures of the old and new testaments, believing them to be the revealed mind and will of God containing the precious and soul-reviving doctrines of justification by the imputed righteousness of Jesus Christ, both personal and passive, apprehended by faith sanctification through God's grace and truth with the final perserverance and continuation of the saints in grace, and for a more full declaration of our faith we refer to the old and new testaments.

And being constituted into a Church, congregationally being Baptists on confession of our faith in Jesus Christ, by the decent immersing of our whole body under the water in the name of the Father and of the Son and of the Holy Ghost Do agree to submit ourselves to the ordinances and discipline of this Church as a part of Christ's visible kingdom, agreeing that being blessed with the adding of grace of God's Holy Spirit we will act towards one another as brethern in Christ to hold communion together in the worship of God in the celebration of his ordinances with a due and becoming respect of all commands as we shall be directed by the word and Spirit of God, and we are for the aforesaid purpose to attend our meetings unless providentially hindered and the reason to be rendered to the Church when called for, to watch over each other in the fear of God, to prove and admonish in Christian Charity and brotherly love, not discovering the infirmities of another out of the community where it may be avoided nor to any in the community except by the gospel rule and according to the best light we have or shall have from the holy scriptures, to endeavor to maintain an unspotted life and conversation at home and abroad and to communicate of our worldly substance according to our several abilities as shall be the glory of God in decent support of the Church and ministry. And not to remove our abode out of the bounds of this Church till an orderly application for dismission by the same.

In witness of which mutual consent and agreement we have hereunto set our hands this eleventh day of June in the year of our Lord 1785.—
Source: *Typescript Minutes*, Whitesburg (formerly Bent Creek) Baptist Church, Whitesburg, Tennessee, June 1785.

Covenant 30: 1797 Covenant of Dumplin Creek Baptist Church, Jefferson City, Tennessee

July the 30, 1797, Jefferson County about Dumplin Creek, we, the Baptist Church of Christ, believing it to be our duty to pay a true respect to the law of love and gospel ordinances instituted and commanded in God's word for the better regulation of our conduct toward God and each other, solemnly promise by the assistance of the holy spirit the serious regard to the following particulars: First, to strive together for the truth of the gospel and the purity of the gospel institutions desiring for the grace of God to live and die in the faith of God's Elect, seriously adhearing to the glorious doctrine of grace as effectual calling by the Holy ghost, justification by the imputed Righteousness of Christ, progressive sanctification by the grace of God imparted, the final preservation of the saints in grace, water baptism by immersion to such and only such as profess their faith in Christ professing to walk in newness of life. Then believing that there will be a Resurrection of the dead of the just and unjust and that the resurrection of the just will be to everlasting happiness and the Resurrection of the unjust will be to everlasting misery.

. . . We promise also to take the holy scriptures of the old and new testament which we believe to be the written word of God as our Rule and guide and in particular with respect to church government, keeping the unity of the spirit in the bonds of peace, bearing with one anothers weakness and not willingly suffer sin to lay upon a brother but deal with

him as follows for private trespasses agreeable to our Lord's directions in
Matthew the eighteenth ch. 15th, 16th, 17th verses; and for public transgressions a public satisfaction as becometh those who give themselves to
the Lord and one another to walk in church fellowship.

We promise to endeavor to support the worship of God in the world
and ordinances and to watch over one another in love and solemnly to
renounce all evil words and actions, foolish talking, jesting, cursing, lying, malacious anger, extortion and fraud of every kind, covetousness,
drunkness and keeping evil company and to abstain from sinful whispering, back biting, all wilful hypocrisy and dishonesty, all excess or superfluity to the gratification of pride and also resist from gaming, wagering,
singing of carnal songs and all Carnal myrth, fidling, dancing and vain
recreation and all sinful contentions and not wink at the disorder of and
under our care but prudently use the Rod of correction when necessary
and not neglect family devotion. We are to mind our own business and
not indulge Sloth, nor will we go to law with each other and if God
should bestow on any of us the ministerial gifts we promise not to hide
them nor to exercise them publically without the approbation of the
church.

We do therefore desire to give up ourselves to the Lord and to one
another to walk in humility in the command and ordinances of the Lord
all the days of our lives and for acceptance at last we desire to depend
entirely on the virtue and spotless Righteousness of our adorable and
Divine Redeemer the Lord Jesus Christ. AMEN.—Source: Glenn A.
Toomey, *The Romance of a Sesquicentennial Church: The Dumplin
Creek Baptist Church of Christ, Jefferson City, Tennessee* (n.p., 1947), 13-
15. Used by permission.

Covenant 31: 1798 Covenant of Philadelphia Baptist Association
(Written by Samuel Jones)

We, whose names are under written, being desirous to be constituted a
church of Jesus Christ, in this place, and having all due knowledge of one
another in point of a work of grace on our hearts, religious principles,
and moral characters, and being desirous of enjoying the privileges that
appertain to the people of God in a church relation, do, in the name of
the Lord Jesus, voluntarily and freely give ourselves up to the Lord, and
to one another, according to his word, to be one body under one head,
jointly to exist and act by the bands and rules of the gospel, and do prom-

ise and engage to do all things, by divine assistance, in our different capacities and relations that the Lord has commanded us, and requires of us: particularly to deny ourselves, take up our cross, follow Christ, keep the faith, assemble ourselves together, love the brethren, submit one to another in the Lord, care one for another, bear one another's burdens, endeavour to keep the unity of the spirit in the bond of peace, and, finally, to honour, obey, and maintain them that may have the rule over us in the Lord.

This is the Covenant we solemnly enter into, in the fear of God, humbly imploring the Divine assistance and blessing that we may be built up and established to the glory of God, the advancement of the Redeemer's interest, and the comfort and edification of our own souls, through the infinite riches of free grace, which is in Jesus Christ our Lord: and now, to the only wise God, Father, Son, and Holy Spirit, be worship, honour, power, glory, dominion, and obedience rendered, now and ever more. Amen.—Source: Samuel Jones, *A Treatise of Church Discipline and a Directory* (Philadelphia: S. C. Ustick, 1798), 9-10.

Covenant 32: 1798 Covenant of Lower Banister Baptist Church, Pittsylvania County, Virginia

We . . . being inhabitants of Pittsylvania and Halifax Counties in the State of Virginia on Banister River and its adjacent waters, being previously baptized upon a profession of our faith in Christ Jesus and having previously given ourselves to the Lord and to each other in our Constitution as here recorded, do think proper at this time to ratify and confirm the same by entering into this our church covenant, declaring ourselves to be of the faith and order of the United Baptists of Virginia—

1. We believe that the church of Jesus Christ in this world is not national but congregational, being a body of faithful men and women called out from the world and bound together for mutual support, comfort and edification of each other according to the Word of God, and in such a body are set thrones, even thrones of the house of David. Jesus Christ is the supreme head and lawgiver of his church, and his laws, their rule, are the sacred key whereby they can shut and none can open and open and none can shut. Therefore they have the sole right and privilege in all cases whatsoever to govern themselves as a religious body by the sole direction of their divine lawgiver, and no man nor set of men, either priest, bishop, councils, synods, presbyteries, nor associations, have any

power to impose church laws on any church or to lord over God's heritage; yet behold such assemblies not only lawful but very useful whenever they act as advisory councils, agreeable to the Word of God; we therefore think it not only our duty and privilege to fill up our places in our Baptist associations but also to pay a due respect to their godly counsels and admonitions, believing that in the multitude of the counselors there is safety.

2. We believe it to be our duty to keep and maintain a Christian discipline amongst us agreeable to the Holy Scriptures and for this purpose we agree to watch ourselves and each other that our lives and conversations may be as becometh the Gospel of Christ, to endeavor to hold up the light of the glorious Gospel before a benighted world, to keep up and preserve the Ordinances of the Lord Jesus, according to the purity and simplicity of the Gospel and earnestly contend for the faith once delivered to the saints, and like true yokefellows in the bonds of the Gospel we agree to stand or fall herein together, believing that the Lord is able to hold us up and give us an inheritance amongst his saints in light.

3. Church meetings of business shall be regularly and statedly appointed by the church, but on extraordinary occasions they may be appointed by the minister in conjunction with the deacons, or by the deacons themselves in case of the absence or disability of the minister, in all of which cases notices shall be generally and publicly given so that nothing be done in a private or clandestine manner.

4. Church meetings shall be faithfully attended by all members in general but more particularly by the males. Every matter coming before the church shall fairly and deliberately be considered and orderly preserved by every debate carried on with coolness and moderation.

5. Every matter of debate respecting the government, order and discipline of the church shall be fairly determined by a majority of the male members present and the government in every respect given up to them.

6. Every matter respecting the fellowship, or dismissing, receiving, restoring, excommunicating, etc., to be finally determined by a majority of both males and females, in all of which cases the minority shall submit.

7. And in order that the black members that are or which may be amongst us should not be neglected, church meetings shall be appointed for them occasionally on Sundays in order to settle any matter that may arise amongst them, and some of the white members to attend with them for to instruct them in the discipline of the church.

8. Every motion made and seconded shall be attended to except the

motion be withdrawn by those who made it, and every query presented to the church shall not be debated unless the church agree to take it up.

9. A clerk shall be chosen by the suffrage of the church who shall keep a record of their proceedings, etc.

10. Amendments or additions to this compact may be made at any time by a majority.—Source: William L. Lumpkin, "Early Virginia Baptist Church Covenants," *The Virginia Baptist Register* (1977), 780-82. Used by permission.

Covenant 33: 1803 Covenant of Kehukee Baptist Association *(North Carolina)*

FORASMUCH as Almighty God, by his grace, has been pleased to call us (whose names are underneath subscribed) out of darkness into his marvellous light, and all of us have been regularly baptized upon a profession of our Faith in Christ Jesus, and have given up ourselves to the Lord, and to one another, in a gospel church way, to be governed and guided by a proper discipline agreeable to the word of God: We do therefore, in the name of our Lord Jesus, and by his assistance, covenant and agree to keep up the discipline of the church we are members of, in the most brotherly affection towards each other, while we endeavour punctually to observe the following rules, viz.

1st. In brotherly love to pray for each other, to watch over one another, and if need be, in the most tender and affectionate manner to reprove one another. That is, if we discover any thing amiss in a brother, to go and tell him his fault according to the direction given by our Lord in the 18th of Saint Matthew's gospel; and not to be whispering and back-biting. We also agree, with God's assistance, to pray in our families, attend our church meetings, observe the Lord's day and keep it holy, and not absent ourselves from the communion of the Lord's supper without a lawful excuse; to be ready to communicate to the defraying of the churches expences, and for the support of the ministry; not irregularly to depart from the fellowship of the church, nor remove to distant churches without a regular dismission.

These things we do covenant and agree to observe and keep sacred, in the name of, and by the assistance of, the Holy Trinity. Amen. Signed by the mutual consent of the members whose names are underneath subscribed.—Source: Lemuel Burkitt and Jesse Read, *A Concise History of the Kehukee Baptist Association, from Its Original Rise to the Present*

Time (Halifax, N.C.: A. Hodge, 1803), 30-31.

Covenant 34A: Prose Edition: 1806 Covenant of
Peter Philanthropos Roots *(New York)*

We do now, in the presence of God, angels and men, without the least known reserve, devote ourselves to God, choosing the Father, Son and Holy Ghost to be our God and portion for time and eternity; promising most solemnly to make his word the rule of our faith and practice.

We covenant to take heed to ourselves, to our temper, conversation and company. Not to indulge passionate, revengeful anger; but to maintain a peaceful, quiet deportment, at home and abroad. Not to allow ourselves in lacivious talking, foolish jesting, evil speaking, nor tavern haunting; but to have our conversation and company as becometh the gospel of Christ.

We promise to keep a faithful watch over each other, to provoke one another to love and good works, to be tender of the persons, characters and estates of all who are united with us; to be just in all our dealings, both among ourselves and towards all men, and to do good to all men as we have opportunity; especially to the household of faith.

We covenant religiously to observe the Lord's day, not to allow ourselves in unnecessary worldly business nor conversation; but constantly to devote the first day of the week to the public and private duties of religion, not forsaking the assembling of ourselves together as the manner of some is.

We promise to practise secret prayer; and while, or whenever we are heads of families, we covenant to maintain the worship of God morning and evening in our houses, daily to attend to the scriptures for the instruction of our families, and to use our earnest endeavors to bring up those under our care in the nurture and admonition of the Lord.

We covenant to attend to the appointments of the church, to be at the meetings in good season, statedly to unite with our brethren in observing the communion supper, and all the ordinances of Christ's house; to maintain gospel discipline, to seek the prosperity of this particular church, and the good of the Redeemer's kingdom in general.

And should we ever be removed to any other place, so that we cannot enjoy the ordinances of Christ in this particular church, we will endeavour, as soon as we have opportunity, to be united with some other church of the same faith and order. And we solemnly covenant, in whatever part of the world we may live, to devote ourselves to God, and to seek the prosperity of Zion, so far as our abilities and opportunities permit, to the end of our days.

Looking to God for his assistance, we severally and unitedly make this solemn covenant. In witness whereof we now say—AMEN.—Source: Peter P. Roots, *A Confession of Faith and Church Covenant* (Utica, N.Y.: Printed by Asahel Seward for Peter P. Roots, 1806), 11-13.

Covenant 34B: Verse Edition: 1806 Covenant of Peter Philanthropos Roots *(New York)*

1. Our solemn cov'nant now we make,
O may we ne'er this cov'nant break,
May God, and men, and angels see,
And witness our sincerity.

2. The Father, Son, and Spirit now,
Our God and portion we avow:
We'll love his name, obey his laws,
And seek to build the christian cause.

3. The scriptures we will daily read,
And to this light give earnest heed;
Our children in the righteous way
We'll strive to teach, and with them pray.

4. No frothy wit, nor tattling vile,
Shall waste our time, our hearts beguile;
In conversation we will try
Those who us hear to edify.

5. To one another we'll be kind,
Each other's good will daily mind;
To all men we'll be just and true,
Nor hold from them their proper due.

6. The church appointments we'll attend,
The Lord's day too in worship spend;
To discipline we will submit.
O may we ne'er these vows forget.

7. Revengeful anger we'll suppress,
'Tis very wrong we do confess;

In love and peace to all we'll speak.
O may we ne'er this cov'nant break.

CONCLUSION

New rules we do not mean to make,
The Bible rules we only take,
And shew by this our script'ral creed,
In Bible truth we are agreed.

Source: Peter P. Roots, *A Confession of Faith and Church Covenant* (Utica, N.Y.: Printed by Asahel Seward for Peter P. Roots, 1806), 18-19.

Covenant 35: 1832 Covenant of I. Person

As we trust we have been brought by divine grace to receive the Lord Jesus Christ, and by the influences of his spirit to give ourselves up to him: so we do now solemnly covenant with each other to walk together in brotherly love watching over each other with Christian care and faithfulness, to admonish and entreat one another as occasion may require, participating in each others joys, and sympathizing with each other in sorrow.

We also engage unitedly to strive for the support of a faithful evangelical ministry of the gospel among us, and that we will not forsake the assembling of ourselves together for worship, and especially for the great duty of prayer, that we will endeavor to bring up such as may at any time be under our care in the nurture and admonition of the Lord, and by a pure and lovely example strive to bring our kindred and acquaintances to the Saviour, to holiness and eternal life; that we will seek divine aid to enable us to live circumspectly in the world, remembering that as we have voluntarily been buried in baptism and have been raised from the emblematical grave, so there is on us a special obligation henceforth to lead a new life, to deny ungodliness and worldly lusts, to avoid unnecessary labour, traveling and worldly conversation on Lord's days, to watch not only against the most gross evils, but also against foolish talking and jesting, vain disputing about words and things which gender strife, disregarding promises, tattling and backbiting, spending time idly at public houses, or places of amusement, betting any wager, playing at any game or enticing others thus to idle away their time.

We also engage to seek through life amidst evil report and good report to live to the glory of Him who hath called us out of darkness into his marvelous light, praying the Lord would prepare and strengthen us for every good work to do his will, working in us that which is well pleasing in his sight through Jesus Christ, to whom be glory for ever and ever, Amen.—Source: Charles Riley MacDonald, "The New Hampshire Declaration of Faith" (Th.D. diss., Northern Baptist Theological Seminary, 1939), 82.

Covenant 36: 1833 Covenant of
New Hampshire Baptist Convention

Having been, as we trust, brought by divine grace to embrace the Lord Jesus Christ, and to give up ourselves wholly to Him; we do now solemnly and joyfully covenant with each other, to walk together in Him with brotherly love, to His glory as our common Lord. We do, therefore, in His strength engage,

That we will exercise a mutual care, as members one of another, to promote the growth of the whole body in christian knowledge, holiness, and comfort; to the end that we may stand perfect and complete in all the will of God.

That to promote and secure this object, we will uphold the public worship of God and the ordinances of his house; and hold constant communion with each other therein; that we will cheerfully contribute of our property for the support of the poor, and for the maintenance of a faithfull ministry of the gospel among us.

That we will not omit closet and family religion at home; nor allow ourselves in the too common neglect of the great duty of religiously training up our children, and those under our care, with a view to the service of Christ, and the enjoyment of heaven.

That we walk circumspectly in the world, that we may win their souls; remembering that God hath not given us the spirit of fear, but of power and of love and of a sound mind; that we are the light of the world and the salt of the earth, and that a city set on a hill cannot be hid.

That we will frequently exhort, and if occasion shall require, admonish one another, according to Matthew 18th, in the spirit of meekness; considering ourselves lest we also be tempted, and that as in baptism we have been buried with Christ, and raised again; so there is on us a special obligation henceforth to walk in newness of life.

And may the God of peace, who brought again from the dead our Lord Jesus, that great Shepherd of the sheep, through the blood of the everlasting covenant, make us perfect in every good work to do his will;

working in us that which is well-pleasing in his sight through Jesus Christ: to whom be glory forever and ever. Amen.—Source: *A Short Summary and Declaration of Faith of the Baptist Church in* [blank space for a church to write in its location] *to Which Is Added the Church Covenant* (Concord, N.H.: Stevens & Young, January 20, 1833), 14; (Concord, N.H.: Young and Worth, January 20, 1833), 14.

Covenant 37: 1838 Covenant of James Allen, Avery Briggs, and E.C. Messinger *(Massachusetts)*

In the presence of God, his holy angels, and this assembly, you do now solemnly avouch the Lord Jehovah, Father, Son, and Holy Ghost, to be your God; the object of your supreme affection, and your portion forever. You cordially acknowledge the Lord Jesus Christ in all his mediatorial offices, Prophet, Priest and King, as your only Saviour, and the Holy Spirit as your Sanctifier, Comforter and Guide. You humbly and cheerfully devote yourselves to God in the everlasting covenant of His grace; you consecrate all your powers and faculties to His service and glory; and you promise, that through the assistance of His Spirit, you will cleave to Him as your chief good; that you will give diligent attendance to His word and ordinances, that you will seek the honor and interest of His kingdom; and that henceforth, denying all ungodliness, and every worldly lust, you will live soberly, righteously, and godly in the world.

You do now cordially join yourselves to this Church of Christ, engaging to strive earnestly for its peace, edification, and purity, and to walk with its members in love, faithfulness, circumspection, meekness and sobriety, and contribute your proportion as God shall prosper you, toward the pecuniary support of the gospel ministry. This you severally profess and engage.

In consequence of these professions and engagements, we, the members of this Church, *[Here the hand of fellowship may be presented]* affectionately receive you to our communion, and in the name of Christ declare you entitled to all its privileges. We welcome you to this fellowship with us in the blessings of the Gospel, and on our part engage to watch over you, and seek your edification as long as you shall continue with us. And hereafter you can never withdraw from the watch and communion of saints, without a breach of covenant.

And now, beloved in the Lord, let it be impressed on your minds that you have entered into solemn obligations from which you can never escape. Wherever you go, these vows will be upon you; they will follow you to the bar of God, and will abide upon you to eternity. You can never be as you have been. You have unalterably committed yourselves, and henceforth you must be the servants of God. Hereafter the eyes of the world will be upon you, and as you demean yourself, so religion will be honored or dishonored; if you walk worthily of your profession you will be a credit and comfort to us, but if otherwise, it will be an occasion of grief and reproach. But, beloved, we are persuaded better things of you, and things which accompany salvation, though we thus speak. May the Lord guide and preserve you till death, and at last receive you and us to that blessed world where our love and joy shall be forever perfect. Amen.—Source: John Allen, Avery Briggs, and E. C. Messinger, *A Summary of Christian Belief and Church Covenant* (Boston: James Loring, 1838), 6-8.

Covenant 38: 1841 Covenant of Kennebec *(Maine)* Baptist Association

Having, as we trust, been enabled, through divine grace, to give ourselves up to the Lord Jesus Christ in an everlasting covenant, we do now give ourselves to one another, relying upon the Spirit of grace to enable us to perform our vows.

We promise, in the presence of the Omniscient God, that so far as he shall enable us, we will turn from the path of sin, and walk in the ways of holiness, all the days of our lives.

We will endeavor to subdue all evil dispositions, passions and practices—to put away all unholy desires—to guard against wandering thoughts—to abstain from secret sins; and to live soberly, righteously, and godly in the world.

We engage to regard each others' spiritual and temporal welfare—to walk together in brotherly love—to exercise Christian watchfulness over each other, administering encouragement, reproof, or admonition, as the case may require, with all meekness and affection, forbearing one another, and forgiving one another; that we will regard each other's reputation; and particularly, that we will not speak evil one of another; but will sympathize in each other's joys and sorrows, and bear with kindness each other's burdens.

We solemnly engage to submit ourselves to the government of Christ in his church, agreeably to his direction contained in the New Testament;

both yielding to and maintaining that Christian discipline which is demanded for the peace and purity of the body; to walk together in a constant and devout attendance on all the ordinances and institutions which Christ has appointed; to be present, so far as our health and other circumstances will admit, at all meetings of the church, whether for preaching, prayer or conference.

We also engage, according to our ability, to bear our proportion of those expenses which may be deemed necessary for the relief of the poor, the support of the ministry, and other necessary charges of the church; to unite our prayers with our alms for the salvation of men, and the extension of the Redeemer's kingdom on earth.

We further engage that, the grace of God helping us, we will walk circumspectly before the world, avoiding its corrupt sentiments and wicked practices, and giving practical evidence that we have not received the grace of God in vain.

With an humble reliance on the strength of Omnipotence, we take upon ourselves these covenant vows; with a devout hope that we may perform them, and that our relations as Christian brethren, may conduce to our mutual happiness on earth, and to our preparation for a more pure and perfect union in Heaven.—Source: *Minutes,* Kennebec (Maine) Baptist Association, 1841, 15-16.

Covenant 39: 1846 Covenant of
Maine Baptist Convention

Having, as we trust, been influenced by divine grace to love God and to embrace the Lord Jesus Christ as our Saviour; and feeling that we are under the strongest obligations to obey his commands, we do now, in the presence of the all-seeing God, solemnly covenant with each other, that, as God shall enable us, we will walk together in brotherly love; that we will exercise a christian care and watchfulness over each other according to the nature of the case, and the rule of the gospel; that we will participate in each other's joys, and endeavor with sympathy to bear each other's burdens and sorrows; that we will cheerfully bear our part in supporting the public means of grace; that we will hold communion together in the worship of God, and in the ordinances and discipline of his church; that we will seek divine aid to enable us to deny ungodliness and every worldly lust and to walk circumspectly before all men; and that, through life, we will strive, amidst evil report and good report to live in the glory

of Him who hath called us out of darkness into his marvellous light.—
Source: *Minutes,* Bowdoinham (Maine) Baptist Association, 1848, 21.

Covenant 40: 1847 Covenant of William Crowell's
The Church Member's Manual

As we trust we have been brought by Divine grace to embrace the Lord
Jesus Christ, and by the influence of his Spirit to give ourselves up to
Him, so we do now solemnly covenant with each other, as God shall
enable us, that we will walk together in brotherly love; that we will exercise a christian care and watchfulness over each other, and faithfully
warn, rebuke, and admonish one another, as the case shall require; that
we will not forsake the assembling of ourselves together, nor omit the
great duty of prayer, both for ourselves and for others; that we will participate in each other's joys; and endeavor with tenderness and sympathy
to bear each other's burdens and sorrows; that we will seek Divine aid to
enable us to walk circumspectly and watchfully in the world, denying
ungodliness and every worldly lust; that we will strive together for the
support of a faithful evangelical ministry among us; and, through life,
amidst evil report and good report, seek to live to the glory of Him who
hath called us out of darkness into his marvellous light.—Source: William Crowell, *The Church Member's Manual* (Boston: Gould, Kendall &
Lincoln, 1847), 231-32.

Covenant 41: 1853 Covenant of J. Newton Brown's
The Baptist Church Manual

Having been led, as we believe, by the Spirit of God to receive the Lord
Jesus Christ as our Saviour; and, on the profession of our faith, having
been baptized in the name of the Father, and of the Son, and of the Holy
Ghost, we do now, in the presence of God, angels, and this assembly,
most solemnly and joyfully enter into covenant with one another, as one
body in Christ.

We engage, therefore, by the aid of the Holy Spirit, to walk together in
Christian love; to strive for the advancement of this church, in knowledge, holiness, and comfort; to promote its prosperity and spirituality; to
sustain its worship, ordinances, discipline, and doctrines; to contribute
cheerfully and regularly to the support of the ministry, the expenses of
the church, the relief of the poor, and the spread of the gospel through all
nations.

We also engage to maintain family and secret devotion; to religiously educate our children; to seek the salvation of our kindred and acquaintances; to walk circumspectly in the world; to be just in our dealings, faithful in our engagements, and exemplary in our deportment; to avoid all tattling, backbiting, and excessive anger; to abstain from the sale and use of intoxicating drinks as a beverage, and to be zealous in our efforts to advance the kingdom of our Saviour.

We further engage to watch over one another in brotherly love; to remember each other in prayer; to aid each other in sickness and distress; to cultivate Christian sympathy in feeling and courtesy in speech; to be slow to take offence, but always ready for reconciliation, and mindful of the rules of our Saviour, to secure it without delay.

We moreover engage, that when we remove from this place, we will as soon as possible unite with some other church, where we can carry out the spirit of this covenant, and the principles of God's word.

Prayer

Now the God of peace, who brought again from the dead our Lord Jesus, that Great Shepherd of the sheep, through the blood of the everlasting covenant, make you perfect in every good work, to do his will; working in you that which is well-pleasing in his sight, through Jesus Christ, to whom be glory forever and ever. Amen.—Source: J. Newton Brown, *The Baptist Church Manual* (Philadelphia: American Baptist Publication Society, 1853), 23-24.

Covenant 42: 1858 Covenant of
A Treatise on the Faith of the Freewill Baptists

Sincerely believing that it is the duty of all who love our God and Savior to unite with the visible church of Christ, and believing that we have earnestly sought and obtained the regenerating influences of divine grace through Jesus Christ, and having renounced the world and the things of the world, and having been buried with Christ in baptism, and having adopted the foregoing as our Confession of Faith,

We do now solemnly covenant before God, that we will strive by his assisting grace to exemplify our confession by a practice which shall correspond to all which we have above professed. And we do now give ourselves publicly and renewedly to God, to love and serve him till death— and to his people, to live together with them in brotherly love and union.

And we do solemnly covenant that we will exercise a mutual Christian care and watchfulness over each other, and will faithfully labor for the promotion of each other's spiritual welfare by fervent prayer, faithful admonitions, and affectionate rebukes, if necessary—will endeavor to restore the erring in the spirit of meekness, and labor together by prayer, precept, and example, for the salvation of sinners.

We do covenant that we will contribute of our substance for the support of a faithful ministry among us, and for all other necessary means of grace, and will be benevolent to the needy, and especially to the poor of our own church, and we will, as far as we are able, attend upon the public worship of God and the stated meetings of the church, and will labor for its prosperity and upbuilding in the most holy faith; and will not forsake it in adversity, but will bear each other's burdens, and so fulfil the law of Christ. We will constantly maintain secret and family devotion, and religiously instruct those under our care, and will cordially cooperate with those who minister to us in holy things, and will esteem them highly in love for their work's sake.

We covenant that we will not traffic in, nor use intoxicating drinks, as a beverage, and that we will sustain the other benevolent enterprises of the day, as Missions, Sabbath Schools, Moral Reform, Anti-Slavery, Education, and all others which, in the use of holy means, tend to the glory of God and the welfare of man.

We Covenant and agree that we will love all those who love our Lord Jesus Christ; that we will avoid all vain extravagance and sinful conformity to the world, and will abstain from all sinful amusements, as theatres, dances, gambling, and from all vain festivals; and will refrain from all unchaste and profane conversation, and from the reading of wicked and corrupting publications. We will walk circumspectly towards those who are without, that the cause of God may not be reproached on our account.

And may the God of peace sanctify us wholly, and preserve us blameless to the coming of our Lord Jesus Christ, to join the glorified around the throne of God, in ascribing blessing, and honor, and glory, and power, unto him that sitteth on the throne, and unto the Lamb forever and ever. Amen.—Source: *A Treatise on the Faith of the Freewill Baptists: With an Appendix Containing a Summary of Their Usages in Church Government*, 6th ed. (Dover: Freewill Baptist Printing Establishment, 1858), 46-49 of appendix.

Covenant 43: 1859 Covenant of Edward T. Hiscox's
The Baptist Church Directory

Having been, as we trust, brought by divine grace to embrace the Lord Jesus Christ, and to give ourselves wholly to him, we do now solemnly and joyfully covenant with each other, TO WALK TOGETHER IN HIM, WITH BROTHERLY LOVE, to his glory, as our common Lord. We do, therefore, in his strength, engage—

That, we will exercise a Christian care and watchfulness over each other, and faithfully warn, exhort, and admonish each other, as occasion may require:

That, we will not forsake the assembling of ourselves together, but will uphold the public worship of God, and the ordinances of his house:

That, we will not omit closet and family religion at home, nor neglect the great duty of religiously training our children, and those under our care, for the service of Christ, and the enjoyment of heaven:

That, as we are the light of the world, and salt of the earth, we will seek divine aid, to enable us to deny ungodliness, and every worldly lust, and to walk circumspectly in the world, that we may win the souls of men:

That, we will cheerfully contribute of our property, according as God has prospered us, for the maintenance of a faithful and evangelical ministry among us, for the support of the poor, and to spread the Gospel over the earth:

That, we will, in all conditions, even till death, strive to live to the glory of him, who hath called us out of darkness into his marvellous light.

And may the God of peace, who brought again from the dead our Lord Jesus, that great Shepherd of the sheep, through the blood of the everlasting covenant, make us perfect in every good work, to do his will, working in us that which is well pleasing in his sight, through Jesus Christ; to whom be glory, forever and ever. Amen.—Source: Edward T. Hiscox, *The Baptist Church Directory* (New York: Sheldon & Co., 1859), 176-77.

Covenant 44: 1868 Covenant of Citadel Square Baptist Church, Charleston, South Carolina *(Apparently Written by Richard Furman)*

Whereas, it is the incumbent duty of those who are favored with the dispensation of the grace of God, to embrace his covenant, acknowledge his government, profess his name, and unite together in the faith and fellowship of the gospel, we do now, in the presence of the great eternal God, who knows the secrets of all hearts, and before angels and men, acknowledge ourselves as under the most solemn obligations to be the Lord's, and we accordingly covenant and agree:

1. That we will take the only living and true God, one God in three persons, Father, Son and Holy Ghost, to be our God.

2. We unreservedly and solemnly give up ourselves, both soul and body, and all we possess, to Almighty God to be ordered, directed and disposed of by him, according to the counsel of his holy will. And this we do, in humble dependence on the grace of the Holy Spirit, to aid and support us in these sacred engagements, and hoping for acceptance and salvation through the merit and mediation of our Lord Jesus Christ.

3. We take the Scriptures of the Old and New Testament to be our rule of faith and practice, in the great concerns of religion, and the general affairs of life; and particularly in the services and business of the church.

4. We promise to maintain communion and fellowship with each other, in the public worship of God, according to the various ordinances of the gospel, "not forsaking the assembling ourselves together, as the manner of some is," but embracing all regular, convenient seasons, for this purpose, as the providence of God shall permit.

And also to exercise mutual forbearance, and love; praying for and sympathizing with each other, in the various circumstances of life, and using every laudable endeavor to provoke to love and good works.

5. We promise to pay a respectful regard to the advice and admonition of the church, and to be subject to its discipline, as directed by the Word of God, and conducted in the spirit of the gospel.

6. We promise to contribute according to our ability, for the support of public worship and the relief of the poor in the church; to use our influence to forward and promote the interests of the Redeemer's Kingdom in the world; to conduct ourselves with uprightness and integrity, and in a peaceful and friendly manner, towards mankind in general, and towards Christians of all descriptions in particular; and also to pay a conscientious regard to civil government, and give it our support as an ordinance of God.

This covenant we make with the free and full consent of our souls, hoping through rich, free and boundless grace, we shall therein be accepted of God unto eternal life, through Jesus Christ our Lord:—to

whom be glory and majesty, power and dominion everlasting. Amen.
Question—Do you approve of and embrace this Covenant?
Answer—I do.

The candidate shall then receive from the Pastor the right hand of fellowship, be admitted to the Lord's table, and be entitled to all the rights and privileges of members, consistent with their respective stations.—Source: *Minutes,* Citadel Square Baptist Church, Charleston, South Carolina, June 1868, 20-22.

Covenant 45: 1871 Covenant of
The Baptist Praise Book: For Congregational Singing

As we trust we have received, through Divine Grace, the Lord Jesus Christ, and given ourselves wholly to him, and on profession of our faith have been buried with him in baptism and thus united to his church, we do now solemnly and joyfully covenant with each other, and, by the aid of the Holy Spirit, engage—

That we will walk together with brotherly love, exercising a Christian care and watchfulness over each other, participating in each other's joys, and, with tender sympathy, bearing one another's burdens and sorrows:

That we will not forsake the assembling of ourselves together at the Communion and other appointed meetings, but seek and pray for the spirituality, harmony, and prosperity of this church; sustain its worship, ordinances, discipline and doctrines; and give its claims a sacred pre-eminence over all organizations of human origin:

That we will cheerfully contribute of our means, as God has prospered us, for the support of faithful and evangelical ministry among us; for the relief of the poor; and for spreading the gospel over the earth:

That we will maintain private and family devotions; religiously educate the children committed to our care; and endeavor, in purity of heart and newness of life, and good-will toward all men, to exemplify and commend our holy faith, win souls to the Saviour, and hold fast our profession till he shall come and receive us unto himself.

[Relying on the grace of God, do you thus covenant and promise?]

And now the God of peace, who brought again from the dead our Lord Jesus, that Great Shepherd of the sheep, through the blood of the everlasting covenant make us perfect in every good work to do his will, working in us that which is well-pleasing in his sight, through Jesus Christ; to whom be glory for ever and ever. Amen.—Source: Richard Fuller,

Thomas Armitage, Basil Manly, Jr., and others, *The Baptist Praise Book: For Congregational Singing* (New York: A.S. Barnes & Co., 1871), viii.

Covenant 46: 1870s Covenant of Bethany Swedish Baptist Church, Moline, Illinois

Having experienced salvation through believing in our Saviour Jesus Christ and His Atonement for our sin, we desire to wholly serve Him and give ourselves on the altar, and we therefore solemnly and with joy make a covenant with each other to walk together with Him in brotherly love and glorify His name who is our common Lord and Saviour. This we promise to do in His power.

We will promote and take part in the public meetings of the Church and the ordinances that God has given to His Church.

We will not forsake our private and family devotions, nor forget to give our children instructions in the Bible and its Godgiven truth. This we should do with joy and in obedience to Christ's command.

As we are the light of the world and the salt of the earth we will, through the power of God, forsake ungodliness and worldly lust and walk Godly and righteously in this world, and try to influence others to follow our example to seek salvation and a Godly life.

We will with thankfulness give of our earthly possessions accordingly as God has prospered us to promote the truth as it is given to us in the Bible and help to bring the Word to the end of the earth.

We also will help the poor in any way we can.

We will in all circumstances, even unto death, strive to live a life that will glorify Him who has called us out of darkness into His glorious light.

"Now the God of peace that brought again from the dead our Lord Jesus, the great Shepherd of the sheep through the blood of His everlasting covenant, make you perfect in every good work to do His will, working in you that which is pleasing in His sight through Jesus Christ; to Him be glory forever and ever."—Amen.—Source: Covenant included in letter from G. David Guston, archivist, Baptist General Conference, St. Paul, Minnesota, December 9, 1987. The original date of the covenant is not given, but the copy provided appears in the eightieth anniversary booklet of the church and is described as having been "written by Rev. Olof Lind[h] and subscribed to by the original Swedish Baptist Church." Norris Magnuson, chairman, Baptist General Conference Historical Committee, stated in a letter of January 22, 1988, that the covenant "was probably written by the early 1870s, when he [Lindh] was pastor there [Moline, Illinois]."

Covenant 47: 1881 Covenant of William Cathcart's
The Baptist Encyclopaedia

First. We believe that the Holy Scriptures were given by inspiration of God, and that they are the only certain rule of faith and practice.

Second. Whereas various interpretations of the Sacred Word have been given by different denominations of professed Christians, we hereby declare that the foregoing Articles of Faith (the covenant follows the articles) express our views of the meaning of the Word of God, which Holy Word we promise to search diligently and to make the man of our counsel.

Third. We agree to contribute towards the support of the worship of God in our own church, and to spread the knowledge of Jesus in our own country and throughout the world according to our ability.

Fourth. We hereby covenant and agree to walk in love and to live in peace, to sympathize with each other under all conditions and circumstances in life, to pray with and for one another, and to exhort and stir up each other unto every good word and work.

Fifth. We solemnly promise, by the assistance of the Holy Spirit, to watch over each other with all kindness and Christian affection; not suffering sin to rest upon a brother, but as far as God in his providence shall make it known to us, we will, in all cases of offense, take our Lord's direction in the 18th chapter of Matthew, which says, "Moreover, if thy brother shall trespass against thee, go and tell him his fault between thee and him alone; if he shall hear thee, thou hast gained thy brother. But if he will not hear thee, then take with thee one or two more, that in the mouth of two or three witnesses every word may be established. And if he shall neglect to hear them, tell it unto the church: but if he neglect to hear the church, let him be unto thee as an heathen man and a publican." And we will urge our utmost endeavors to maintain a scriptural discipline in the church.

Sixth. Moreover, we covenant to meet on the first day of the week for public worship, and to fill up our places at all the appointed meetings of the church, as God shall give us health and opportunity. All and each of these duties we freely and most solemnly promise (by the assistance of the great Head of the church) to observe, until we are planted in the glorious church above.—Amen.—Source: William Cathcart, ed., *The Baptist Encyclopaedia* (Philadelphia: Louis H. Everts, 1881), 283.

Covenant 48: 1889 Covenant of
Free Baptist Cyclopaedia: Historical and Biographical

Believing that the union of Christians in a visible church is sanctioned by the teachings of Christ and the practice of his apostles, that it is adapted to promote piety and increase Christian influence, we do now heartily enter into covenant before god [sic], and with each other.

We will constantly strive to maintain true piety in our hearts, to keep ourselves in vital communion with God, and commend religion to others, not only in words, but by means of a devout spirit and a holy example, always careful of each other's reputation and usefulness.

We will watch over each other in the spirit of true charity, seeking to bear each other's burdens, assist the needy, strengthen the weak, encourage the despondent, sympathize with the sorrowful, reprove the erring, win back the straying to duty, aid in maintaining wholesome discipline, receive Christian admonition and reproof in meekness, keep the unity of the spirit in the bond of peace, and cheerfully submit to such regulations as the majority may approve. We will contribute, according to our ability, for the support of a faithful ministry; maintain secret and family prayer, and aid, by our presence and otherwise, in sustaining public and social worship, and in giving success to the various means of grace.

We will give an active and consistent support to the great causes that aim to promote morality and Christian progress, such as Home-culture, Temperance, Sabbath-schools, Education and Missions. We will refuse all sanction to the sale and use of intoxicating liquors as a beverage, and to those worldly indulgences and amusements which tend to lessen true piety in ourselves, or weaken Christian influences over others, so that the cause of religion be not reproached on our account.

We will everywhere hold Christian principle sacred, and Christian objects supreme, counting it our chief business in life to spread Christian knowledge and diffuse the Christian spirit in society and among all the nations of the earth, constantly praying and toiling that the kingdom of God may come, and His will be done on earth as it is done in heaven.

May He who has promised his help enable us to keep this covenant, grant us grace to be faithful in all things, until He shall gather us to himself, and crowns us with final victory. Amen.—Source: G. A. Burgess and J. T. Ward, *Free Baptist Cyclopaedia: Historical and Biographical* (n.p.: Free Baptist Cyclopaedia Co., 1889), 138-39.

Covenant 49: 1895 Covenant of
Church Book Alphabetically Arranged and Record Book
(Probably Written by James Robinson Graves)

Thanking God for the light we have received, for the revelation of Jesus which we now enjoy; and hoping that God, for Christ's sake, has pardoned our sins; and having been baptized on a profession of our faith in Christ Jesus into the name of the Father, Son, and Holy Ghost; we do, this day, before God and the world, with deep joy and great solemnity, enter into covenant with one another, as one body in Christ.

We therefore covenant and agree, that, by the aid of the Holy Spirit, we will walk together in love and Christian fellowship. We promise to labor for the advancement and final triumph of the church; to sustain her worship by attending the house of God and supporting the ministry; to guard her ordinances, enforce her discipline, and defend her doctrine.

We also pledge ourselves to walk circumspectly in the world; to be honest, just and faithful in our business relations; and, as God may give us help, we promise to live righteous and holy lives.

We further promise to watch over each other in brotherly love; to visit the sick; to pray for each other and the world; to aid the poor and needy, and to perform such other kind offices as may be well pleasing in the sight of God.—Source: *Church Book Alphabetically Arranged and Record Book* (Louisville, Ky.: Charles T. Dearing, 1895), n. p.

Covenant 50: 1926 Covenant of
A Manual of Seventh Day Baptist Church Procedure

Art. 1. We agree to keep the commandments of God, and walk in the faith of Jesus Christ.

Art. 2. To accept the Holy Scriptures as our rule of faith and practice.

Art. 3. To watch over each other for good, to the intent that we may build up together in Christ, grow in grace and a further knowledge of truth, and be instrumental in bringing men to a saving knowledge of our Lord and Saviour, Jesus Christ.

Art. 4. To faithfully attend the appointments, and bear the burdens and expenses of the church, according as God may give us severally the ability.—Source: William Lewis Burdick and Corliss Fitz Randolph, eds., *A Manual of Seventh Day Baptist Church Procedure*, rev. ed. (Plainfield, N.J.: American Sabbath Tract Society, 1926), 39. Used by permission.

Covenant 51: 1949 Covenant of Chickasawhatchee Primitive Baptist Church, Dawson, Georgia

We do solemnly promise that we will be faithful in the study of God's Word, and prayer; that we will attend all our church meetings when possible to do so; that we will labor unitedly and zealously for the Master's Cause; seeking at all times His Glory, and the advancement of His Kingdom, and that we will strive daily to crucify the flesh and live such lives that we may be a light unto the world and show forth the praises of HIM who has called us out of darkness into His marvelous light.

We promise that we will ever labor for the peace and fellowship so necessary for the best interests of the Church, making whatever personal sacrifices that may be necessary; that we will lovingly watch over each other for good, and whenever any shall go astray either in faith or practice, we will kindly, lovingly, and faithfully seek to save such a one from the error of his way, that he may enjoy richly the blessings of God's House and the sweet joys of salvation, and that none of God's children be lost to our church.

We promise to contribute freely of our carnal things for the support of the Church, and that each will give as the Lord has prospered him that our ministry may give themselves wholly to the work whereunto God has called them.

And for Grace, to enable us to live and labor, we do most earnestly pray.—Source: *Chickasawhatchee Primitive Baptist Church, Dawson, Ga., May 1, 1949, Membership List, Church Covenant, Articles of Faith, Articles of Decorum* (no reference data given).

Covenant 52: 1949 Covenant of *Doctrines and Usages of General Baptists and Worker's Handbook*

Having given ourselves to God, we now give ourselves to His church and covenant with it and with each other, as also with God—

1. That we will forsake all unrighteousness, even the appearance of evil. We will abstain from all questionable pursuits and pleasures; we will forego all hurtful habits; we will avoid all evil associations; and we will touch not, taste not, handle not, any unclean thing.

2. That we will follow earnestly after righteousness and true holiness in the fear and love of God. We will seek first the kingdom of God and His righteousness, trusting that all needful and helpful things will be added to us; we will seek entire consecration to God; we will live a life of prayer; we will seek the constant abiding of the Divine life within us: and we will be satisfied only when we have evidence that we please God and are accepted of Him.

3. That we will faithfully improve all the means of grace. We will attend and support the services of the church, the preaching, the social services, the business meetings; we will contribute freely of our means for the advancement of the Gospel; and we will cooperate with our brethren in every enterprise having for its end the glory of God and the salvation of men.

4. That we will be Christ-like in all our deportment. We will be tender and affectionate toward each other; we will be careful of each other's reputation, thinking no evil, and backbiting not with our tongues; we will return good for evil; we will be just and honest, truthful and honorable in all our dealings; we will do unto others as we would be done by; we will be meek, loving and forgiving as we desire and hope to be forgiven.

5. We will be faithful, Christian workers. We will do whatever Christian work comes to hand, shunning no cross, shirking no duty; we will even seek opportunities to do good, glorify God and save souls; we will study to win our associates, our neighbors, our families, all whom we may influence to become Christians: we will count it more than our meat and our drink, more than all things else, to do the will of our Father in heaven, to lead souls from sin and death, and lead them to God and heaven.—Source: *Doctrines and Usages of General Baptists and Worker's Handbook*, rev. ed. (Poplar Bluff, Mo.: General Baptist Press, 1949), 9. Used by permission. This covenant also appears in *General Baptist Hymn Book* (Poplar Bluff, Mo.: General Baptist Education and Publications, Inc., 1965), 416.

Covenant 53: 1969 Covenant of Franklin M. Segler's
The Broadman Minister's Manual

Having been led by the Spirit of God to receive Jesus Christ as Saviour and Lord by faith, and having publicly confessed him by baptism in the name of God the Father, Son, and Holy Spirit, we freely and joyfully enter into covenant with one another as one body in Christ.

We pledge, therefore, by the aid of God's Spirit, to live together in Christian love; to work for the advancement of God's kingdom through this church in knowledge, holiness, and mutual care; to support its ministry by a faithful stewardship of money, time, and talents; and to sustain its worship, ordinances, doctrines, and disciplines.

We also pledge to maintain family and private worship, to rear our children in the nurture and spirit of the Lord; to seek the salvation of all members of our own families and of our acquaintances; and to strive for maturity in ourselves and in our fellow Christians.

We further pledge to follow Christian principles of morality in our daily living; to be ethical in our dealings and faithful in our commitments; to promote the unity of fellowship by proper attitudes and careful speech; and to be zealous in our efforts toward the advancement of the kingdom of God here and throughout the world.—Source: Franklin M. Segler, *The Broadman Minister's Manual* (Nashville: Broadman Press, 1969), 147-48. Used by permission.

Covenant 54: 1969 Covenant of R. Lofton Hudson

We believe that we are God's children. He has come near to us. We have felt his presence and received Christ as our Lord, our close friend, our helper, the Higher Power to which we respond.

Therefore, we belong to one another, we need brothers and sisters as well as a Father and Mother (Holy Spirit). We commit ourselves to accepting one another in all of our uniqueness, without respect to race or class, in our estrangements and separation and aloneness.

We commit ourselves to getting with as many of the world's needs as we can focus on and find time and energy for. The sick, the twisted and damaged souls, the ignorant who do not know of God's grace and truth (reality), the fearful who have given up on humanity, and the hopeless who have decided that it is better to give up than to dream the impossible dream. To these we commit ourselves.

We commit ourselves to attacking the problems of the government and the world. Other continents, Russia, Communist China, the power structures in our country in our own political set-up—these are all our concern. We do not know where we should focus at any given moment, so we leave ourselves open to the leadership of God's Spirit and of our intuitions.

We commit ourselves to our families, to those closest to us. We will try to peel off our pretenses and our facades and be frank, open, honest, and sincere. We hope to do more than guess at one another. In the milieu of flowing circumstances we trust that we can touch one another in meaningful ways. In this we find community, comaraderie, togetherness and communion. We may even love one another in a mature way.

In this world, in our human condition, we commit ourselves to healthy human relations, to caring for one another without fostering dependency, to learn to live with hostility and rejection without becoming paranoid, to be free to be loving persons without thinking that every person will love us back, to become morally and spiritually self-responsible without developing a pseudo-autonomy which leaves us alone and isolated. We acknowledge our need for one another and for God.

We commit ourselves to the God who makes himself known through the Bible, through Christ, through nature, through his mysterious Spirit, through beauty and great music and art, and through the mind of man. Let us leave him free to act and ourselves free to react to his overtures.— Source: R. Lofton Hudson, "Our Outdated Church Covenant," *Home Missions,* March 1969, 39. Used by permission.

Covenant 55: 1969 Covenant of Gerald Phillips

In response to the leadership of the Holy Spirit of God I have received Jesus Christ as my personal Saviour and Lord and have professed this faith publicly by testimony and by baptism in the name of the Father, Son and Holy Spirit. Therefore, before God and fellow-believers of this assembly I now with joy and deliberate purpose unite my life with others of like faith in a covenant relationship that will make us one body in Christ.

I commit myself to try to live before all men a life free of pretense and hypocrisy, a life that is frank, open, honest and sincere. I pledge myself to make every effort to discipline my own life so as not to bring reproach through word, action or attitude on my Lord, my church or myself. To encourage an atmosphere of mutual trust and meaningful togetherness I further pledge myself to try to love every member of this fellowship and to seek means to express that love always and under all circumstances.

In my personal ministry to others of this body I will be sensitive to needs and will share, comfort, console, encourage and aid them as needs demand and circumstances permit. I pledge myself to look for the best in others and to be slow to be offended by word, action or attitude that may seem unchristian and to seek a quick, Christian solution to any breach of fellowship as Christ has instructed us.

Because of my love for Christ and my need for Christian community I will actively do my part in this church to sustain, develop and enrich its worship, proclamation of the gospel, Christian education and ministry to people. I will give generously that the local and worldwide ministries of this church may be carried out.

In order to maintain a regenerate membership I will help my church receive and baptize only such persons as can give evidence of a personal experience with Christ in salvation. I will support my church in its efforts to maintain unity, guard the purity of its teaching, protect its integrity and promote the holiness of its members through a loving, Bible-centered discipline of its members.

To keep my own life spiritually fresh I commit myself to a regular, personal devotional life. I will make Bible study, prayer and Christian training a part of the life of my family wherever possible. And I will try at all times and places, as the Holy Spirit aids, to be a living and verbal witness of new life in Jesus Christ.

As a demonstration that Christian fellowship is vital to my life and witness I will, upon leaving this church, as soon as possible, unite with some other church where I can carry out the spirit of this covenant and the principles of God's Word.—Source: Gerald Phillips, "Church Covenant," *Illinois Baptist,* June 25, 1969, 2. Used by permission.

Covenant 56: 1971 Covenant of
James E. Fitch and John G. Mitchell's
Developing a Church Covenant:
An Expression of Personal Commitment

We covenant with God our Father:

We accept, O Lord, your forgiveness for the sins we have committed, and pray that you will stop their harmful effects; we covenant with you, to be forgiving persons.

We thank you, O Lord, for touching our hearts and lives with your healing; we covenant with you, to be healers to others.

We thank you, our Father, for making us aware of your presence; we covenant with you, to watch for, wait upon, and depend on your help daily in our lives.

We thank you, O Lord, for making us aware of who we are, and for helping us to understand others; we covenant with you, to be understanding persons.

We thank you, O Lord, for accepting us as persons, when we are so far from being holy and righteous; we covenant with you, to be persons who accept others even when they do not measure up to our standards.

We thank you, O Lord, for being interested in our lives; we covenant with you, to let your son Jesus be our Lord.

We recognize, O Lord, the steadfastness of your faithfulness to us; we return that commitment and dedicate our lives to you and your service.

We thank you, O Lord, for breaking some of the sinful bonds on our lives; we covenant with you to be Christian toward those who are not experiencing this freedom.

We thank you, O Lord, for loving us when we do not deserve your love; we covenant with you, to love others as you have loved us.

We covenant with one another:

Because God has accepted me, I accept you, my brethren, into my life and into my care. I covenant to accept you as you are, and hope that we can grow together to be mature children of God.

Because I have experienced the forgiveness of God in my life, I covenant with you, as a brother in Christ, to forgive you, even when I feel the pain you may cause me.

Because I know God's help and support in my life, I covenant, my brethren, to support you to the best of my abilities, in times of your grief, stress, and sickness.

Because we are members of Christ's body, the church, I covenant with you to share life and service with you, with all of its joys and sorrows. I covenant to be concerned about you and your family. I promise to defend you as brethren from those who would deny you their love and respect. I covenant to be honest with you, even when it may be painful to us both.

I covenant to respond when you try to help me. I promise to trust that you act from a concern for me.

I covenant with you, that henceforth, I will commit my life to be your friend in Jesus Christ, the one who has touched us all and given our lives meaning.

We covenant together:

To apply our faith in all aspects of our lives;

To strive for a more perfect society in keeping with the Spirit of God;

To be faithful stewards of our time, influence, abilities, and possessions; to use them wisely and fully;

To assemble ourselves together regularly for worship, study, witness, and fellowship;

To pray for one another, and care for one another;

To encounter God daily through reading the Scriptures and prayer; and to be faithful to this fellowship of Christians. Amen.—Source: James E. Fitch and John G. Mitchell, *Developing a Church Covenant: An Expression of Personal Commitment* (Nashville: Sunday School Board, Southern Baptist Convention, 1971), 29-30. Used by permission. Reprinted in Howard B. Foshee, *Broadman Church Manual* (Nashville: Broadman Press, 1973), 30-32.

Covenant 57: 1972 Covenant of Baptist Church of the Covenant, Birmingham, Alabama

I covenant before God, with this pastor, and congregation to do the following:

1. I will be faithful in attendance in worship and training.

2. I covenant to involve myself in at least one major ministry of the church.

3. I covenant to give of my means sacrificially, with the tithe as the basic guideline.

4. I covenant to live ethically and morally so that the cause of Christ is not weakened and this church shamed.

I am committed to an interracial, intercultural, and international church. I am committed to an innovative church—one that is warmly evangelical and socially concerned. I will strive mightily to assist the church to be a faithful people of God.—Source: Covenant enclosed in a letter from J. Herbert Gilmore, Jr., pastor, March 1, 1973.

Covenant 58: 1972 Covenant of *A Manual of Procedures for Seventh Day Baptist Churches* (A Mid-Twentieth-Century Covenant Adopted by Bay Area, California, Seventh Day Baptist Church)

For the glory of God and Christ Jesus,
In the service of our fellow men,
For the blessing of all men, our brothers,
Solemnly and joyfully
We united to advance in Christian experience through
The Bay Area Seventh Day Baptist Church.

We covenant together:
To give mutual assistance in our Christian life,
To watch over one another for good,
To worship and work together in love and harmony,
To live so we may share in bringing the Kingdom of God closer to
fulfillment.
We cherish liberty of thought
As an essential condition for the guidance of the Holy Spirit, and
Therefore have no binding creed; we do still resolve that
We shall each search the Scriptures and pray without ceasing, that
We may continue to strengthen our Christian Faith and
Grow in Grace.
Source: Wayne R. Hood, ed., *A Manual of Procedures for Seventh Day Baptist Churches* (Plainfield, N.J.: Seventh Day Baptist General Conference, 1972), 98-99. Used by permission.

Covenant 59: 1976 Covenant of
First Baptist Church, Decatur, Georgia

As members of the First Baptist Church of Decatur we joyfully confess our faith in God as revealed in Jesus Christ and affirm Him as the source of our life and hope. We, therefore, freely give allegiance to His church in whose fellowship we strive to grow in faith and understanding and we dedicate ourselves to the service of God in the world—recognizing in ourselves and affirming in others God's gifts of identity and individual worth. As members of this particular community of faith we make these solemn commitments:

I will sustain the public worship of God in word and symbol, celebrating His glory and remembering His grace.

I will be a faithful steward, devoting my time, talents and possessions to the enrichment and extension of ministry that addresses itself to the needs of the total person.

I will be diligent in the study of the Scriptures, patiently searching their teachings for divine instruction and guidance.

I will seek to live according to the pattern of Jesus Christ, measuring my attitudes and actions toward others by His love.

I will sustain and nourish this fellowship of believers, encouraging each person in the pilgrimage of faith.

I will share in Christ's mission to the world, seeking through word and deed to make His love known to all people.

Relying on the guidance and power of the Holy Spirit we seal this covenant with one another and with God as we pray:

Eternal Father, Creator of all life, grant us Your presence and strength as we engage in fulfilling this commitment, through Jesus Christ, our Lord and Saviour. Amen.

Source: Hettie Pittman Johnson, *The Church Expanding: The Story of the First Baptist Church, Decatur, Georgia, 1862-1987* (Decatur: First Baptist Church, 1987), 236. Used by permission.

Covenant 60: 1983 Covenant of Chevis F. Horne

We are people whom Christ has set free. We belong, not to ourselves, but to our Liberator. We are God's people. We praise him "who loves us and has freed us from our sins by his blood."

Being led, as we believe by the Holy Spirit, and in order to use our freedom responsibly, we do most solemnly enter into covenant with one another under God. We shall make over and over again the earliest Christian confession: Jesus Christ is Lord. We shall be faithful in proclaiming the good news of Jesus Christ, in prayer, in the study of God's Word, the practice of Christian stewardship, and the nurturing of the Christian fellowship. We shall love, accept, affirm, and pray for one another. There will be no cheap person among us and no friendless person in our midst. We want the doors of our church to be as wide as the love of Christ.

We shall be especially concerned about our families, that they be Christian, that a faithful love exist between husband and wife and that our children be wanted, loved, and cared for.

Knowing that we are dependent on the church which is the body of Christ the way the hand depends on the physical body, we promise to be vitally connected with our church here and wherever we may live.

With the benediction on Sunday, we shall not leave the church within these sacred walls. We shall be the church in the world! We shall go, all of us, into the world as ministers of Christ. We shall speak the reconciling word and do the reconciling deed.

We shall reach across barriers, keep open communication, and care for people the way Christ has cared for us. We shall seek economic justice so that the good life will be within the reach of everyone. We shall try to overcome racial prejudice and all conditions that demean and cheapen human life.

We shall abstain from the use of drugs while being concerned about those who are the victims of drugs.

We who have been so richly blessed will share our affluence with the poor, hungry, and starving of our world.

We shall be the careful keepers of the good earth, passing it unspoiled to those who will come after us.

We shall say and do those things that make for peace in a world where the threat of nuclear war falls like an ominous shadow.

We would live in such a way that people can see Jesus Christ in us, recognizing him as the one who loves them, would save them, and cannot give them up. Amen.—Source: Chevis F. Horne, "Is It Time for a New Church Covenant?" *The Baptist Program*, April 1983, 19. Used by permission.

Covenant 61: 1987 Covenant of First Baptist Church *(North American Baptist Conference)*, Lodi, California

By the help and guidance of the Holy Spirit we covenant:

1. To walk together in Christian love.

2. To exercise Christian care and watchfulness over one another.

3. To pray with and for one another, sharing our burdens, sorrows and joys.

4. To be thoughtful and courteous to one another, to be slow to take offense, and to be quick to forgive and to seek forgiveness.

5. To guard the spiritual and scriptural purity, peace and prosperity of the Church and its growth in scriptural knowledge and godliness.

6. To assist, as the Lord enables, in the work of the Church, and to promote its usefulness as a witness to the saving grace of God in Christ Jesus.

7. To contribute, as the Lord directs, to the financial support of the Church, the relief of the needy, and the evangelization of all people.

8. To love and to pray for all believers in the Lord Jesus Christ.

9. To engage regularly in personal Bible reading and prayer, and to establish family devotions where possible.

10. To bring up such children as may be entrusted to our care in the

nurture and admonition of the Lord.

11. To walk circumspectly in the world, to provide things honest in the sight of all men, to be faithful in engagements, exemplary in deportment, denying ungodliness and worldly lusts.

12. To endeavor by example, by word and by prayer, to win others to an acceptance of Jesus Christ as Savior and Lord.

Source: Covenant included in a letter from Ilse Mollenhauer, secretary to John Binder, executive director, North American Baptist Conference, Oakbrook Terrace, Illinois, February 18, 1988.

Covenant 62: 1988 Covenant of Halawa Heights Baptist Church, Honolulu, Hawaii

Having been led, as we believe by the Spirit of God, to receive the Lord Jesus Christ as our Saviour and, on the profession of our faith, having been baptized in the name of the Father, and of the Son, and of the Holy Spirit, we do now, in the presence of God, and this assembly, most solemnly and joyfully enter into covenant with one another as one body in Christ.

To give willingly, generously and regularly of our time, talents, and money to support and advance the work of the Kingdom of God through this church and our denomination at home and abroad;

To faithfully attend the worship services and Christian training opportunities provided by this church;

To strengthen our spiritual lives through daily family devotions and individual Bible study;

To nurture our children in the counsel of the Lord;

To avoid all things that would impair our bodies, minds and influence, or would in any way weaken our witness for Christ;

To faithfully care for one another in times of sickness and distress;

To uphold each other in prayer;

To cultivate kindness, patience and forgiveness;

To witness to the unsaved of the redeeming love of God through Jesus Christ.

Should we leave this place, we will, as the Lord leads, unite with another church, where we can carry out the spirit of this covenant and the principles of God's Word.—Source: Included in letter from Dan H. Kong, executive director-treasurer, Hawaii Baptist Convention, March 10, 1988.

Section C: Covenants of Baptists in Canada
(See ch. 5 for history and interpretation of this section.)

Covenant 63: 1800 Covenant of Old Canning Baptist Church, Queen's County, New Brunswick

We do here in the presence of the great eternal omniscient God, who knows the secrets of all hearts, and in the presence of angels and men acknowledge ourselves to be under the most solemn covenant with God to be for him and no other. And we do now renew our covenant with him.

1st We take the only living and true God to be our God, one God in three persons. The Father, Son, and Holy Ghost.

2nd We take the Holy Scriptures of the Old and New Testaments to be the revealed mind and will of God, and promise through the existence of the Holy Spirit to make them the rule of our lives. Acknowledging ourselves by nature children of wrath and our hope of mercy with God is only through the righteousness of Jesus Christ apprehended by faith.

3dly We now call heaven and earth to witness that without the least reservation we give up ourselves, soul, and body and all that we have and are to this one God through Jesus Christ to be entirely at his disposal. Boath ourselves, our names and estates. As God shall see most for his own glory, that we will do faithfully by the help of God's Spirit whatsoever our consciences influenced by the word and Spirit of God directs us to be duty, tho' it be never contrary to nature boath as to duties to God or man.

4thly And we do also by the assistance of divine grace unitedly give up ourselves to one another in covenant, promising by the help of the grace of God, to act towards one another as brothers in Christ, watching over one another in the love of God, even to watch against foolish talking and jesting which is not convenient, and every thing that does not become the followers of the Holy Spirit of God. And seek the good of each other and the church universal for the glory of God, and to hold communion one with another in the worship of God, according to Christ's visible kingdom so far as the providence of God admits of the same. And submitting ourselves to the discipline of this church as part of Christ's mistical body according as we shall be guided by the word and Spirit of God. And by the help of divine grace still to be working for a greater sight from God which is contained in the sacred Scriptures, believing that there is greater misteries to be unfolded and further light to shine in the church beyond what they have ever yet attained too. Looking and watching for the glorious day when the Lord Jesus Christ will take to himself his great power and reign from sea to sea and from the rivers to the end of the earth. And this covenant we make with the free and full consent of souls, believing that through rich, free and boundless grace it is owned of God and ratifyed in heaven before the throne of God and the Lamb. Amen. Even so come Lord Jesus. Amen and Amen.—Source: I. E. Bill, *Fifty Years with the Baptist Ministers and Churches of the Maritime Provinces of Canada* (St. John, New Brunswick: Barnes and Co., 1880), 595-96.

Covenant 64: 1809 Covenant of Oxford Baptist Church, Upper Canada (Ontario)

We do now in the presance of the omnipotent God of Elect angels and men avouch the Lord Jehovah To Be our onley Lord and Sovrign and give up our Selves to his Service without Resurvation taking his Holy word for the Rule of our Conduct and by the assistance of Devine Grace promising to Observe all Commands Institution Enjoined on us therin as far as we shall Understand them that we will as far as Divine Providence permits Constantley attend the Publick Worship of God and ordinences of the Gospel in this Church and Extende a Faithful watch over all its members also in Each private Relation use our influence to promote Piety and famely religion by Reding the Scripters prayer and Christian Conversation Submiting to the Laws of Christ in the Disciplline of his Hous[.]

[We] promis to abstain from and wach against Convitiousness Defraud Idleness foolish Jesting reviling and Evil Speaking with whatsoever is unbecoming the Christian Profession Den[y]ing unGodliness worldley Lusts that we will Live Soberley Seking the Advancement of the Kindom of God in the general Good humbly trusting in the Righteousness of our Glorious Redeemer for the Holey Spirit to Sanctify and enable us to presevier In Holiness Until the Coming of our Lord and Saviour Jesus Christ to whome Be honor and power Everlasting amen.—Source: F. W. Waters, "Pioneer Baptist Creeds and Covenants in Upper Canada and Lower Canada," *Canadian Baptist Home Missions Digest* 6 (1963-1964): 218-19. Used by permission.

Covenant 65: 1827 Covenant of
Halifax Baptist Church, Nova Scotia

As we trust that we have been brought by divine grace to receive the Lord Jesus Christ, and by the influences of his Spirit to give ourselves up to him, so we do now solemnly covenant with each other, as God shall enable us, to walk together in brotherly love; that we will exercise a Christian care and watchfulness over each other, and faithfully admonish and entreat one another, as occasion may require; that we will not forsake the assembling of ourselves together, nor neglect the great duty of prayer for ourselves and for others, that we will endeavor to bring up such as may at any time be under our care, in the nurture and admonition of the Lord, and, by a pure and lovely example, to win our kindred and acquaintances to the Saviour, to holiness, and to eternal life; that we will participate in each other's joys, and endeavor with tenderness and sympathy to bear each other's burdens and sorrows; that we will seek divine aid to enable us to live circumspectly and watchfully in the world, "denying ungodliness and worldly lusts," and remembering that, as we have voluntarily been buried by baptism, and have been raised up from the emblematical grave, so there is on us a special obligation henceforth to lead a new and holy life; that we will strive together for the support of a faithful, evangelical ministry among us; and, through life, amidst evil report and good report, seek to live to the glory of him who hath called us out of darkness into his marvellous light.—Source: *Origin and Formation of the Baptist Church, in Granville-Street, Halifax, Nova-Scotia, Constituted on the 30th of September, A. D. 1827* (Halifax: Printed at the Nova-Scotia Office, 1828), 30-31.

Covenant 66: 1843 Covenant of
Long Point Baptist Association *(Ontario)*

As we hope that we have been brought by Divine Grace to believe in the Lord Jesus Christ, and by the influence of the Holy Spirit to give ourselves soul and body to him, and to the Eternal Father, so we do now, in the presence of God and the holy Angels, solemnly covenant with each other, as the Lord shall enable us, to endeavor to walk together and watch over one another in Christian Love; to regard the Holy Scriptures as the rule of our faith and practice; to stand fast in one spirit, with one mind striving together for the faith of the gospel; and to maintain its ordinances, discipline and public institutions, as far as we have ability.

We engage as members of the visible Church of Jesus Christ, to cultivate communion and fellowship with each other, in the public and social worship of God and the ordinances of the Gospel; "not forsaking the Assembling ourselves, as the manner of some is" but embracing all regular convenient seasons for the purpose as the Providence of God shall permit; to pray for, and sympathise with each other, in the various circumstances of life; and to use every endeavor to "provoke to love and good works," and bring up our children, and those that are placed under our care, in the nurture and admonition of the Lord.

We engage individually, to pay a respectful regard to the advice and admonitions of the Church, and to be subject to its discipline, as directed by the word of God, and conducted in the spirit of the Gospel.

This Covenant we make with the free and full consent of our own souls, hoping through rich, free and boundless grace, we shall therein be accepted of God unto eternal life, through Jesus Christ, our Lord, to whom be glory for ever and ever—Amen.—Source: *Minutes,* Long Point Baptist Association (Ontario), 1843, 14-15.

Covenant 67: 1855 Covenant of Free Christian Baptist General Conference, New Brunswick

Having been brought as we humbly trust by Divine grace to embrace the LORD JESUS CHRIST, and accept him as our Saviour, and believing that the interest of His Kingdom require our united efforts, we do therefore give ourselves up to Him, and agree with each other, to walk together in him, with brotherly love, seeking our duty to God, to one another, and to the world: and in view of these we adopt the following as our Church Covenant:—

1. That we will exercise a mutual care as members one of another—striving to keep the unity of Spirit in the bonds of peace—to promote the growth of the whole body in Christian knowledge, holiness, and comfort; and to labour together by prayer, precept, and example, for the salvation of sinners.

2. We agree to exert our influence for the constant maintenance of the public and social worship of God, and the ordinances of his house, also contribute of our substance according to our ability and circumstances for the support of a faithful ministry and all other necessary expenses of the church.

3. We who are heads of families will maintain constant prayer in our

households; we will also maintain secret prayer, and to the utmost of our ability we will endeavour to train our children and those under us, for usefulness in the world in the service of Christ, and the enjoyment of Heaven.

4. We agree to attend to the utmost of our power the Sabbath, Conference, Prayer, and other meetings of the church. In every Conference meeting we attend, we will report ourselves to the church, and in no meeting will we wilfully grieve the Holy Spirit of God—we will labour for the prosperity of the church, and its up-building in the most holy faith—not forsaking in adversity, but bear each others burdens, and so fulfil the law of Christ.

5. We will attend to the ordinance of the Lord's Supper as we may have opportunity, or as it may be administered by those over us in the Lord.

6. We will not use intoxicating drinks ourselves, nor allow them to be used in our families, nor furnish them for persons in our employment, except for Medical, Chemical, or Mechanical purposes. We will not buy nor sell these articles, nor give our influence for the traffic in them, only for the purposes above named.

7. We will frequently exhort, and if occasion require, admonish each other according to Matt. 18th, in the spirit of meekness—we will walk circumspectly in the world that we may win souls—we will have a general interest for the cause of God, and will strive to promote those enterprises which have for their object its advancement, among which are Sabbath Schools, Bible Societies, Missions, &c.— We will co-operate with our overseers in the promotion of every good work, and to the utmost of our power seek the eternal well-being of all mankind.

8. We agree to the annexed directory of principles and rules, as guiding to our faith, in doctrine; and our practice, in matters of church government. And finally, we commit ourselves to God and to the word of his grace, and may the God of peace, who brought again from the dead our Lord Jesus Christ, that great Shepherd of the sheep, through the blood of the everlasting Covenant, make us perfect in every good work to do his will—building us up also, upon the foundation of the Apostles and Prophets, Jesus Christ himself being the chief corner stone in whom the whole building fitly framed together, shall grow into an holy temple in the Lord, that we may be builded together, for an habitation of God through the Spirit.—Amen.—Source: *Minutes,* Free Christian Baptist General Conference of New Brunswick, 1855, 30-31.

Covenant 68: 1945 Covenant of Primitive Baptist Conference of New Brunswick, Maine, and Nova Scotia .

1. We solemnly covenant before God, that we will strive, by His assisting grace, to exemplify our profession by a corresponding practice. We covenant and agree, as members of the Church, and as Christians, to watch over each other in love, for mutual upbuilding in Gospel Faith, endeavoring to keep the unity of the Spirit in the bond of peace, to be careful of each other's reputation; to confess our faults one to another; to strengthen the feeble, and kindly admonish the erring; and to labour together for the building up of the Church and the denomination, and the salvation of sinners.

2. We promise that we will faithfully and constantly maintain secret and family prayer, and religiously instruct those under our care.

3. We covenant and agree to use our influence to sustain the regular public worship of God, contributing according to our ability and circumstances for the support of the Ministry and other Church expenses among us; that we will be benevolent to the needy, and especially to the poor of our own church.

4. We also promise that, so far as we shall be able, we will attend upon public worship, the social meetings of the Church, and report ourselves regularly at the monthly conference; and that we will walk in all the ordinances of the Lord's house.

5. We covenant and agree that we will abstain from all vain amusements and sinful conformity to the world; that we will not traffic in, use, nor furnish to others, intoxicating drinks as a beverage; and that we will sustain the benevolent enterprises of our denomination and the Church—Missions, Education, Sabbath schools, Moral Reform, and all others which tend to the glory of God and the welfare of men.

And may the God of Peace sanctify us wholly and preserve us blameless unto the coming of our Lord Jesus Christ; that we may join the glorified around the throne of God in ascribing blessing and honour and glory and power to Him that sitteth on the throne, and unto the Lamb forever. Amen.—Source: *Constitution and By-Laws of the Primitive Baptist Conference of New Brunswick, Maine, and Nova Scotia,* 1945 (no other data given).

Covenant 69: 1986 Covenant of New Covenant
Baptist Church, Winnipeg, Manitoba

Having been led, as we believe, by the Spirit of God to receive the Lord Jesus Christ as our Saviour, and on the profession of our faith, having been immersed in the name of the Father, and of the Son and of the Holy Spirit, we do now, in the presence of God, most solemnly and joyfully enter into covenant with one another as one body of Christ.

In agreement with the Scriptures that we are not our own and have been bought with the price of Christ's blood, we covenant to seek first the kingdom of God and His righteousness, with the confidence that He who began a good work in us will perfect it until the day of Christ Jesus. We accept the Bible as our sole authority, believing that all Scripture is inspired by God and profitable for teaching, for reproof, for correction, for training in righteousness; that we, as the people of God may be adequately equipped for every good work.

Just as Christ showed concern for His mother even from the cross, we covenant together to put our religion into practice by meeting the spiritual, physical and emotional needs of our family members, for to deny these responsibilities is to contradict the very message we proclaim.

As one body of Christ we shall grow in all ways into Him who is the Head, by whom we are fitted and joined together. Each separate part will work according to its function, adding its own strength so that we grow, building ourselves up in love. In order to keep the body healthy and functioning, we covenant to:

1. love one another, considering others as more important than ourselves;
2. pray for one another, bearing one another's burdens;
3. regularly assemble together in order to:
   a) admonish and encourage one another;
   b) worship in Spirit and in Truth;
   c) sustain the two ordinances of Christ; and
   d) cheerfully support the extension of the kingdom of God.

As one body filled by one Spirit, we covenant to live and walk by Him maintaining the Unity of the Spirit and Bond of Love.

In order to fulfill Christ's desire that we be effective salt and light in the world, we covenant together to live lives that are innocent and pure, use speech and conduct that honours God, look for opportunities to talk about Him, and always be prepared to explain the hope of our calling. We also covenant together to fulfill Christ's Great Commission by making disciples of all peoples, both as a church and in cooperation with others.—Source: Covenant included in a letter from Allen Schmidt, executive director-treasurer, Canadian Convention of Southern Baptists, Cochrane, Alberta, April 28, 1988.

Covenant 70: 1980s Covenant of
Faith Baptist Church, Calgary, Alberta

Having been led, as we believe, by the Spirit of God, to receive the Lord Jesus Christ as our Saviour,

And on profession of our faith, having been baptized in the name of the Father, and of the Son, and of the Holy Spirit,

We do now in the presence of God and this assembly, most solemnly and joyfully enter into covenant with one another as one body in Christ.

Because we believe that Jesus is the Christ, the Son of the Living God, we will seek to bring every phase of our lives under his Lordship.

We unreservedly and with abandon commit our lives and destiny to Christ promising to give him priority in all the affairs of life. We will seek first the kingdom of God and his righteousness.

We fully commit ourselves to use our time, energy, and money to become informed, mature Christians, and to seek the salvation of our family and acquaintances.

We will seek to be Christ-led in all relations with our fellowmen, with other nations, groups, classes, and races.

We pledge to be faithful in the corporate gathering of this church, to sustain its worship, ordinances, discipline, and doctrine.

We believe that God is the total owner of our lives and resources. We give God the throne in relation to material aspects of our lives. Because God is a lavish giver, we too shall be lavish and cheerful in our regular gifts to the church.

We promise to watch over one another in brotherly love; to remember one another in prayer; to help one another in time of sickness and trouble; to show Christian character in our speech and in our concern for others; and to be not easily offended and always ready to settle differences, remembering Christ's command to do so quickly.

We commit ourselves to glorify God in adoration and sacrificial service through the church, and to be God's missionaries in the world, bearing witness to God's redeeming grace in Jesus Christ.

Moreover, when we move away, we will seek, as soon as possible, to unite with another church that carries out the principles of God's Word and the spirit of this covenant.—Source: Covenant included in a letter from Allen Schmidt, executive director-treasurer, Canadian Convention of Southern Baptists, Cochrane, Alberta, April 28, 1988.

Section D: Covenants of Baptists in Other Countries
(See ch. 5 for history and interpretation of this section.)

Covenant 71: 1796 Covenant of George Liele (Jamaica)

1. We are of the Anabaptist persuasion because we believe it agreeable to the Scriptures. Proof:—(Matt. iii. 1-3; 2 Cor. vi. 14-18.)

2. We hold to keep the Lord's Day throughout the year, in a place appointed for Public Worship, in singing psalms, hymns, and spiritual songs, and preaching the Gospel of Jesus Christ. (Mark xvi. 2, 5, 6; Col. iii. 16.)

3. We hold to be Baptised in a river, or in a place where there is much water, in the name of the Father, and of the Son, and of the Holy Ghost. (Matt. iii. 13, 16, 17; Mark xvi. 15, 16; Matt. xxviii. 19.)

4. We hold to receiving the Lord's Supper in obedience according to His commands. (Mark xiv. 22-24; John vi. 53-57.)

5. We hold to the ordinance of washing one another's feet. (John xiii. 2-17.)

6. We hold to receive and admit young children into the Church according to the Word of God. (Luke ii. 27-28; Mark x. 13-16.)

7. We hold to pray over the sick, anointing them with oil in the name of the Lord. (James v. 14, 15.)

8. We hold to labouring one with another according to the Word of God. (Matt. xviii. 15-18.)

9. We hold to appoint Judges and such other Officers among us, to settle any matter according to the Word of God. (Acts vi. 1-3.)

10. We hold not to the shedding of blood. (Genesis ix. 6; Matt. xxvi. 51-52.)

11. We are forbidden to go to law with another before the unjust, but to settle any matter we have before the Saints. (1 Cor. vi. 1-3.)

12. We are forbidden to swear not at all [sic]. (Matt. v. 33-37; Jas. v. 12.)

13. We are forbidden to eat blood, for it is the life of a creature, and from things strangled, and from meat offered to idols. (Acts xv. 29.)

14. We are forbidden to wear any costly raiment, such as superfluity. (1 Peter iii. 3, 4; 1 Timothy ii. 9-10.)

15. We permit no slaves to join the Church without first having a few lines from their owners of their good behaviour. (1 Peter ii. 13-16; 1 Thess. iii. 13.)

16. To avoid Fornication, we permit none to keep each other, except they be married according to the Word of God. (1 Cor. vii. 2; Heb. xiii. 4.)

17. If a slave or servant misbehave to their owners they are to be dealt with according to the Word of God. (1 Tim. i. 6; Eph. vi. 5; 1 Peter ii. 18-22; Titus ii. 9-11.)

18. If any one of this Religion should transgress and walk disorderly, and not according to the Commands which we have received in this Covenant, he will be censured according to the Word of God. (Luke xii. 47-48.)

19. We hold, if a brother or sister should transgress any of these articles written in this Covenant so as to become a swearer, a fornicator, or adulterer; a covetous person, an idolater, a railer, a drunkard, an extortioner or whoremonger; or should commit any abominable sin, and do not give satisfaction to the Church, according to the Word of God, he or she, shall be put away from among us, not to keep company, nor to eat with him. (1 Cor. v. 11-13.)

20. We hold if a Brother of Sister should transgress, and abideth not in the doctrine of Christ, and he, or she, after being justly dealt with agreeable to the 8th article, and be put out of the Church, that they shall have no right or claim whatsoever to be interred into the Burying-ground during the time they are put out, should they depart life; but should they return in peace, and make a concession so as to give satisfaction, according to the word of God, they shall be received into the Church again and have all privileges as before granted. (2 John i. 9-10; Gal. vi. 1, 2; Luke xvii. 3, 4.)

21. We hold to all the other Commandments, Articles, Covenants, and Ordinances, recorded in the Holy Scriptures as are set forth by our Lord and Master Jesus Christ and His Apostles, which are not written in this Covenant, and to live to them as nigh as we possibly can, agreeable to the Word of God. (John xv. 7-14.)—Source: Ernest A. Payne, "Baptist Work in Jamaica Before the Arrival of the Missionaries," *The Baptist Quarterly*

7 (January 1934): 24-26. Used by permission.

Covenant 72: 1879 Covenant of the Union
of the Baptist Churches of France

In consequence of the truths which we fully receive and which are expressed in the following articles, and of the conviction which we have that we have been brought by the grace of God to receive the Lord Jesus Christ and to give ourselves to Him, relying upon His aid we together make a solemn covenant, and promise:

That we will walk together in brotherly love, as is becoming to the members of a Christian church; that we will exercise an affectionate watchfulness over one another and that we will warn one another and exhort one another mutually and faithfully on all occasions, in order to stimulate one another to charity and to good works;

That we will never neglect the assembling of ourselves for mutual edification, nor fail to pray for one another and for all;

That we will always exert ourselves to bring up the children who have been committed to us in the discipline of the Lord, nourishing them with His Word, and that we will give to all our kinsmen and friends the example of pure conduct in order to bring them to the love of the Savior, to holiness and to life eternal;

That we will rejoice in the happiness of each other and will strive with tenderness and sympathy to bear one another's burdens and sorrows;

That we will live with circumspection in the world, renouncing impiety and worldly lusts and setting a good example, remembering that, since we have been voluntarily buried in baptism and raised with Christ, a special obligation rests upon us henceforth to lead a new and holy life;

That we will do all that is in our power to contribute of our means to the faithful preaching of the gospel in the midst of us;

That according to our power and in all circumstances, as worthy stewards of the Lord, we will do good to all men, and especially in aiding the propagation of the gospel in its primitive purity and power throughout the whole earth.

Finally, that, during the whole course of our earthly pilgrimage, in evil report and in good report, we will seek humbly and ardently to live for the glory of Him who has called us from darkness into His marvelous light.—Source: W. J. McGlothlin, *Baptist Confessions of Faith* (Philadelphia: American Baptist Publication Society, 1911), 356.

Covenant 73: 1895 Covenant of Hwe Ching
Baptist Church, Hwe Ching, China

We, the constituents of the Hwe Ching Baptist Church of Christ, Believing in the one only True God, existing in three Persons, the Father, the Son and the Holy Spirit, and in Jesus Christ, as the Son of God, who, for the sins of the world became incarnate, died upon the cross, rose again from the dead, and ascended into Heaven; Believing also in the Holy Scriptures of the Old and New Testaments as the revealed will and word of God, and the only rule of faith and practice in matters of religion, wherein we are taught the immortality of the soul, man's corruption by nature, Redemption by the death of Jesus Christ, Regeneration and Sanctification by the Spirit of God, the Resurrection from the dead, the Final Judgment, Eternal Life of the Righteous and Eternal Punishment of the wicked;

Having ourselves been regenerated, as we trust, through Divine Grace, by the power of the Holy Spirit, and having been immersed in obedience to the command of Jesus Christ our Lord, upon our profession of faith in him, into the name of the Father and of the Son and of the Holy Spirit;

Do now mutually covenant

1. That we, brethren and sisters, servants of one Lord, unite together as a *Church of Jesus Christ,* according to the pattern set forth in the New Testament.

2. That we will worship together regularly as such church, not forsaking the assembling of ourselves together. Heb. 10:25.

3. That we will celebrate the ordinances appointed by Jesus Christ, *according to the order set forth by Christ* and *his Apostles in the New Testament.* (1 Cor. 11:23-26)

4. That we will abstain from every form of idolatrous worship, whether directed to images or tablets or to Heaven & Earth, such as burning of paper and incense to the dead, or to demons, bowing to tablets or to the bodies of the dead, or such like worship; and that, so far as we are able to prevent it, we will not allow any such worship in our homes. (I Cor. 10:14, I Thess. 5:22)

5. That we will in our lives, and in the management of our families, not be conformed to the world, but being transformed by the renewing of our mind, we will seek to know and to do the will of God. In all things we will make the word of God our standard of truth and of duty. (Rom. 12:2, II Tim. 3:15, 16)

6. That we will train our children in the fear of God, teaching them carefully concerning God, concerning Jesus Christ, concerning the Holy Spirit, and concerning prayer, praying for them, and endeavoring to lead them to the Saviour. (Prov. 22:6, Eph. 6:4)

7. That we will ever pray for one another, for the church, and for the extension of the Gospel into the regions beyond; in meekness and love exhorting one another if we see any falling into sin; And in every possible way we will strive to strengthen each other in the way of life. (Matt. 28:19-20; Gal. 6:1, I Thess. 5:25, II Thess. 3:1, Col. 1:9-12)

8. That when rebuked for sin by our Pastor or by our brethren, we will accept it kindly, and strive to amend where we have really been wrong. (II Cor. 7:9-11)

9. That we will cheerfully contribute of our substance for the support of the Gospel at home and abroad, realizing that all we have and are belong to Christ. (Gal. 6:6, II Cor. 9:6-11)

10. That we will deal with offenders faithfully, according to the manner prescribed in the word of God. (Matt. 18:15-17, II Thess. 3:6)

Unto all the above we solemnly covenant in the presence of the Father and of the Son and of the Holy Spirit. *Amen!*—Source: "Organization of the Hwe Ching Baptist Church, October 27th 1895," in Southern Baptist Historical Library and Archives (Nashville, Tennessee), Peyton Stephens Papers, Archive 602, folder 15.

Covenant 74: 1948 Covenant of
Baptist Union of Victoria (Australia)

Believing that God has led us by His Spirit to receive Jesus Christ as Lord and Saviour, and, on profession of our faith, to be baptised in the Triune Name, and to unite together in the fellowship of our Church:
WE COVENANT—
by the power of the Holy Spirit—
to walk and work together in Christian love,
to watch over, and pray for, and encourage one another,
to guard each other's reputation,
to bear each other's burdens,
to share each other's joys and sorrows,
to cultivate Christian courtesy and sympathy,
to be slow to take offence, and ready always for reconciliation.
WE COVENANT—

to seek together the extension of God's Kingdom and the building up of Christ's Church,

to seek the growth of our Church in knowledge and holiness,

to give our Church a place in our affection and prayers above other organisations,

to maintain, and engage in, the worship and service of our Church,

to be loyal in attendance at the Lord's Day services and at other meetings,

to contribute to the support of our Church as God prospers us,

to increase the influence of our Church in the community.

WE COVENANT—

to spread the Gospel of Christ at home and abroad,

to seek the salvation of others, our families, our friends, our neighbours and those about us,

to walk discreetly before the world,

to act kindly and justly to all,

to endeavour, by purity of heart and good will to men, to exemplify and commend our faith,

to be ready to give an answer to those who seek of us a reason for our hope.

WE COVENANT—

to maintain our own personal devotional life,

to study God's Word diligently,

to be constant in prayer,

to guide and nurture our children in the faith by personal example and precept.

WE COVENANT—

when we remove from the district, to unite, as soon as possible, with some other Church where we can carry out the spirit of this Covenant, and the principles of God's Word.

Source: Covenant included in letter from Howard Crago, archivist for the Baptist Union of Victoria, December 9, 1987.

Covenant 75: 1954 Covenant of Baptist Convention of the Republic of Cameroon (Africa)

Since we have received the Lord Jesus Christ as Saviour and have been baptized, we now before God and his Church agree:

To walk together in Christian love,

To worship and pray together,

To be willing to help in all Church work,

To give cheerfully our tithes and offerings for the work of the Church and the spread of the Gospel,

To help the old, the sick, and the troubled in our Church and in the Town,

To have family prayers,

To teach our children about Jesus Christ,

To witness to members of our family, friends, and to strangers,

To be honest and faithful in all our dealings,

To keep from all types of immorality in our thoughts, our speech, and our actions,

To keep ourselves free from the power of strong drink,

To speak only that which is true and helpful,

To be slow in anger and quick to forgive,

To be ready to serve in another Church of the same faith when leaving this one.

Oh God, help us by your power to keep these promises. Amen.

Source: Covenant included in a letter from Sampson E. Khama, Southwest Province, Republic of Cameroon, Africa, December 8, 1987.

Covenant 76: 1962 Covenant of Mt. Roskill Baptist Church, Auckland, New Zealand

Being called of God into the fellowship of His people and into the membership of this Church, I pledge myself by the grace of God to strive:

(1) To live at all times such a life as becomes a true Christian and a member of the Church.

(2) To take an active and earnest part in the life and work of the Church, regularly attending its services of worship as far as I am able, and being willing to help in whatever way I can.

(3) To be faithful in prayer for the Church and its witness in the community.

(4) To share conscientiously in contributing to the funds of the Church according to my means.

(5) To do all in my power to deepen and enrich the spirit of fellowship in the Church, always endeavouring to refrain from uncharitable thoughts or words and ever seeking to develop the Spirit of love in this brotherhood of Christ's people.

(6) To share by life and word in the supreme task of the Church, namely, witnessing to the saving and keeping power of Jesus Christ our Lord.—Source: Photocopy provided in a letter from Stan Edgar, secretary, New Zealand Baptist Historical Society, Auckland, New Zealand, February 2, 1988.

Covenant 77: 1960s Covenant of Rosebank Union Baptist Church, Johannesburg, South Africa

1. Realising my guilt before God, I have confessed and renounced my sin before Him and received the Lord Jesus Christ, who bore my sin on the cross, as my personal Saviour (Rom. 3:19, 23; 5:8; 1 Pet. 2:24; John 1:12).

2. I acknowledge the Lord Jesus Christ as Lord of all my life and seek to confess Him before others (Rom. 10:9).

3. I trust in the power of the Holy Spirit, who lives in me, to keep me and lead me in the way of holiness and love in all relationships of life (John 14:26; 16:13; Rom. 8:2; Gal. 5:22-23).

4. I accept the Bible as the inspired Word of God and as my final authority in all matters of faith and conduct (2 Tim. 3:16).

5. I recognise my responsibility to make diligent use of the means of grace, and to be regular in my attendance at the services of the Church and at the Lord's Table (1 Thess. 5:17; 1 Pet. 2:2; 2 Pet. 3:18; Heb. 10:25; 1 Cor. 11:26).

6. I recognise my responsibility to pray regularly for the work of this Church, for its Ministers, officers and members (Eph. 6:18-19).

7. I recognise my financial responsibility to participate in the worship and witness of the Church by systematic giving as the Lord may prosper me (1 Cor. 16:2; 2 Cor. 9:7).

8. I recognise my responsibility by all means to serve the Lord through His Church and to extend His Kingdom here and throughout the world (Matt. 28:19-20; Rom. 12:6-13).

9. Conscious that in my own strength I cannot please God, I now, in complete dependence on Divine grace, accept and affirm this covenant.

Signature:

Date:

Source: Sydney Hudson-Reed, *Lantern on the Skyline: Seventy Years of Service for Christ at Rosebank Union Church* (Roodepoort, South Africa: Roodepoort Mission Press, 1978), 95-96.

Covenant 78: 1974 Covenant of
Manual for the Baptist Union of Sweden
Translated by David Lagergren

The leader says:

The church is the body of Jesus Christ. It consists of persons who have accepted in faith and obedience the calling of God through the gospel to forgiveness of sins and eternal life. They have thereby entered into a new and holy fellowship with God and with each other. They are, through the Holy Spirit, born anew to a living hope and proclaim together with all who are called and sanctified a unity which is thus described by the apostle: *one* Lord, *one* faith, *one* baptism, *one* God who is the Father of all.

I ask you:

Do you confess Jesus Christ as Lord and Saviour and is it your wish to unite into a church of God according to the model of the New Testament?

Do you wish to let yourselves be built up to become a holy temple in the Lord, and do you promise to hold on to the apostles' teaching, the fraternal fellowship, the breaking of bread and the prayers?

Do you promise to be obedient to the commission of the Lord: Go out and make disciples of all nations, baptizing them in the name of the Father and of the Son and of the Holy Spirit?

As you have accepted the blessings and obligations inherent in the church fellowship, and renewed your confession of Him who is the Lord of the church, I declare, in the name of God, the Father, and of the Son and of the Holy Spirit the church of [church inserts its name here] founded. May the God of hope fill you with all joy and peace in believing, so that by the power of the Holy Spirit you may abound in hope.—Source: Covenant included in a letter from David Lagergren of Stockholm, Sweden, March 17, 1988.

Covenant 79: 1985 Statement of Church Member Obligations of All-Union Council of Evangelical Christians-Baptists *(USSR)*

Church members must preserve obedience and trust in the Lord (1 Sam. 15:22-23; Rev. 2:10) and live in peace and mutual love with each other.

"Our thanks are always due to God for you, brothers. It is right that we should thank Him, because your faith increases mightily, and the love you have, each for all and all for each, grows ever greater" (2 Thes. 1:3;

Jn. 13:34-35; 1 Jn. 3:11; 1 Pet. 1:22; Jn. 15:12-17).

Each church member is obliged to obey ministers (1 Pet. 5:5; Heb. 13:17), give them honor (1 Tim. 5:17), pray for them (Col. 4:3), and preserve the church unity (Phil. 1:27; 2:2; Rom. 15:5-6; 17:7).

Church members should zealously participate in church life and material ministry.

"So that there might be no sense of division in the body, but that all its organs might feel the same concern for one another. If one organ suffers, they all suffer together. If one flourishes, they all rejoice together" (1 Cor. 12:25-26; Rom. 12:13; 2 Cor. 9:7-8; Heb. 13:16).

Each church member is called to attend worship services and decently participate in the Lord's Supper.

"Let us not stay away from our meetings, as some do" (Heb. 10:25; Ps. 16:3; 27:4; 122:1; 1 Cor. 11:26-28; Acts 2:42).—Source: "Statement of Faith of Evangelical Christians-Baptists" (approved in 1985 in Moscow at the 43rd Congress as auxiliary material for the spiritual education of believers), 22-23.

Epilogue: Suggested Guidelines for Writing and Using Church Covenants Today

A church covenant creatively written and wisely used can help a Baptist congregation nurture a regenerate and disciplined membership. That possibility alone suggests the merit of taking a new look at the potential benefits of covenants for Baptists. A covenant is not a panacea for solving all the problems surrounding the meaning and practice of responsible church membership. But when placed in context with other key New Testament convictions which help safeguard the integrity of the church, such as believer's baptism and church discipline, an innovative and biblically based statement of church member obligations can help a congregation learn more fully what it means to be the regenerated people of God. Thus, this chapter presents some practical guidelines to assist a church in writing and using its own covenant.

Covenant-making has a strong biblical basis and is theologically sound. We must covenant with God because, as the Bible records, He has covenanted with us. The theology behind a Baptist church covenant is that God's initiative in our favor demands our initiative in His favor. A primary value of writing and using covenants today is that they give Baptists a way to express their loyalty to God in the context of church membership.

True, the New Testament does not specifically command that each congregation prepare and/or use a covenantal document. But the New Testament does speak at length about the covenantal values of healthy Christian relationships and conduct, both among fellow Christians and among non-Christians (see ch. 1 for a fuller discussion of biblical backgrounds for covenanting). Therefore, a church-approved covenant which magnifies New Testament teachings regarding relationships and conduct within the community of the "new covenant" has a legitimate place in the Baptist experience.

Covenants have wide historical precedents among Baptists. Past experiences tell contemporary Baptists that many advantages can emerge from responsible preparation and implementation of covenants. Most important, a covenant helps preserve a regenerate church membership. Faithful commitment to the contents of a biblically based covenant can constructively influence the creation and maintenance of a disciplined church membership. A covenant also deepens a church's fellowship.

A covenant can lead a church to a keener understanding of its vital commitments. Through a covenant a church clarifies the spiritual and ethical expectations which it believes the Bible requires of church members. Standards for Christian maturity can become clearer. A covenant establishes a sense of dedication to the common goals and responsibilities of a church, and it can increase church members' loyalty to God and the church.

A covenant can serve as a major instructional tool for a congregation by highlighting New Testament fundamentals of churchmanship and insisting on more careful attention to them. As a teaching device, a covenant does not supplant the Bible; rather, it elevates basic principles of biblical ethics to a conspicuous place in church members' lives. The Bible is the sole written authority for Baptist faith and practice; a responsible covenant recognizes and builds upon this reality.

Perhaps the best approach is for each church to write its own covenant. Several values result when a church accepts this challenge. A personally written covenant more adequately reflects the unique needs and expectations of that church. A church can create a covenant that expresses its own priorities and clearly states its commitments. A covenant constructed around the specific moral and spiritual expectations of a congregation will be a more viable and useful document. Preparing an individualized covenant contributes to congregational renewal. The process of thinking through, struggling with, and writing down essential biblical disciplines in a covenantal format leads a church into progressive patterns of life-style and ministry. A church that writes its own covenant will likely have stronger covenant practices.

A church which relies on the internal creativity of its membership in preparing a covenant will probably experience far more covenantal values than a church which perfunctorily adopts a uniform covenant from an external source. In fact, distinct liabilities can result from merely accepting a prepackaged standard covenant. And, unfortunately, use of this form of covenant is the predominant pattern in modern Baptist life, at least in the United States.

At times, the tendency to accept uniform covenants possibly represents a misunderstanding of Baptist polity and practice which provide each church complete liberty to design its own covenant. The trend more likely reflects an ecclesiastical laziness. Churches find it easier and more convenient to neglect the covenant idea or to adopt a uniform covenant than to engage in the work required to write their own. Church manuals, hymnals, and other literature which suggest specific covenants may contribute to the weakening of congregational discipline by making it unnecessary for churches to deal seriously with the unique covenantal responsibilities to which they are willing to pledge themselves.

Another disadvantage of using standard covenants is that their language and content may be outdated for the requirements of individual congregations. To illustrate, an extremely popular covenant uses out-of-date words such as "circumspectly" and "deportment." It fails to make explicit that its promises should be made to God as well as to fellow church members, thereby weakening the essential theological thrust of a biblically based covenant. And it gives uneven attention to crucial social issues and principles. While expressing an abhorrence for "the sale and use of intoxicating drinks," most versions of the covenant make no reference to other critical ethical concerns, such as drugs, pornography, sex, racial attitudes, and war and peace. Thus, the covenant does not provide basic guidance for Christian conduct regarding some of the key problems of contemporary times.

A third liability of accepting uniform covenants is the tendency of Baptists to ascribe too much authority to them. The inclusion of J. Newton Brown's 1853 covenant in literally millions of copies of church manuals, hymnals, and periodicals magnified the alleged authority of the covenant out of proportion. This tacit acceptance of a particular covenant by Baptist publishers has led many Baptists to view it as the official covenant for Baptist churches. To the contrary, a covenant has authority only when a church votes to give it authority. Model covenants printed in Baptist literature deserve no special status. Every Baptist church has absolute freedom to prepare its own covenant and should exercise this privilege to achieve maximum covenantal benefit. A Baptist church is under no obligation to use a covenant which comes from a source outside its own membership. Baptist publishers can help churches more by sponsor-

ing the concept of writing personalized covenants than by merely sponsoring uniform covenants.

How to Prepare a Church Covenant

Every church can profit by writing out the nature of its covenantal
relationship in a formal statement of pledges. This process focuses increased attention on church members' responsibilities to God and one
another and on biblical patterns of Christian conduct. The following
step-by-step procedure can help a church design an acceptable covenant.

1. *Create interest in writing a covenant by demonstrating its potential
values.*—A pastor can do this through a series of sermons on the covenant idea—exploring biblical, historical, theological, and practical aspects of the topic. Deacons can assist by writing, adopting, and using a
deacons' covenant. Diaconal commitment to covenantal relationships
provides a model by which the larger congregation can place renewed
emphasis on its own disciplines. A church study group might devote several sessions to examining the church covenant concept. This group becomes an interest center from which a broader look at covenants by the
entire church evolves. Once a church becomes aware of the values of
covenanting, it will be more willing to examine its own covenantal status
and consider the preparation of a personalized covenantal document.

2. *Appoint a church covenant committee.*—The pastor, deacons, or a
study group cannot assume the prerogative to prepare a covenant for the
church. Apart from official approval by the church, any covenant will
have limited appeal to the greater congregation. A better approach is for
the church in business session—as the result of a recommendation from
the church staff, church council, deacons, or some other group—to elect
a church covenant committee. This committee will coordinate the development of a covenant and will suggest ways for the church to use it on an
ongoing basis. This committee will be responsible to the church at every
level of its functioning.

Since the new committee will assist in preparing a *church* covenant, it
should be composed of a broad spectrum of the total church membership. Representatives of both sexes and of various age levels should be
placed on the committee. Each member of the committee should be a
committed and active member of the church. Since the committee will be
preparing a document intended to nurture integrity in church membership, all committee members should possess impeccable moral and spiri-

tual credentials.

3. *Carefully examine available covenants.*—Read the covenants printed in chapter 6 of this book. Review the kinds of subjects treated in them. Assess the strengths and weaknesses of the covenants studied. Evaluate the various structures and writing styles reflected in the covenants. Consult with churches which recently have gone through the process of developing their own covenants, and learn from their experiences.

4. *Adopt principles by which the content of the covenant will be determined.*—The committee needs to establish at the outset that nothing will be placed in the covenant which does not have a biblical foundation. This will guarantee that the covenant will magnify basic teachings of the Bible relating to Christian conduct. A covenant does not create new tasks for Christians; it summarizes biblical responsibilities and applies them to contemporary life.

The committee needs to work against designing the covenant around negative features of non-Christian conduct that are to be avoided; covenants based on that approach do not offer affirming guidance. Instead, concentrate on positive features of Christian conduct that are to be imitated; covenants rooted in this pattern elevate the ethical truths of the Bible and encourage adherence to them.

Should a covenant focus mainly on general or specific responsibilities? The committee has to resolve this question early. A covenant which is extremely specific in naming personal sins to avoid, all the social issues which need attention, and other detailed matters runs the risk of being too legal, long, and narrow in scope and application. And a covenant which is overly general can be so ambiguous as to be meaningless. Perhaps the following guideline can help in structuring a covenant. A covenant ought to be specific enough to state concrete commitments, disciplines, and expectations, but it should be general enough to allow for flexibility in interpretation. This approach will state the position of the church on matters of conduct and, at the same time, give priority to the Baptist concepts of soul competency and the priesthood of all believers.

Include in a covenant biblical emphases that are basic and universal for Christian life. "Trifling things and customs based upon peculiar cultural conditions ought not to be included in its obligations."[1] Treat the individual elements of a covenant as biblical principles which guide conduct, not as rules which govern it. The strength of a covenant does not lie in a legalistic attachment to its wording but in a reliance upon the biblical principles which lie beneath the wording.

5. *Define and write the contents of the covenant.*—Open the covenant with a clear statement that its vows are intended to be made both to God and to other church members. Then consider including a brief doctrinal statement. Although a covenant is concerned primarily with conduct, it ideally has a strong biblical and theological foundation, since one's actions relate closely to one's beliefs. Then devote the bulk of the covenant to conduct.

The contents of a covenant should be comprehensive in scope. A healthy covenantal agreement needs to present principles for conduct that apply to all phases of life. Early English Baptist covenants emphasized conduct relating to church fellowship, church discipline, worship and personal devotion, and pastoral and lay care. These same concerns are basic to many modern covenants. A social consciousness pervades some of the best contemporary covenants. As a minimum, covenants need to include pledges relating to personal life, family life, social life, church relationships and commitments, ministry concerns for others, and moral and spiritual integrity under the lordship of Christ. The authority of the Bible, a sound sense of preventive discipline, and a responsible view of church membership should underlie the written expression of all these concerns.

Each covenant committee needs to word its covenant in its own unique and creative way, utilizing the creative interaction of all committee members. In the course of several meetings, the committee will probably prepare and revise three or four preliminary drafts of the covenant before finalizing the one to present to the church. This final draft should use words understandable by young church members while expressing content that will challenge even the most mature members. If this does not seem possible, the committee may wish to prepare and recommend two covenants similar in content but different in wording—one for children and the other for youth and adults.

6. *Secure congregational input and approval.*—Joint participation by church members in forming a covenant will give it its deepest meaning for a church. One writer correctly claimed that "a covenant will have more meaning and value if its content is designed by members of the congregation. When each sentence and paragraph has been carefully weighed and discussed, a covenant will have greater significance and enduring value."[2]

The committee will find it helpful to print copies of the preliminary draft for each church member. Accompanying the draft should be a brief

statement of the principles upon which it is based. Members should be
encouraged to study the draft carefully and write down any responsible
criticisms. The committee will receive the evaluations, weigh them carefully, prepare a second draft incorporating the best suggestions, distribute this draft to the church staff and selected other church leaders for
further suggestions, modify the statement as needed, and then write a
final draft for presentation to the church in an official business session.
The final draft should be distributed to church members well in advance
of the business meeting designated for its discussion. Verbal discussion in
the meeting may lead to additional alterations in the contents. Then the
vote should be taken.

Congregational involvement in forming a covenant, such as that just
described, will help make certain that the covenant finally adopted is a
church covenant, not a committee covenant.

7. *Print and circulate the covenant.*—Initial distribution should occur
in various ways. Incorporate the covenant into the bulletin of a Sunday
morning worship service in which the congregation dedicate themselves
to voluntary faithfulness in meeting the requirements of the covenant.
Print the new covenant in the church newsletter. A handy procedure is to
print the covenant on small cards. Each card should contain the name of
the church, its location, the date of the covenant's adoption, and the text
of the covenant. Give copies to all members, including nonresidents, with
a statement describing the development and purpose of the covenant.
Other cards can be attached to the inside covers of hymnals so that they
will be available as worship aids.

8. *Periodically revise the covenant.*—Even after a church writes and
approves a covenant, it should subject the document to continuing modification. No church covenant has canonical status, in spite of the tendency of many Baptists to ascribe definitive authority and official standing to selected uniform covenants. A progressive principle needs to be
built into the making of each covenant. New illumination by the Holy
Spirit, fresh insights into the meaning of the Bible, and the need to keep
the language and content of a covenant updated are a few of the factors
which may necessitate periodic alteration of a covenant.

Ways to Use a Church Covenant

A church which disciplines itself to write and adopt a covenant needs
to plan responsible ways to use it. The occasional public reading of a

covenant is inadequate. Covenantal relationships ought to permeate church life more thoroughly than that, and many possible approaches can help deepen mutual commitments of church members to God, one another, and biblical ethics. At whatever cost, a church should reject legalistic and creedalistic applications of its covenant.

Every regenerated Christian who joins a Baptist church automatically assumes essential responsibilities to God, the church, and the world. These duties are integral to individual discipleship and to the nature and mission of the church and cannot be treated casually, postponed, or ignored. Rather, service and contributions to God, the church, and the world must have high priority in the life of each member. The accomplishing of such ministries and disciplines as regular attendance in Bible study and worship, responsible stewardship, sensitive caring, and exemplary living is foundational to committed discipleship. Careful use of a covenant is one way to help assure that these and other ministries and disciplines will become fully activated and effective.

Perhaps the best approach to covenantal practices is one that is continuing and comprehensive for all members. Church members of all ages should sense the gravity of covenantal pledges and the need to live up to the biblical principles that support them. A church will do well to place on its present members the same covenantal expectations that it intends to present to future members. Failure to do this will create a double standard of ethics for members and falsify the legitimacy of covenanting as being applicable to the whole church. Covenantal practices require full participation by all members.

Six possible ways to use covenants relate to baptism, the Lord's Supper, church discipline, constituting new churches, special covenant meetings, and living out the contents of a covenant. Suggestions for each use follow.

1. *Baptismal Pledges.*—Church covenants deserve increased attention in the context of baptism. By its very nature, baptism is an act of initiation into the church and includes vows to God and the church. Baptism should be an active expression of a Christian's intention to live out the moral and spiritual agreements inherent in regeneration.

Early Baptists often related baptism and covenants. John Smyth, leader of the earliest known Baptist congregation, formed in Amsterdam about 1609, wrote in that year that "the true forme of the Church is a covenant betwixt God & the Faithful made in baptisme" and that "the covenant is this: I wilbe their Father . . . & wee shalbe his sonnes calling him Father by the Spirit, whereby we are sealed . . . ."[3] In 1675 Henry D'Anvers, an English Baptist, stated that "Baptism is no other, than our Mystical *Marriage* . . . and *striking* of a Covenant (the Essentials of Marriage) betwixt Christ and a believer . . . ."[4] John Taylor, a frontier Baptist in America, witnessed in about 1770 the baptizing of over fifty people by Samuel Harris, a Separate Baptist, at Harper's Ferry, Virginia, at which time a church covenant was read.[5]

Spiritual benefit resides in providing opportunity for a person to verbalize his or her allegiance to the contents of a church's covenant as part of the baptismal experience. By responding affirmatively to covenantal questions asked by the pastor while standing in the baptismal waters, the one about to be baptized shares actively in the covenantal process. This can help strengthen his or her faith and cement a personal bond to God and the church.

Attempt to maximize participation in the baptismal covenant. The one who baptizes can facilitate this by addressing alternate covenantal questions to the congregation and to the person about to be baptized. Through such questioning, those involved unite themselves to God and one another in the context of mutual support. Immersion completes the initial phase of covenanting for the new church member.

2. *The Lord's Supper and Covenants.*—The covenantal motif is central to the New Testament approach to the Lord's Supper. A Baptist scholar observed, "The Lord's Supper [is] a covenant meal in which the Lordship of Christ and our commitment to do his will are brought again and again to the worshiping congregation."[6] In one sense the covenant idea is foundational to all the other meanings of the Lord's Supper. Baptist history is filled with examples of churches using covenants in the setting of the Lord's Supper. Even church covenant meetings, which flourished among Baptists in the 1800s, were intended to prepare church members for participation in the Lord's Supper.

Practical action incorporates meaningful covenanting into the Lord's Supper. To begin with, church leaders can use prebaptismal classes, new member orientation classes, and other instructional settings to educate a congregation on the covenantal character of the ordinance and on the contents of the church's covenant. This is important since the Lord's Supper helps the Christian community renew the vows made in baptism.

If a church celebrates the Lord's Supper in the same worship service in which it baptizes new members, then the covenantal themes of the two ordinances can be tied together. After the persons baptized and the congregation verbalize mutual vows in the baptismal setting, the Lord's Supper can include a presentation of framed copies of the church's covenant to each person who has been baptized and shared in his first Lord's Supper. (If a church celebrates baptism and the Lord's Supper in separate worship services, the Supper can still include a presentation of framed covenants to members receiving the bread and cup for the first time.) The pastor can then give a covenantal charge to the congregation which can include a reading of the church covenant, either in unison or responsively. This will regularly remind the congregation of its covenant pledges.

3. *Church Discipline and Covenants.*—The time is ripe for a disciplinary reawakening in Baptist life. The New Testament contains a large amount of information on church discipline. The following guidelines for approaching discipline may be helpful.

Come to terms with frequently raised objections to a disciplined church membership. Avoid the extreme of converting church discipline into legalism. Take discipline seriously in order to make it successful. State the church's disciplines in a written covenant. Construct church discipline on a solidly biblical basis. View discipline as the task of the entire congregation. Place primary emphasis on the formative phase of discipline, rather than on the corrective. Assist a wayward member best by helping him or her solve a problem, not by excluding the person from membership, although exclusion does have a biblical basis and may be necessary in extreme situations. Apply corrective church discipline with therapeutic intentions and with the hope of redemption and reconciliation, or not at all.

Baptists have tended to maintain a close relationship between church discipline and church covenants. Each church needs to arrive at its own understanding of how to relate the two today. A written covenant can identify key nurturing disciplines of church life, such as participation in worship, prayer, Bible study, giving of money, service, and witness. In a covenant these and other disciplines are placed before the congregation in baptism, the Lord's Supper, and other settings. The disciplines can eventually occupy a prominent place in the lives of members.

The disciplinary value of a covenant exists mainly in an alliance with preventive discipline rather than with reformative discipline, although, at times, the latter is essential, too. The covenantal practice of providing disciplines by which church members can live out their Christian commitments most meaningfully deserves to be restored for the advantage of the church and its members. Since discipline in its preventive and corrective applications is an essential guardian of the regenerate quality of church life, a healthy reunion of discipline and covenants in Baptist life may lead to church renewal.

4. *Constituting New Churches.*—Another way to implement covenants is in forming new churches. The church covenant idea is integral to the nature of a church and is basic to the essence of congregational life. Many major Baptist confessions of faith include the covenantal idea in their definitions of the church.

An important Baptist church manual has quite helpfully labeled three stages comprising the constitutive development of a church. First, Baptists become a church *"essential"* when they formally express in a covenant their intention to be a church. Second, they become a church *"completed"* after adopting a constitution and electing officers. Third, they become a church *"recognized"* after admission into a Baptist association.[7] The reader quickly sees that a church covenant is critical to the first stage of organizing a new church and thus supports the other stages.

An illustration of a new church making a covenant the heart of its constitutive procedure appears in the earliest records of the First Baptist Church of Warren, Rhode Island. Formed on November 14, 1764, on a day set aside for fasting, the service of organization included prayers, a sermon, and the presentation, reading, and signing of a covenant. The assisting minister, James Manning, who became the first pastor of the church, then asked the persons who had signed the covenant whether they received it as the "plan of union in a church relation, which question was answered by them all in the affirmative, standing up."[8]

A church covenant is not a document whose primary value comes from a one-time use in forming a church and then being placed in a cornerstone only to be rediscovered by a later generation of members. Rather, a covenant is a living agreement whose biblical principles offer continuing sustenance for a church genuinely trying to be regenerate. Baptist history validates this possibility.

5. *Special Covenant Meetings.*—Special meetings can highlight important covenantal emphases. A church may want to consider sponsoring an annual church covenant day or more frequent covenantal events. Many Baptist churches in the past held monthly covenant meetings on a weekday prior to the Sunday on which they observed the Lord's Supper. The meetings had at least four purposes. They prepared church members for participation in the forthcoming Lord's Supper, reminded members of covenantal obligations, gave members an opportunity to share meaning-

ful spiritual experiences of the previous month, and provided members with a regular time to renew and strengthen covenantal pledges. "The recovery of such a practice today could help to impress upon us the significance of our covenant obligations and prepare us for a more meaningful celebration of the Lord's Supper."[9]

The neglect of covenant meetings today is probably due, in part, to the multiplication of other church meetings. Prayer meetings, business meetings, and committee meetings, for example, occupy much of the time formerly given to covenantal emphases. This could be changed, however. In preparation for the Lord's Supper, the prayer meeting on the Wednesday night (or other night) preceding this event could easily be reconverted into the covenant meeting it once was among many Baptists. In the covenant meeting, a church could read and study its covenant and grasp its meaning for the Lord's Supper and for daily living.

In his 1898 book, *The Covenant and the Covenant Meeting*, Augustine Carman described the covenant meeting as "the heart of the devotional life of a Baptist church."[10] Perhaps a church today could recapture some of that spirit by using covenant meetings to do such things as: (1) study the biblical background and implications of every element in its covenant; (2) explore in detail the covenantal thrust and values of baptism and the Lord's Supper; (3) hammer out ways of strengthening the regenerate character of church membership; (4) reaffirm the covenantal qualities of congregational life through making continuing commitments to God and one another; and (5) seek direction through extensive sessions of prayer for activating the contents of the covenant in daily life.

6. *Daily Covenantal Relationships.*—The most important way to implement a church covenant is to apply its contents in daily relationships. The biblical obligations voluntarily accepted in becoming a member of a Baptist church require covenantal embodiment and fulfillment in the total affairs of life. A healthy view of a covenant stresses the ethics of church membership. A church which takes a responsible approach to its covenant will try extremely hard to meet in daily relationships the demands of Christian discipline delineated in the covenant. A covenant worth having is a covenant worth living.

A covenant may call for firm attachment to the doctrines and ordinances of a church; regular attendance in Sunday School, training opportunities, and church worship; faithful contributions of time, talents, and money; committed involvement in the ministries of the church; personal attention to living Christlike lives, meeting God in daily prayer and Bible study, and treating our bodies as the temple of the Holy Spirit; nurturing a Christian atmosphere in our homes; exerting a Christian influence upon social problems and the general life of our communities; bearing a Christian witness to non-Christians; and other important moral and spiritual commitments. Therefore, church members in covenant need to apply their fundamental energies to accomplishing these very challenges. The overall quality of a regenerate church membership will surely improve once there is a proper linkup between a statement of ethical intentions and lives of achievement.

Conclusion

An excellent example of a church creatively involved in writing its own covenant and applying many of the principles just described is the Heritage Baptist Church in Cartersville, Georgia. Noting that the church was less than two years old, Clarissa Strickland, the pastor's wife, observed in April 1989 that the church agreed to prepare its own written covenant in order to forge an identity that would shape its sense of mission and approach to ministry. Emphasizing that writing original covenants may be more palatable to churches that stress relationships than to churches which focus more heavily on doctrine, she noted that "covenant" continues to provide a workable biblical model for shaping relationships with God, one another, and the environment. However, those relationships respect human freedom, since God calls (and does not coerce) people into covenant.[11]

Strickland reported further that in seeking guidance from other churches regarding the preparation of a covenant, her church learned that some other churches have written their own and that a renewed interest in covenants exists among some Southern Baptist churches. Then in an incisive, challenging, and perhaps prophetic summary, she identified the values which her church has already experienced through engaging in a covenant-writing process:

> The process of covenantal reclamation is one which is just beginning and one which requires reassertion of the initiative of local churches.
> As for my church, as we eagerly await the first written draft from our covenant committee after months of study, introspection, talking, listening and praying, it has already been an experience of personal renewal. We have rediscovered some of our Baptist heritage, and have been compelled to look deeply within at our personal and corporate

commitments to God and to each other.

And even as Jeremiah's vision of the new covenant was of one which would not be written on stone, but on the hearts of God's people, it is our hope that God will continue to lead us into areas of growth and change, in which we shall experience continuing newness of life and relationship.[12]

When the formation of a church covenant excites a congregation to reaffirm the Lordship of Christ, to establish renewed commitment to New Testament standards for a regenerate church membership, to inject a disciplined attachment to biblical ethics into their conduct, and to probe the best that our Baptist heritage has to offer regarding freedom and accountability, then the effort involved in writing and using the covenant translates into meaningful relationships. And the church becomes a covenant community.

Notes

Foreword

1. J. K. Zeman, *Baptist Roots and Identity* (Brantford, Baptist Convention of Ontario and Quebec, 1978), 4.
2. Donald F. Durnbaugh, *The Believers' Church* (New York: Macmillan Co., 1970), 33.
3. Norman H. Maring and Winthrop S. Hudson, *A Baptist Manual of Polity and Practice* (Valley Forge: Judson Press, 1963), 15.
4. Robert G. Torbet, *A History of the Baptists*, rev. ed. (Valley Forge: Judson Press, 1963), 487.
5. William L. Lumpkin, *Baptist Confessions of Faith*, rev. ed., (Valley Forge: Judson Press, 1969), 119.
6. J. B. Moody, *The Distinguishing Principles of Baptists* (Nashville: Folk & Browder, 1901), 7; J. D. Freeman, "The Place of Baptists in the Christian Church," in *Proceedings, Baptist World Congress, 1905* (London: Baptist Union Publication Department, 1905), 27; E. Y. Mullins, *The Axioms of Religion* (Philadelphia: American Baptist Publication Society, 1908), 56-57.
7. J. W. MacGorman, "Vanishing Baptist Distinctive," *The Christian Index*, July 18, 1957, 6.
8. William Henry Brackney, *The Baptists*, Denominations in America Series, ed. Henry Warner Bowden (Westport, Conn.: Greenwood Press, Inc., 1988), 50.
9. *Annual*, Southern Baptist Convention, 1937, 89; Thomas Elliott Huntley, *Huntley's Manual for Every Baptist* (St. Louis: Central Service Publication, 1963), 70-71; Robert T. Handy, "American Baptist Churches in the U.S.A.," *Encyclopedia of Southern Baptists*, 1982, 4:2081; Henry Webb, Editorial Note, *The Deacon*, January-March 1979, 48; Brightie E.

White, Jr., "A Covenant for the Pastor-Church Relationship," *The Baptist Program*, December 1982, 5-7; James C. Barry and Fred L. Kelly, *How to Lead a Congregation to be the People of God: A Guide for Shared Ministry Worship Planning* (Nashville: Convention Press, 1986); Jim Osborn, "Your Marriage as a Covenant with God," *Church Training*, February 1988, 24.
10. Lumpkin, *Baptist Confessions of Faith*, 396.
11. Maring and Hudson, 72-73.
12. James Leo Garrett, "Seeking a Regenerate Church Membership," *Southwestern Journal of Theology* 3 (April 1961): 32.
13. Terri Lackey, "Interest Surges in Religion While Ethics Level Declines," *Baptist Press*, December 18, 1987, 6.
14. J. Herbert Gilmore, "The Disciplined Church," *Now* 3 (Winter 1973): 11.
15. *Minutes*, Meredith Baptist Association (New Hampshire), 1846, 13.

Chapter 1

1. Delbert R. Hillers, *Covenant: The History of a Biblical Idea* (Baltimore: John Hopkins Press, 1969), 171.
2. Harold Henry Rowley, *The Covenanters of Damascus and the Dead Sea Scrolls* (Manchester, England: Manchester University Press, 1952), 135-36.
3. *Manual of Discipline* 1:16f., in Theodore H. Gaster, trans. and ed., *The Dead Sea Scriptures* (Garden City, N.Y.: Doubleday & Co., 1956), 40-41.
4. *Manual of Discipline* 5:7-20 in ibid., 47-48.
5. *Manual of Discipline* 6:23-7:25 in ibid., 51-55.
6. *Zadokite Document* 6:11-7:6a, in ibid., 68-69; 15:1-16:20 in ibid., 84-85.
7. R. A. Barclay, "New Testament Baptism an External or Internal Rite," in *Initiation*, ed. C. J. Bleeker, Studies in the History of Religions, vol. 10 (Leiden: E. J. Brill, 1965), 178.
8. Maurice Goguel, *L'eucharistie des Origines a Justin Martyr* (Paris: Librairie Fischbacher, 1910), 90.
9. William Melmoth, trans., *The Letters of Caius Plinius Caecilius Secundus*, ed. F. C. T. Bosanquet, Bohn's Classical Library (London: George Bell and Sons, 1903), 395.
10. E. Glenn Hinson, "Baptism in the Early Church History," *Review and Expositor*, 65 (Winter 1968): 23-24.

11. Ibid., 26.

12. Gregory Dix, trans. and ed., *The Treatise on the Apostolic Tradition of St. Hippolytus of Rome, Bishop and Martyr*, 2d ed. (London: Society for the Publication of Christian Knowledge, 1968), 34-35; James Cooper and Arthur John Maclean, trans. and eds., *The Testament of Our Lord* (Edinburgh: T. & T. Clark, 1902), 126; *Apostolic Constitutions* IV. xli. in *The Ante-Nicene Fathers*, 7:476.

13. *Apostolic Constitutions* IV. xli. in *The Ante-Nicene Fathers*, 7:476.

14. Gregory Nazianzen, *Oration on Holy Baptism* VIII in *A Select Library of Nicene and Post-Nicene Fathers of the Christian Church* (2nd series), 7:362.

15. John Chrysostom, *Baptismal Homily* 1. 16; 2. 17; 2. 18; 3. 20; in *Ancient Christian Writers*, 31:29, 50, 63.

16. Dix, 40.

17. Saint Cyprian, *Epistle* 57. 2. in *The Fathers of the Church*, 51:159.

18. Cooper and Maclean, 128.

19. Oliver J. Thatcher and Edgar H. McNeal, eds., *A Source Book for Mediaeval History* (New York: Charles Scribner's Sons, 1905), 485-87.

20. Henry Bettensen, ed., *Documents of the Christian Church*, 2d ed. (London: Oxford University Press, 1963), 162, 180.

21. B. J. Kidd, ed., *Documents Illustrative of the History of the Christian Church* (London: Society for the Publication of Christian Knowledge, 1941), 3:66-67.

22. Harold S. Bender, "The Anabaptist Vision," *The Recovery of the Anabaptist Vision*, ed. Guy F. Hershberger (Scottdale, Pa: Herald Press, 1957), 43.

23. George Huntston Williams and Angel M. Mergal, eds., *Spiritual and Anabaptist Writers*, The Library of Christian Classics, vol. 25 (London: SCM Press, 1957), 45.

24. Lumpkin, *Baptist Confessions of Faith*, 22, 26.

25. Gunnar Westin and Torsten Bergsten, eds., *Balthasar Hubmaier: Schriften*, Quellen zur Geschichte der Taufer, Band IX (Heidelberg: Gutersloher Verlagshaus Gerd Mohn, 1962), 349-50.

26. Ibid., 361-62.

27. Robert A. Macoskey, "The Contemporary Relevance of Balthasar Hubmaier's Concept of the Church," *Foundations* 6 (April 1963): 116.

28. John C. Wenger, "The Theology of Pilgrim Marpeck," *The Mennonite Quarterly Review* 12 (October 1938): 246-47.

29. Williams and Mergal, 187.

30. Cornelius Krahn, *Dutch Anabaptism: Origin, Spread, Life and Thought (1450-1600)* (The Hague: Netherlands: Martinus Nijhoff, 1968), 194.

31. Dietrich Philips, *Enchiridion or Hand Book of the Christian Doctrine and Religion*, trans. A. B. Kolb (Elkhart, Ind.: Mennonite Pub. Co., 1910), 454-55.

32. Lowell Hubert Zuck, "Anabaptist Revolution Through the Covenant in Sixteenth Century Continental Protestantism" (unpublished doctor's dissertation), abstract in *Dissertation Abstracts* 29 (October 1968):1289-A.

33. Raymond A. Parker, "Church Covenant, Baptist," *Encyclopedia of Southern Baptists*, 1958, 1:283.

34. Albert Peel and Leland H. Carlson, eds., *The Writings of Robert Harrison and Robert Browne*, Elizabethan Nonconformist Texts, vol. 2 (London: George Allen and Unwin, 1953), 422; Albert Peel, *The Brownists in Norwich and Norfolk about 1580* (Cambridge: University Press, 1920), 11, 253-54.

35. Leland H. Carlson, ed., *The Writings of Henry Barrow, 1587-1590*, Elizabethan Nonconformist Texts, vol. 3 (London: George Allen and Unwin, 1962), 84.

36. Leland H. Carlson (ed.), *The Writings of Henry Barrow, 1590-1591*, Elizabethan Nonconformist Texts, vol. 5 (London: George Allen and Unwin, 1966), 8.

37. B. R. White, *The English Separatist Tradition from the Marian Martyrs to the Pilgrim Fathers*, Oxford Theological Monographs (New York: Oxford University Press, 1971), 83-84; Leland H. Carlson, ed., *The Writings of John Greenwood and Henry Barrow, 1591-1593*, Elizabethan Nonconformist Texts, vol. 6 (London: George Allen and Unwin, 1970), 301.

38. Champlin Burrage, *The Early English Dissenters in the Light of Recent Research (1550-1641)* (Cambridge: University Press, 1912), 1:138.

39. Lumpkin, *Baptist Confessions of Faith*, 92.

40. Harold Paget, ed., *Bradford's History of the Plymouth Settlement, 1608-1620* (New York: E. P. Dutton & Co., 1920), 7.

Chapter 2

1. Walter H. Burgess, *John Smith the Se-Baptist, Thomas Helwys, and the First Baptist Church in England, with Fresh Light upon the Pilgrim Fathers' Church* (London: James Clarke & Co., n.d.), 87-88.

2. W. T. Whitley, ed., *The Works of John Smyth, Fellow of Christ's*

College, 1594-8 (Cambridge: University Press, 1915), 1:252, 254.

3. Ibid., 2:645.

4. Thomas Grantham, *The Paedo-Baptists Apology for the Baptized Churches, Shewing the Invalidity of the Strongest Grounds for Infant Baptism Out of the Works of the Learned Assertors of That Tenent* (n.p., 1671), 2-5.

5. Lumpkin, *Baptist Confessions of Faith*, 119.

6. John Murton, *A Description of What God Hath Predestinated Concerning Man in His Creation, Transgression, & Regeneration, as Also an Answere to John Robinson Touching Baptisme* (n.p., 1620), 169-70.

7. Adam Taylor, *The History of the English General Baptists* (London: T. Bore, 1818), 1:411.

8. Champlin Burrage, *The Church Covenant Idea: Its Origin and Its Development* (Philadelphia: American Baptist Publication Society, 1904), 149.

9. John Spilsbury, *A Treatise Concerning the Lawfull Subject of Baptisme* (London: n.p., 1643), 41.

10. Hanserd Knollys, *A Moderate Answer unto Dr. Bastwicks Book; Called, Independency Not Gods Ordinance* (London: Iane Coe, 1645), 18-20.

11. Thomas Colyer [Collier], *Certain Queries: Or, Points Now in Controvercy Examined, and Answered by Scripture, for the Satisfaction of All Those That Desire Information in the Truth* (n.p., 1645), 7-8, 10.

12. Benjamin Keach, *The Glory of a True Church, and Its Discipline Display'd* (London: n.p., 1697), 5.

13. Lumpkin, *Baptist Confessions of Faith*, 165, 286.

14. Charles B. Jewson, "St. Mary's, Norwich," *The Baptist Quarterly*, 10 (July 1940): 170, 230-32.

15. D. Hugh Matthews, "Church Covenants in Wales," unpublished manuscript, February 19, 1988, 1.

16. Edward Bean Underhill, ed., *Records of the Churches of Christ, Gathered at Fenstanton, Warboys, and Hexham, 1644-1720*, The Hanserd Knollys Society, vol. 9 (London: Haddon, Brothers, and Co., 1854), 289-90.

17. Burrage, *The Church Covenant Idea*, 154.

18. James Ford, "A Seventeenth Century Baptist Church: Bromsgrove," *Transactions of the Baptist Historical Society*, 1 (1908-9): 102-3.

19. Jewson, 230-32.

20. Ernest A. Payne, *College Street Church, Northampton, 1697-1947*

(London: Kingsgate Press, 1947), 9.

21. Lumpkin, *Baptist Confessions of Faith*, 210-11.

22. Matthews, 1.

23. Ibid.

24. Jewson, 232.

25. Horton Davies, *The English Free Churches*, The Home University Library of Modern Knowledge, 2d ed. (London: Oxford University Press, 1963), 38.

26. Burgess, 83.

27. "Church Covenants," *The Baptist Quarterly*, 7 (January 1935): 229.

28. Davies, 38.

29. Benjamin Keach, *The Glory of a True Church*, 74.

30. Edward Terrill, *The Records of a Church of Christ Meeting in Broadmead, Bristol, A.D. 1640 to A.D. 1688*, ed. Nathaniel Haycroft (London: J. Heaton & Son, 1865), 78.

31. Benjamin Keach, *The Glory of a True Church*, 74.

32. "Church Covenants," 230.

33. William Winterbotham, *A History of the Baptized Church, Meeting at Shortwood, in the Parish of Gloucestershire* (London: J. S. Hughes, 1820), 47-49.

34. "Church Covenants," 233.

35. Burrage, *The Church Covenant Idea*, 160.

36. Elias Keach, *The Glory and Ornament of a True Gospel-constituted Church* (London: n.p., 1697), 5-6.

37. Burrage, *The Church Covenant Idea*, 219.

38. 'Church Covenants," 234.

39. Matthews, 2.

40. "The Welsh Letter on Church Discipline," in John Rippon, *The Baptist Annual Register for 1790, 1791, 1792, and Part of 1793* (London: John Rippon, 1790s), 66.

41. Matthews, 2.

42. The covenant of this church appears in ibid.

43. Ibid., 4.

44. The covenant of this church appears in ibid.

Chapter 3

1. Burrage, *The Church Covenant Idea*, 182.

2. Williston Walker, *A History of the Congregational Churches in the United States*, The American Church History Series, vol. 3 (New York:

Christian Literature Co., 1894), 217.

3. See the listing of sources in Charles W. Deweese, "The Origin, Development, and Use of Church Covenants in Baptist History," (Ph.D. diss., The Southern Baptist Theological Seminary, 1973), 71.

4. H. Shelton Smith and others, eds., *American Christianity: An Historical Interpretation with Representative Documents* (New York: Charles Scribner's Sons, 1960), 1:112.

5. Williston Walker, *The Creeds and Platforms of Congregationalism* (New York: Charles Scribner's Sons, 1893), 143.

6. Smith, 129, 132.

7. J. R. Graves, ed., *Historical Facts Versus Historical Fictions* (Memphis: J. R. Graves & Son, 1890), 133, citing the "Manuscript of John Comer." Comer was pastor of the Newport Church from 1726 to 1729.

8. *Minutes,* First Baptist Church, Charlestown (Boston), Massachusetts, March 1665.

9. Morgan Edwards, *Materials Towards a History of the Baptists in America* (Philadelphia: Joseph Crukshank and Isaac Collins, 1770), 1:109.

10. Norman H. Maring, *Baptists in New Jersey: A Study in Transition* (Valley Forge: Judson Press, 1964), 18.

11. *Records of the Welsh Tract Baptist Meeting, Pencader Hundred, New Castle County, Delaware, 1701 to 1828* (Wilmington: Historical Society of Delaware, 1904), 1:26, 30.

12. Maring, 18-19.

13. *History of Baptist Churches in Maryland Connected with the Maryland Baptist Union Association* (Baltimore: J. F. Weishampel, 1885), 23.

14. *Minutes,* Salem Baptist Church, Marlboro County, South Carolina, August 1812.

15. Alvah Hovey, *A Memoir of the Life and Times of the Rev. Isaac Backus* (Boston: Gould and Lincoln, 1859), 117.

16. *Minutes,* Backus Memorial Baptist Church, Middleborough, Massachusetts, January 1756.

17. Isaac Backus, *A History of New England: With Particular Reference to the Denomination of Christians Called Baptists,* ed. David Weston, 2d ed. (Newton, Mass.: Backus Historical Society, 1871), 2:303-4.

18. *Minutes,* Bowdoinham (Maine) Baptist Association, 1805, insert.

19. G. W. Paschal, "Morgan Edwards' Materials Towards a History of the Baptists in the Province of North Carolina," *The North Carolina Historical Review* 7 (July 1930): 384.

20. Robert I. Devin, *A History of Grassy Creek Baptist Church, from Its Foundation to 1880, with Biographical Sketches of Its Pastors and Ministers* (Raleigh: Edwards, Broughton & Co., 1880), 43, 53; George Washington Paschal, *History of North Carolina Baptists* (Raleigh: Edwards & Broughton Co., 1930), 1:401-2.

21. John Taylor, *A History of Ten Baptist Churches, of Which the Author Has Been Alternately a Member* (Cincinnati: Art Guild Reprints, 1968 [originally 1823]), 5-7.

22. A. F. Spalding, *The Centennial Discourse on the One Hundredth Anniversary of the First Baptist Church, Warren, R. I., November 15, 1864* (Providence: Knowles, Anthony & Co., 1865), 14. Spalding printed the text of the original church record which dealt with the organizing process.

23. *A Confession of Faith . . . Adopted by the Baptist Association, Met at Philadelphia, September 25, 1742* (Philadelphia: Anderson and Meehan, 1818), 78.

24. Ibid., 91.

25. Ibid., 94-95.

26. William L. Lumpkin, "Early Virginia Baptist Church Covenants," *The Virginia Baptist Register* (1977), 773.

27. James Leo Garrett, Jr., *Baptist Church Discipline* (Nashville: Broadman Press, 1962), 28.

28. Ibid., 30.

29. Samuel Jones, *A Treatise of Church Discipline, and a Directory. Done by Appointment of the Philadelphia Baptist Association* (Philadelphia: S. C. Ustick, 1798), iii, 8-10.

30. William H. Brackney, ed., *Baptist Life and Thought: 1600-1980* (Valley Forge: Judson Press, 1983), 126.

31. W. O. Carver, *History of the New Salem Baptist Church, Nelson County, Kentucky, 1801-1901* (n.p., n.d.), 3-4; *Minutes*, Taylorsville Baptist Church, Taylorsville, Kentucky, July 1828.

32. Brackney, ed., *Baptist Life and Thought*, 47.

33. Morgan Edwards, *The Customs of Primitive Churches* (n.p., 1774), 5.

34. Ibid., 5, 67, 77.

35. David Thomas, *The Virginian Baptist: Or a View and Defence of the Christian Religion, As It Is Professed by the Baptists of Virginia* (Baltimore: Enoch Story, 1774), 25-26.

36. Lemuel Burkitt and Jesse Read, *A Concise History of the Kehukee Baptist Association, from Its Original Rise to the Present Time* (Halifax,

N.C.: A. Hodge, 1803), 30-31.

37. Wiley W. Sammons, *Identity of the True Baptist Church. Vol. II, Doctrine, Precept & Practice from 1765-1979 in East Tennessee, North Carolina and Alabama* (Thornton, Ark.: Cayce Pub. Co., 1979), 238-39.

38. Burkitt and Read, 174-75.

39. Paschal, *History of North Carolina Baptists*, 1:215.

40. Bill J. Leonard, "The Use of Covenants in Southern Baptist History," *Search*, 16 (Fall 1985): 37. Used by permission.

41. *Minutes*, Severn's Valley Baptist Church, Severn's Valley, Kentucky, August 1844.

42. See Deweese, "The Origin, Development, and Use of Church Covenants," 313, for a copy of the Taylorsville version.

43. Z. T. Cody, *History of the Mays Lick Baptist Church* (Maysville: Ky.: G. W. Oldham, 1890), 3, 7.

44. *Minutes*, Sharon Baptist Church, Concord, Kentucky, March 1825.

45. Peter P. Roots, *A Confession of Faith and Church Covenant* (Utica: N.Y.: Printed by Asahel Seward for Peter P. Roots, 1806), title page.

46. John Peck and John Lawton, *An Historical Sketch of the Baptist Missionary Convention of the State of New York* (Utica, N.Y.: Bennett & Bright, 1837), 197-98.

47. Three such covenants from New York (1797 and 1816) and West Virginia (1805) appear in typescript copy provided in a letter from Don A. Sanford, historian, Seventh Day Baptists of USA and Canada, Janesville, Wisconsin, December 23, 1987.

48. Roots, 19.

49. Lewis Halsey, *History of the Seneca Baptist Association: With Sketches of Churches and Pastors* (Ithaca: N.Y.: Journal Association Book and Job Printing House, 1879), 122.

50. Glenn A. Toomey, *The Romance of a Sesquicentennial Church: The Dumplin Creek Baptist Church of Christ, Jefferson City, Tennessee* (n.p., 1947), 14.

51. John Buzzell, *The Life of Elder Benjamin Randal, Principally Taken from Documents Written by Himself* (Limerick: Hobbs, Woodman & Co., 1827), 132.

52. Ibid., 132-36.

53. Lumpkin, "Early Virginia Baptist Church Covenants," 775.

54. *Minutes*, Eastern Maine Baptist Association, 1826, 6.

55. Lumpkin, "Early Virginia Baptist Church Covenants," 787-88.

Chapter 4

1. Burrage, *The Church Covenant Idea*, 201.

2. Charles Riley MacDonald, "The New Hampshire Declaration of Faith" (Th.D. diss., Northern Baptist Theological Seminary, 1939), 66.

3. *Proceedings*, Baptist Convention of the State of New Hampshire, 1830, 8.

4. Ibid., 1831, 7.

5. William Hurlin and others, *The Baptists of New Hampshire* (Manchester, N.H.: New Hampshire Baptist Convention, 1902), 52. This work contains the minutes of the convention board for the years under discussion.

6. *Proceedings*, Baptist Convention of the State of New Hampshire, 1832, 6.

7. Hurlin, 53.

8. Ibid., 53-54.

9. Ibid., 54-55.

10. Ibid., 55.

11. E.g., two editions were published at Concord, one by Stevens & Young and the other by Young and Worth. Chase & Dunlap are identified as the stereotypers in each.

12. "Baptists," *Encyclopedia of Religious Knowledge*, ed. J. Newton Brown (Brattleboro, Vt.: Fessenden and Co., 1835), 191-92.

13. Edward C. Starr, ed., *A Baptist Bibliography* (Chester, Pa.: American Baptist Historical Society, 1953), 3:199-200.

14. MacDonald, 77.

15. Lewis A. Myers, *A History of New Mexico Baptists* (Albuquerque: Baptist Convention of New Mexico, 1965), 48.

16. See the covenant, e.g., in William Crowell, *The Church Member's Manual* (Boston: Gould, Kendall & Lincoln, 1847), 231.

17. Starr, 5:197.

18. *The Articles of Faith and Covenant in Use Among Regular Baptist Churches* (Detroit: Michigan Christian Herald Print, 1880), 10-12.

19. *Minutes*, Maine Baptist Convention, 1844, 5; 1846, 5.

20. *Minutes*, Bowdoinham Baptist Association, 1848, 21; 1805, 2-4; *Minutes*, Hancock Baptist Association, 1850, 24; 1851, 20; *Minutes*, Kennebec Baptist Association, 1858, 15; 1841, 15-16; *Minutes*, Penobscot Baptist Association, 1849, 28; 1850, 29; 1851, 31; *Minutes*, Lincoln Baptist Association, 1851, 20; 1852, 16; 1853, 20; 1854, 17; *Minutes*,

Waldo Baptist Association, 1854, 15; *Minutes,* Washington Baptist Association, 1858, 15.

21. William Crowell, *The Church Member's Hand-Book: A Guide to the Doctrines and Practice of Baptist Churches* (Cincinnati: D. Anderson, 1849), 29.

22. Starr, 5:196-97.

23. William Henry Brackney, *The Baptists,* Denominations in America, Number 2 (Westport, Conn.: Greenwood Press, 1988), 136.

24. Ibid., 48.

25. J. Newton Brown, *A Baptist Church Manual* (Valley Forge: Judson Press, 1985), cover.

26. See Charles W. Deweese, "Southern Baptists and Church Covenants," *Baptist History and Heritage,* 9 (January 1974): 6-7, for a list of fourteen manuals which printed Brown's covenant. To that list, add the following six manuals: (1) R. H. Boyd, *Boyd's National Baptist Pastor's Guide and Parliamentary Rules* (Nashville: National Baptist Publishing Board, 1900; 25th ed., 1983), 15-16; (2) L. G. Jordan, *The Baptist Standard Church Directory and Busy Pastor's Guide* (Nashville: Sunday School Publishing Board, National Baptist Convention, U.S.A., 1928, reprinted 1988), 37-38; (3) Ralph M. Johnson and R. Dean Goodwin, *Faith and Fellowship of American Baptists* (New York: Council on Missionary Education of the American Baptist Convention, 1954), 62; (4) Franklin M. Segler, *The Broadman Minister's Manual* (Nashville: Broadman Press, 1969), 146-47; (5) Howard B. Foshee, *Broadman Church Manual* (Nashville: Broadman Press, 1973), 26-28; (6) W. A. Criswell, *Criswell's Guidebook for Pastors* (Nashville: Broadman Press, 1980), 101.

27. Hugh Wamble, "Church Covenants," unpublished manuscript, November 1961, 11.

28. R. Lofton Hudson, "Our Outdated Church Covenant," *Home Missions,* March 1969, 38.

29. Reagan Frazier, Sunday School Board, telephone call, January 9, 1989.

30. F. M. McConnell, *The Agreements and Differences Between the Two General Baptist Bodies in Texas* (Dallas: Irwin Printing Co., n.d.), 14.

31. The Baptist Bible Union of America, *Confession of Faith* (n.p., 1923), 36.

32. H. Leon McBeth, *The Baptist Heritage: Four Centuries of Baptist Witness* (Nashville: Broadman Press, 1987), 756.

33. Brackney, *The Baptists*, xxi.

34. *Proceedings*, Southern Baptist Convention, 1927, 38-39.

35. "Church Covenant Month," *Biblical Recorder*, March 9, 1927, 6; "Church Covenant," *The Baptist Courier*, March 3, 1927, 1; Arch C. Cree, "Via the Church Covenant," *The Christian Index*, March 24, 1927, 7; J. A. McCord, "March Church Covenant Month," *The Illinois Baptist*, March 5, 1927, 2; "March Is Church Covenant Month," *The Word and Way and Central Baptist*, March 3, 1927, 1; "Church Covenant," *Baptist New Mexican*, February 24, 1927, 5.

36. Davis C. Woolley, letter to C. B. Arendall, Jr., November 6, 1961.

37. See Deweese, "Southern Baptists and Church Covenants," 9, for a list of twelve books and booklets (excluding the church and ministers' manuals included in endnote 26), seven periodical articles and curriculum studies, and a tract. To this list can be added (1) the chapter titled "Our Church Covenant" in Sadie Tiller Crawley, *The Meaning of Church Membership* (Nashville: Sunday School Board, SBC, 1928; reset 1949); (2) the chapter titled "Your Church and Its Covenant" in Harold L. Songer, *In Covenant: An Introduction to Church Membership for Adults* (Nashville: Church Training Department, Sunday School Board, SBC, 1970); and (3) the unit by Charles W. Deweese titled "Covenant—The Basis of Church Membership" in *Living in Covenant* (Nashville: Sunday School Board, SBC, 1977).

38. Allen Adcox, Sunday School Board, telephone call, January 9, 1989.

39. J. R. Hobbs, *The Pastor's Manual* (Nashville: Sunday School Board, SBC, 1924), 218.

40. *1985-86 Sunday School Publishing Board Catalog of Publications,* 8.

41. Jordan, 37-38.

42. See these changes, e.g., in Boyd, 15-16.

43. Ibid., title page.

44. Ibid., 15.

45. G. David Guston, letter to Charles W. Deweese, December 9, 1987.

46. Attachments to ibid.

47. Ilse Mollenhauer (secretary to John Binder), letter to Charles W. Deweese, February 18, 1988, covenants attached.

48. Wayne C. Clark, *The Meaning of Church Membership* (Valley Forge: Judson Press, 1950; 14th printing, 1969), 47-48.

49. Deweese, "The Origin, Development, and Use of Church Covenants, " 199, 203. For complete results of survey, see 194-242.

50. *Minutes*, First Baptist Church, Weston, West Virginia, September

1867, 23-24.

51. *Annual,* Southern Baptist Convention, 1970, 74, 78.

52. Edward T. Hiscox, *The New Directory for Baptist Churches* (Philadelphia: American Baptist Publication Society, 1894; reprint, Grand Rapids, Mich.: Kregel Publications, 1970), 7.

53. Edward T. Hiscox, *The Star Book on Baptist Church Polity* (New York: Ward & Drummond, 1880), i.; idem, *The New Directory for Baptist Churches,* 562-63; idem, *The Standard Manual for Baptist Churches* (Philadelphia: American Baptist Publication Society, 1890; reprinted 1949); 2, 74-76; idem, *The Hiscox Guide for Baptist Churches* (Valley Forge: Judson Press, 1964), 201-2; idem, *The Hiscox Standard Baptist Manual* (Valley Forge: Judson Press, 1965), 143-44.

54. See, e.g., W. B. Boggs, *The Baptists: Who Are They? And What Do They Believe?* 4th ed. (Philadelphia: America Baptist Publication Society, 1898), 166-67; S. H. Ford, *Baptist Waymarks* (Philadelphia: American Baptist Publication Society, 1903), 183-84; J. T. Mann, *Baptist Churches: Their Ordinances and Practice,* 3d ed. (n.p., n.d.), 145; J. T. Mann, *"The First Church,"* 3d ed. (Americus, Ga.: Americus Printing Co., 1904), 181-82; E. Y. Mullins, *Baptist Beliefs* (Louisville: Baptist World Pub. Co., 1913), 95-96. The two works by Mann omitted Hiscox's last paragraph and added new paragraphs.

55. Robert A. Baker, *Her Walls Before Thee Stand: Centennial Story, First Baptist Church, Texarkana, Texas, 1877-1977* (n.p., n.d.), 27, 149.

56. *Minutes,* Old Colony Baptist Association (Massachusetts), October 1836, 7; October 1837, 7.

57. John Allen, Avery Briggs, and E. C. Messinger, *A Summary of Christian Belief and Church Covenant* (Boston: James Loring, 1838), 4-8.

58. *Minutes,* Kennebec Baptist Association (Maine), 1841, 7, 15-16; 1858, 4, 15.

59. *Minutes,* Citadel Square Baptist Church, Charleston, South Carolina, June 1868, 14-15.

60. *Minutes,* First Baptist Church, Livingston, Alabama, November 1871, 15-18.

61. Baker, 56-57.

62. Foshee, 30-32.

63. Frederick A. Agar, *The Deacon at Work* (Philadelphia: Judson Press, 1923), 82; *Proceedings,* Southern Baptist Convention, 1927, 39; James Edgar Dillard, *We Southern Baptists, 1937-8* (Nashville: Executive Committee, SBC, 1938), 22; Mitchell Bronk, "The Covenant, the

New Hampshire Confession, and J. Newton Brown," *The Watchman-Examiner*, November 16, 1939, 1244; Clifton J. Allen, "Let Us Covenant Together," *Baptist Adult Union Quarterly* 27 (January-March 1956): 36; G. Allen West, "Honestly Now, Are You Keeping the Covenant?" *The Baptist Training Union Magazine* 31 (March 1956): 48; William L. Hendricks, "The Church Covenant: Is It Accurate? Is It Adequate?" *The Baptist Program* 37 (February 1961): 24; Cecil M. Hyatt, " 'How Can the Church Covenant Be Made Relevant to the Contemporary Christian Life?' " *The California Southern Baptist*, October 6, 1966, 3; Segler, *The Broadman Minister's Manual*, 146; Songer, *In Covenant*, 28.

64. Crowell, *The Church Member's Manual*, 230.

65. Maring and Hudson, *A Baptist Manual of Polity and Practice*, 73, 207.

66. "Baptists," *Encyclopedia of Religious Knowledge*, 191.

67. Crowell, *The Church Member's Manual*, 112; J. M. Pendleton, *Church Manual: Designed for the Use of Baptist Churches* (Philadelphia: American Baptist Publication Society, 1867), 7-8; Jordan, 17; Wayne R. Rood, ed., *A Manual of Procedures for Seventh Day Baptist Churches* (Plainfield, N.J.: Seventh Day Baptist General Conference, 1972), 96.

68. Maring and Hudson, 62.

69. [William Crowell], "Advantages of the Baptist Church Polity," *The Christian Review* 11 (May 1846): 65.

70. Davis C. Woolley, letter to Mrs. W. M. Bush, October 17, 1968.

71. *Minutes*, Meredith Baptist Association, 1842, 11; *Minutes*, Kennebec Baptist Association, 1850, 10-11; *Minutes*, Washington Baptist Association, 1858, 12.

72. Crowell, *The Church Member's Manual*, 72.

73. See Deweese, "The Origin, Development, and Use of Church Covenants," 158, for a list of seven such manuals.

74. Boyd, 11.

75. Hendricks, 27.

76. Maring and Hudson, 73.

77. *Minutes*, Milford (New Hampshire) Baptist Association, 1846, circular letter; reprinted in "Covenant Obligations," *The Biblical Recorder*, January 16, 1847, 1.

78. Francis Wayland, *Notes on the Principles and Practices of Baptist Churches* (New York: Sheldon, Blakeman & Co., 1857), 331.

79. Edward T. Hiscox, *The Baptist Church Directory* (New York: Sheldon & Co., 1859), 39.

80. Augustine S. Carman, *The Covenant and the Covenant Meeting* (Philadelphia: American Baptist Publication Society, 1898), 31-33.

81. Hiscox, *The New Directory for Baptist Churches*, 249.

82. Carman, 27, 39.

83. Ibid., 28-31.

84. Hiscox, *The New Directory for Baptist Churches,* 251.

85. Albert W. Wardin, *Baptists in Oregon* (Nashville: Curley Printing Co., 1969), 15.

86. Boyd, 32; Jordan, 27, 172.

87. Jordan, 172; Johnson and Goodwin, 60.

88. Carman, 8; Burrage, *The Church Covenant Idea*, 219.

89. Leland D. Hine, *Baptists in Southern California* (Valley Forge: Judson Press, 1966), 71; Maring, 287; "Church Covenant Month," *Biblical Recorder*, March 9, 1927, 6.

90. Maring and Hudson, 72-73.

91. Theodore Gerald Soares, *A Baptist Manual: The Polity of the Baptist Churches and of the Denominational Organizations* (Philadelphia: American Baptist Publication Society, 1911), 41; Roy M. Reed, *Christian Engagements: A Study of the Church Covenant* (Texarkana, Ark-Tex: Baptist Sunday School Committee of the American Baptist Association, 1962), 7.

92. William Warren Sweet, *The Story of Religion in America*, rev. ed. (New York: Harper & Row, 1950), 332, 345, 372.

93. Hendricks, "The Church Covenant," 29; Hudson, "Our Outdated Church Covenant," 38-39.

94. Deweese, "The Origin, Development, and Use of Church Covenants," 169-72.

95. J. Herbert Gilmore, Jr., attachment to letter to Charles W. Deweese, March 1, 1973; Charles A. Chilton, attachment to letter to Charles W. Deweese, November 6, 1987.

96. West, "Honestly Now, Are You Keeping the Covenant?" 4-5, 48; Allen, "Let Us Covenant Together," 36-38.

97. Elizabeth O'Connor, *Call to Commitment: The Story of the Church of the Saviour, Washington, D.C.* (New York: Harper & Row, 1963), 34; Robert H. Zbinden, letter to Charles W. Deweese, March 16, 1973.

98. Hendricks, 24, 27, 29; Chevis F. Horne, "Is It Time for a New Church Covenant?" *The Baptist Program*, April 1983, 5, 19.

99. Horne, 5, 19.

100. Earl Waldrup, *New Church Member Orientation Manual* (Nash-

ville: Convention Press, 1965), v.

101. For a list of these articles, see Deweese, "The Origin, Development, and Use of Church Covenants," 182.

102. Bill J. Leonard, "The Use of Covenants in Southern Baptist History," 39-40.

103. Hudson, "Our Outdated Church Covenant," 39.

104. *Annual*, Southern Baptist Convention, 1970, 74.

105. Cree, 7.

Chapter 5

1. Jarold K. Zeman, "The Changing Baptist Identity in Canada Since World War II," *Celebrating the Canadian Baptist Heritage: Three Hundred Years of God's Providence*, eds. Paul R. Dekar and Murray J. S. Ford (Hamilton, Ontario: McMaster University Divinity College, 1984), 6. Jarold K. Zeman, along with Philip G. A. Griffin-Allwood and George A. Rawlyk, coedited *Baptists in Canada, 1760-1990: A Bibliography of Selected Printed Resources in English* (Hantsport, Nova Scotia: Lancelot Press, 1989), which included a selection of thirty-three entries on confessions of faith and covenants (120-25).

2. *Minutes*, New Brunswick Baptist Association, 1832, 15-16.

3. *Minutes*, Eastern Nova Scotia Baptist Association, 1854, 11.

4. Ibid.

5. "A Declaration of the Faith, Practice, & Covenant of the Churches of Christ Composing the Nova Scotia Baptist Associations" (Halifax: Christian Messenger Office, 1855).

6. *Minutes*, Prince Edward Island Baptist Association, 1869, 3.

7. Isaac Backus, 2:110-11.

8. Ibid.

9. *Minutes*, Cornwallis New Light Congregationalist Church, 1778.

10. "Doctrinal Statement and Church Covenant," Horton Baptist Church, 1807.

11. *Minutes*, Free Christian Baptist General Conference of New Brunswick, 1855, 9, 32.

12. Ibid., 1863, 15.

13. *Free Christian Baptist Handbook* (St. John, New Brunswick: George W. Day, 1873), 20-21.

14. *Minutes*, Free Christian Baptist Conference of Nova Scotia, 1866, 15, 16.

15. Edward Manning Saunders, *History of the Baptists of the Maritime*

Provinces (Halifax: John Burgoyne, 1902), 401.

16. *Minutes,* Western New Brunswick Baptist Association, 1874, 47; *Minutes,* African Baptist Association of Nova Scotia, 1881, 13.

17. *A General Summary of Belief of the Baptists of Prince Edward Island, with the Covenant and Some Important Rules of Order* (St. John, New Brunswick: Christian Visitor Office, 1878), 31-32; *Minutes,* Southern New Brunswick Baptist Association, 1884, 4; Paul H. Prebble, ed., *The Central United Baptist Church at Saint John, N[ew] B[runswick], 1850-1950* (Saint John: Lingley Printing Co., 1950), 68; *Handbook of the United Baptist Convention of the Maritime Provinces* (Toronto: Canadian Branch of American Baptist Publication Society, 1923), 30-31.

18. "Church Covenant," Cornwallis Baptist Church, recorded in the Registry of Deeds for Kings County, March 22, 1849; Henry Melville King, *Historical Discourse Delivered on the Fiftieth Anniversary of the Organization of the Dudley-Street Baptist Church, Boston . . . March 9, 1871* (Boston: Rand, Avery & Frye, 1871), 56.

19. "Meetinghouse Covenant," Digby Joggins Baptist Church, 1833.

20. See, e.g., *Minutes,* New Brunswick Baptist Association, 1832, 14; *Minutes,* Western Nova Scotia Baptist Association, 1863, 18; *Minutes,* Eastern Nova Scotia Baptist Association, 1864, 15-16

21. For illustrations of many of these prints, see Charles W. Deweese, "Church Covenants and Church Discipline Among Baptists in the Maritime Provinces," *Repent and Believe: The Baptist Experience in Maritime Canada,* ed. Barry M. Moody (Hantsport, Nova Scotia: Lancelot Press, 1980), 28-30.

22. *Minutes,* Horton Baptist Church, January 4, 1862.

23. Philip G. A. Griffin-Allwood, "By What Authority?" *The Atlantic Baptist,* July 1988, 16.

24. F. W. Waters, "Pioneer Baptist Creeds and Covenants in Upper Canada and Lower Canada," *Canadian Baptist Home Missions Digest,* 6 (1963-1964): 218.

25. William Gillespie (Guelph, Ontario), letter to Charles Deweese, January 12, 1989, 1. This lengthy letter with numerous covenantal documents attached provides excellent historical analysis of covenantal developments in Ontario in the first half of the 1800s.

26. John Peck and John Lawton, *An Historical Sketch of the Baptist Missionary Convention of the State of New York . . .* (Utica: Bennett & Bright, 1837), 198.

27. Stuart Ivison and Fred Rosser, *The Baptists in Upper and Lower*

Canada before 1820 (Toronto: University of Toronto Press, 1956), 78.

28. Gillespie.

29. *Articles of Faith, Practice, and Covenant: Together with the Marriage Ceremony of the Western Association of the Regular Baptist Churches in Upper Canada* (St. Thomas: Printed for the Association, 1832), 24-25.

30. Gillespie, 2.

31. Ibid., 4. See *Articles of Faith and Practice with the Church Covenant, Approved by the Danville Association and Adopted by the Churches . . .* (Brockville, Upper Canada: William Buell Jr. & Co., 1829).

32. Gillespie, 4-5, including a photocopy of the 1844 associational minutes containing the covenant.

33. Ibid., 4.

34. Ilse Mollenhauer (secretary to John Binder), North American Baptist Conference, letter to Charles W. Deweese, February 18, 1988, covenants attached.

35. Allen Schmidt, Canadian Convention of Southern Baptists, letter to Charles W. Deweese, April 28, 1988, covenants attached.

36. Ibid.

37. Ernest A. Payne, "Baptist Work in Jamaica Before the Arrival of the Missionaries," *The Baptist Quarterly* 7 (January 1934): 20-21, 24.

38. W. J. McGlothlin, *Baptist Confessions of Faith* (Philadelphia: American Baptist Publication Society, 1911), 354.

39. G. Keith Parker, *Baptists in Europe: History and Confessions of Faith* (Nashville: Broadman Press, 1982), 124. A copy of the French Baptist Federation covenant appears on 124-25.

40. Howard Crago, Baptist Union of Victoria (Australia), letter to Charles W. Deweese, December 9, 1987.

41. Samson E. Khama, South West Province, Republic of Cameroon, letter to Charles W. Deweese, December 8, 1987.

42. David Lagergren, Stockholm, Sweden, letter to Charles W. Deweese, March 17, 1988.

43. Stan Edgar, Secretary, New Zealand Baptist Historical Society, letter to Charles W. Deweese, September 2, 1988.

44. Sydney Hudson-Reed, *Lantern on the Skyline: Seventy Years of Service for Christ at Rosebank Union Church* (Roodepoort, South Africa: Roodepoort Mission Press, 1978), 95.

45. "Statement of Faith of Evangelical Christians-Baptists" (Moscow, 1985), provided by Alexei Bichkov through the International Department of the Baptist Union of USSR, 17, 20, 22-23.

46. Alexei Bichkov, The Union of Evangelical Christians-Baptists of USSR, letter to Charles W. Deweese, March 2, 1988.

47. Crea Ridenour, letter to Charles W. Deweese, November 21, 1987.

48. Luis Magin Alvarez, letter to Charles W. Deweese, November 30, 1987.

49. Kate Carter, letter to Charles W. Deweese, March 17, 1988.

50. Jimmie Ross, letter to Charles W. Deweese, February 11, 1988.

51. Ivah T. Heneise, letter to Charles W. Deweese, February 19, 1988.

52. Wallace Turnbull, letter to Charles W. Deweese, January 31, 1988.

53. J. Wayne Jenkins, Germany Baptist Mission, letter to Charles W. Deweese, January 28, 1988, citing Glenn Pinkston.

54. Cathcart, ed., *The Baptist Encyclopedia*, 528.

55. G. Keith Parker, letter to Charles W. Deweese, December 2, 1987.

56. H. Wayne Pipkin, letter to Charles W. Deweese, February 15, 1988.

57. Letters to Charles W. Deweese from Graham Lange (Austria), February 16, 1988; J. Wayne Jenkins (Federal Republic of Germany), January 28, 1988; Ernst Binder (Switzerland), March 28, 1988; Paolo Spanu (Italy), January 20, 1988; Herman G. de Winkel (Netherlands), March 24, 1988; Bent Hylleberg (Denmark), November 13, 1987; Jouko Neulanen (Finland), January 11, 1988.

58. D. W. Bebbington, letter to Charles W. Deweese, January 26, 1988; Peter H. Barber, letter to Charles W. Deweese, February 5, 1988.

59. R. Heaton, letter to Charles W. Deweese, December 17, 1987.

60. *A Manual for Worship and Service* (Canada: All-Canada Baptist Publications for the Baptist Federation of Canada, 1976), 202-3; William H. Jones, *What Canadian Baptists Believe* (Niagara Falls, Ontario: JBTS Publishing House, 1980), 48-49.

61. Zeman, "The Changing Baptist Identity in Canada," 6.

62. Ibid.

63. Ibid.

64. Jones, 48.

Epilogue

1. Maring and Hudson, 73.

2. Allen W. Graves, *A Church at Work* (Nashville: Convention Press, 1972), 18.

3. W. T. Whitley, ed., *The Works of John Smyth*, 2:645.

4. Henry D'Anvers, *A Treatise of Baptism* (London: Elephant and Castle, 1674), 216.

5. John Taylor, *A History of Ten Baptist Churches*, 6-7.

6. Dale Moody, "The Lord's Supper" (undated mimeographed essay), 5-6.

7. Maring and Hudson, 62.

8. Spalding, *The Centennial Discourse on the One Hundredth Anniversary of the First Baptist Church, Warren, R. I.,* 14.

9. Maring and Hudson, 73.

10. Carman, *The Covenant and the Covenant Meeting*, 39.

11. Clarissa Strickland, "Church Covenants Reexamined by Southern Baptist Churches," *SBC Today*, April 1989, 24.

12. Ibid.

Index

Index

235

Church Covenant Meetings, 85-88, 103, 113, 210-11
Church Covenant Month, 68-69
Church Covenant Supplies, 69-70, 71
Church Covenants
  Adaptation to cultural situations, 108
  Attitudes toward, 28-29
  Australia, 107, 108, 110, 198-95
  Austria, 112
  Authority of, 83-84, 90
  Backgrounds (pre-Baptist), 15-23
  Biblical basis, 15-18, 55, 59, 85, 86-87, 200
  Britain, 24-38, 116-32
  British influences on later Baptist practices, 33-37
  Canada, 98-106, 113-14, 182-90
  Chile, 111, 114
  China, 107, 108, 114, 193-94
  Collection of 79 covenants, 115-199
  Colombia, 110
  Congregational input and approval, 205-06
  Countries apparently not using, 112-13
  Decline, 36, 88-91, 97
  Definition, viii, 24, 81-82, 97, 205
  Denmark, 112
  Early Church and Middle Ages, 18-20
  Europe, 112-13
  Federal Republic of Germany, 112
  Finland, 112
  Flexibility in designing, 34
  France, 107, 108, 114, 192
  Frontier, 52-54
  Guidelines for using, 206-12
  Guidelines for writing, 203-06
  Haiti, 111-12, 114
  Ideals, 81-88
  Impact of secularization upon use, 89
  Implications for Southern Baptists, 95-96
  Italy, 112
  Jamaica, 107-09, 114, 190-91
  Latin America, 111
  Legalistic application, 89
  Maritime Provinces (Canada), 99-104, 182-83, 184, 185-87
  Middle Colonies, 41, 43
  Nature, purpose, contents, uses, and values, 29-33, 45, 55, 81-82, 97, 201-02, 203
  Netherlands, 112
  New England, 39-41
  New Hampshire tradition, 61-76, 156-58, 160-62, 164
  New Zealand, 107, 109, 114, 196-97
  Ontario and western provinces (Canada), 104-06, 183, 184-85, 188-90
  Principles for determining contents, 204
  Printing and circulating, 206
  Recent covenants by individuals, 79-80, 176-77, 179-80
  Relation to Christian ethics, iv-x

  Relation to church discipline, 30-31, 35, 36, 38, 48-50, 52, 53-54, 57, 58, 59, 84-85, 88, 103, 113, 209-10
  Relation to confessions of faith, viii-ix, xii, 29-30, 45, 52-53, 55, 90
  Relation to creedalism, 112
  Relation to defining and constituting a church, 48, 49-51, 51-52, 82-84, 97, 210
  Relation to regenerate church membership, v-viii, ix, xi-xiii, 29, 38, 52, 90, 97, 199, 201, 207, 213
  Renewal, 56-57, 59, 91-96, 97
  Republic of Cameroon, 107, 108-109, 114, 195-96
  Revising, 206
  Scotland, 112-13
  Settings for use, 56, 59, 103
  Signing, 25, 26, 28, 32, 34-35, 38, 51, 57, 59, 82, 88
  South Africa, 107, 109, 197-198
  Southern Colonies, 43
  Spain, 111
  Standardization, 36, 60, 88-89, 108, 110-12, 114, 201-02
  Survey regarding use, 74
  Sweden, 107, 108, 109, 114, 198
  Switzerland, 112
  Trends in early America, 54-58
  Use in baptism, 20, 25, 29, 46-47, 207-08
  Use in covenant meetings, 85-88, 103, 113, 210-11
  Use in Lord's Supper, 208-09
  United States, 39-97, 132-82
  USSR, 107, 109-10, 198-99
  Venezuela, 110
  Zimbabwe, 113
Church Manuals, 66, 83, 84-85
Churches, Baptist (Canada)
  Brussels Street (Saint John, New Brunswick), 102
  Central (Edmonton, Alberta), 106
  Charlotteville or Vittoria (Ontario), 104
  Clinton or Beamsville (Ontario), 105
  Community (Red Deer, Alberta), 106
  Cornwallis (Nova Scotia), 101, 103
  Cramahe (Ontario), 105
  Digby Joggins (Nova Scotia), 103
  Discovery (Regina, Saskatchewan), 106
  Faith (Calgary, Alberta), 106, 189-90
  Faith (Penticton, British Columbia), 106
  Gladstone (Vancouver, British Columbia), 106
  Grace (Calgary, Alberta), 106
  Halifax (Nova Scotia), 64, 103, 184
  Horton, First—now Wolfville (Nova Scotia), 99, 100, 101, 104
  Malahide (Ontario), 104
  New Covenant (Winnipeg, Manitoba), 106, 188-89